e re ned on or t

Following the collapse of the Wilhelmine Empire in Germany, a new generation of artists found a fresh environment where they might flourish. Their optimism was accompanied by an equally powerful distrust of the immediate past, for post-romanticism, and ultimately expressionism, served as symbols of a bygone era. Composers, performers, and audiences alike sought to negate their recent past in various ways: by affirming modern technology (electronic or mechanical music, sound recordings, radio, and film), exploring music of a more remote past (principally Baroque music), and celebrating popular music (particularly jazz). The essays contained in this volume address these fundamental themes. Examining the way in which German music was performed, staged, programmed, and received in the 1920s not only offers deeper insight into Weimar culture itself but sheds light on our contemporary musical world.

CAMBRIDGE STUDIES IN PERFORMANCE PRACTICE 3

Music and performance during the Weimar Republic

CAMBRIDGE STUDIES IN PERFORMANCE PRACTICE 3

General editor: PETER WILLIAMS

Editorial board:
OTTO BIBA, ROBERT MORGAN
R. LARRY TODD, ALEXANDER SILBIGER

Already published
1 Perspectives on Mozart performance *edited by* R. LARRY TODD *and*
   PETER WILLIAMS
2 Plainsong in the age of polyphony *edited by* THOMAS FORREST KELLY

CAMBRIDGE STUDIES IN PERFORMANCE PRACTICE 3

Music and performance during the Weimar Republic

edited by
BRYAN GILLIAM

CAMBRIDGE
UNIVERSITY PRESS

Published by the Press Syndicate of the University of Cambridge
The Pitt Building, Trumpington Street, Cambridge CB2 1RP
40 West 20th Street, New York, NY 10011–4211, USA
10 Stamford Road, Oakleigh, Melbourne 3166, Australia

First published 1994

Transferred to digital printing 2001

Printed in Great Britain by Biddles Short Run Books, King's Lynn

A catalogue record for this book is available from the British Library

Library of Congress cataloguing in publication data

Music and performance during the Weimar Republic / edited by Bryan Gillam,
    p.   cm. – (Cambridge studies in performance practice: 3)
Includes bibliographical references and index.
1. Performance practice (Music) – Germany – 20th century.   2. Music–Germany –
20th century – History and criticism.   3. Music and society.
I. Gillam, Bryan Randolph.   II. Series.
ML 457.M86 1994
780'.943'09042 – dc20   93–31382   CIP   MN

ISBN 0 521 42012 1 hardback

SN

CONTENTS

GENERAL PREFACE

No doubt the claim, heard frequently today, that "authentic performance" is a chimera, and that even the idea of an "authentic edition" cannot be sustained for (most) music before the last century or two, is itself the consequence of too sanguine an expectation raised by performers and scholars alike in the recent past. Both have been understandably concerned to establish that a certain composer "intended so-and-so" or "had such-and-such conditions of performance in mind" or "meant it to sound in this way or that." Scholars are inclined to rule on problems ("research confirms the following . . ."), performers to make the music a living experience ("artistry or musicianship suggests the following . . ."). Both are there in order to answer certain questions and establish an authority for what they do; both demonstrate and persuade by the rhetoric of their utterance, whether well-documented research on the one hand or convincing artistic performance on the other; and the academic/commercial success of both depends on the effectiveness of that rhetoric. Some musicians even set out to convey authority in both scholarship and performance, recognizing that music is conceptual *and* perceptual and thus not gainfully divisible into separate, competitive disciplines. In general, if not always, the scholar appears to aim at the firm, affirmative statement, often seeing questions as something to be answered confidently rather than searchingly redefined or refined. In general, with some exceptions, performers have to aim at the confident statement, for their very livelihood hangs on an unhesitating decisiveness in front of audience or microphone. In the process, both sometimes have the effect, perhaps even the intention, of killing the dialectic – of thwarting the progress that comes with further questions and a constant "yes, but" response to what is seen, in the light of changing definitions, as "scholarly evidence" of "convincing performance."

In the belief that the immense activity in prose and sound over the last few decades is not being accompanied by an increasing awareness of the issues arising – a greater knowledge at last enabling the questions to be more closely defined – the Cambridge Studies in Performance Practice will attempt to make regular contributions to this area of study, on the basis of several assumptions. Firstly, at its best, Performance Practice is so difficult a branch of study as to be an almost impossibly elusive ideal. It cannot be merely a practical way of "combining performance and scholarship," for these two are fundamentally different activities, each able to inform the other only up to a certain point. Secondly, if Performance Practice has moved beyond the questions (now seen to be very dated) that exercised performance groups in the 1950s and 60s, it can widen itself to include any or all music written before the last few years. In this respect, such studies are a musician's equivalent to the cry of literary studies, "Only contextualize!," and this can serve as a useful starting-point for the historically-minded performer or the practically-minded scholar. (The Derridaesque paradox that there is no context may have already affected some literary studies, but context is still clearly crucial across the broad field of music, the original comparative literature.) Cambridge Studies in Performance Practice will devote volumes to any period in which useful questions can be asked, ranging from at least Gregorian chant to at least Stravinsky.

Thirdly, Performance Practice is not merely about performing, neither "this is how music was played" nor "this is how you should play it in a concert or recording today." (These two statements are as often as not irreconcilable.) In studying all that we can about the practical realization of a piece of music we are studying not so much how it was played but how it was heard, both literally and on a deeper level. How it was conceived by the composer and how it was perceived by the period's listener are endless questions deserving constant study, for they bring one into intimate contact with the historical art of music as nothing else can. It is the *music* we fail to understand, not its performance as such, if we do not explore these endless questions. As we know, every basic musical element has had to be found, plucked out of thin air – the notes, their tuning, compass, volume, timbre, pace, timing, tone, combining – and they have constantly changed. In attempting to grasp or describe these elements as they belong to a certain piece of music, it could become clear that any modern re-realization in (public) performance is a quite separate issue. Nevertheless, it is an issue of importance to the wider musical community, as can be seen from the popular success of performers and publications (records, journals, books) concerned with "authenticity." In recognizing this practical importance, Cambridge Studies in Performance Practice will frequently call upon authoritative performers to join scholars in the common cause, each offering insights to the process of learning to ask and explore the right questions.

PETER WILLIAMS

PREFACE

The political and economic collapse in the aftermath of World War I catalyzed fundamental changes in German cultural life, especially musical culture. To be sure, great changes were taking place all over Europe, yet nowhere is the search for a modern musical aesthetic better exemplified than during the scientific, political, and cultural experiment called the Weimar Republic. Progressive impulses – in various branches of art and science – doubtless predated the First World War, but they found few open doors during the Wilhelmine era. Only after the breakdown and ultimate overthrow of the Empire could a new generation of artists and intellectuals find an environment in which they might flourish.

Government censorship was lifted in 1918, an early act of the provisional government, and cultural institutions that had operated at the pleasure of the court would now be run by the state.[1] But despite their optimism, artists and intellectuals had to reckon with political insecurity and economic instability during the years following the November Revolution. Their belief in a brighter future was accompanied by an equally powerful distrust of the immediate past, for post-romanticism, and ultimately expressionism, served as symbols of the bygone Wilhelmine era. Composers, performers, and audiences sought to ignore – even negate – their recent past in various ways: by affirming modern technology (electronic and mechanical music, sound recordings, radio, and film), exploring music of a more remote past (principally Baroque music), and celebrating popular music (particularly jazz).

Although today's search for "authenticity" in the performance of historical music might have its roots as early as the late-nineteenth century, it received its first systematic manifestation in early twentieth-century modernism, a time when countless composers and performers alike embraced *Neue Sachlichkeit*: an aesthetic view that sought to strip music of its romantic or ideal pretensions; to emphasize stability and clarity; and to question the role of subjective artistic prerogative versus an objective, infallible musical text. Music, in short, should do little more than express itself. Ernst Toch took this argument to its logical extreme when he foresaw a music where "every trace of spontaneity, of sentiment, of impulse is driven out."

In the general preface, Peter Williams emphasizes that performance practice "is not merely about performing," that the field is as much about musical perception and reception. His observation serves as a basis for this volume, because exploring the way in which German music was performed, staged, programmed, and received in the 1920s not only offers deeper insights into Weimar culture itself but sheds light on our contemporary musical world. And although the issue of musical performance (including staging) is no doubt the interconnecting thread among these essays, a few subcategories weave their way through the volume as well.

Three of these essays (those by Stephen Hinton, Kim Kowalke, and Robert Hill) directly confront performance problems, but in entirely different ways. Hinton's contribution ("*Lehrstück*: an aesthetics of performance") represents the first in-depth study of the *Lehrstück*: a didactic piece that sought to break down barriers between composer, performer, and audience – and, the author asserts, a genre that embodies the political spirit of the Weimar Republic "perhaps more than any other artistic genre." Hinton also traces the origin of the term, which – contrary to conventional wisdom – is not a twentieth-century, Brechtian neologism, but rather a concept going back centuries. Hill's essay ("Overcoming romanticism") recognizes an important post-war change in the relationship between performer, musical text, and audience expectation. The end of the war also marked the end of a "late-romantic" relationship between performer and the score, where inter-pretive values inherited from the nineteenth century had enfranchised artists to transform the musical text as necessary to render fully their understanding of the poetic content of the music. Hill laments that what began in the spirit of *Neue Sachlichkeit* outlived the era; this post-World War One performing aesthetic, which ruled out the expressive manipulation of musical time and operated under the covert assumption of "good musicianship," continues to prevail. Kowalke ("Singing Brecht vs. Brecht singing") addresses more specific performance issues, namely the often discussed, but frequently misunderstood, problem of "Brechtian" performance practice and what it should mean to performers today. At the heart of this study lies the problematic, hard-to-define relationship between poetry and music, but within the context of an epic dramaturgy where text, music, and stage events exist in new relationships.

Christopher Hailey ("Rethinking sound: music and radio in Weimar Germany") explores the burgeoning technology of live and recorded sound with all its technical and aesthetic ramifications for performance and composition. Live radio broadcast offered the unprecedented possibility of a musical performance that could be experienced in various cities and towns – both simultaneously and away from the point of origin. The crude early microphone made large orchestral broadcasts disappointing, and Hailey cogently argues that renewed interest in chamber-music performance and composition in the 1920s cannot be appreciated fully outside of this context. My essay ("Stage and screen: Kurt Weill and operatic reform in the 1920s") explores cinema – a synthesis of art and technology that galvanized change in all branches of German theater. The exponential growth of German cinema in the twenties also paralleled the maturing of Weill as an opera composer. The ways in which his works employ cinematic techniques, or even film footage itself, exemplifies a preoccupation with cinema shared by stage directors and other composers of Weill's generation.

In evaluating the impact of jazz and popular music, J. Bradford Robinson ("Jazz reception in Weimar Germany") asserts that – contrary to popular opinion – Germany's so-called Jazz Age was largely the product of the Weimar media (both print and radio), and what was understood to be jazz was far removed from the original model. Moreover, what musicians knew about jazz came from neither authentic recordings nor live performance, but rather from handbooks such as Alfred Baresel's *Das Jazz-Buch* (1926). Robinson also discusses various responses to jazz among composers, ranging from negative (Schoenberg) to enthusiastic (Krenek), and from playful (Hindemith) to socio-critical (Weill).

A vital, yet often ignored, undercurrent to Weimar musicology and performance is nationalism. The Bach and Handel revivals of the twenties might well be interpreted, in part, as a post-war search for national cultural identity. Some of this nationalism was a benign, unreflective type – a response to wounded national pride – but there was also the reactionary, ideological brand that showed its dark side increasingly as the decade progressed. Pamela Potter ("German musicology and early music performance, 1918–1933") surveys this issue, looking at the aims of a progressive government that tried to forge a relationship between the perceived elitist, non-utilitarian world of musicology and German society at large. By promoting early music performance musicologists could demonstrate their service, indeed relevance, to the broader community. But, as Potter demonstrates, this effort was not without its nationalistic overtones: by and large the performance repertoire and scholarly editions sought to glorify German composers even down to the level of regional (Silesian, Bohemian, etc.) *Kleinmeister*.

Peter Williams' essay ("The idea of *Bewegung* in the German organ reform movement") also explores this issue, but in narrower focus. Williams observes that although the movement earnestly tried to understand the technology and sound of earlier organs, it did so mostly from the standpoint of German instruments, composers, and repertoires. In consonance with Potter, Williams recognizes an unmistakable nationalist-political agenda lurking beneath the surface. Indeed, by the late 1920s the word *Bewegung* had become an essential part of the National-Socialist discourse, which was finding ever greater resonance in the societal mainstream. In 1927 the Nazis held their first rally in Nuremberg, and within six years Hitler was made Chancellor. The Weimar constitution – as well as the cultural aims of the era – would be systematically dismantled.

Through the creation of their own cultural organizations under the control of Joseph Goebbels, the National Socialists sought to redress the "sins" of the past. In music, the nadir was surely the first *Reichsmusiktage* (1938) in Düsseldorf, a massive music festival at which Goebbels, in his inaugural address, warned that the health of German music was in serious danger. The music of the Weimar era, poisoned by foreign "Marxism" and domestic "Jewish elements," had allegedly dealt a serious blow to German art. A large exhibit entitled *Entartete Musik* (Degenerate Music) was organized in conjunction with the festival to help pinpoint these so-called dangerous elements: atonality, jazz, musical Bolshevism, international Judaism, and the like. Musicians who flourished during the Weimar years were now officially deemed "degenerate." By then the doors that had opened up in the early twenties had long since been closed.

I am deeply grateful to the following music publishers for their kind permission to reproduce copyrighted excerpts:

BMG UFA (Wiener Bohême Verlag): Exx. 7.11, 7.12; European American Music Corp.: Exx. 1.1, 5.3, 5.4, 7.7, 7.8, 7.10, 7.15; B. Schott's Söhne: Exx. 2.2; Universal Edition: Exx. 2.1, 2.3, 2.4, 7.1, 7.2, 7.3, 7.4, 7.5, 7.6, 7.10, 7.19, 7.21, 7.23; Musikverlag Zimmermann: Exx. 7.13, 7.17, 7.20, 7.22, 7.24.

I am also indebted to a number of individuals who have been most helpful in preparing this volume. They include Peter Williams, Kathryn Puffett, Isabelle Bélance-Zank, David Farneth, Neil Lerner, and J. Michael Cooper, who prepared the index. My deepest gratitude, however, is reserved for my wife, who – despite her busy schedule as physician and mother – gave me the time I needed to put this volume together.

STAGE AND SCREEN: KURT WEILL
AND OPERATIC REFORM IN THE 1920S

BRYAN GILLIAM

Few artistic media so closely parallel the rise and fall of the Weimar Republic as German silent film, which began to flourish as a medium of international stature shortly after the November Revolution, reached its zenith within two years of the Treaty of Locarno, and became largely irrelevant (with the advent of talking pictures) by the beginning of the next decade. The German film industry was fairly insignificant before the First World War; the war years saw the creation of various film organizations that would help that industry gain international prominence in the 1920s. A remarkable sense of optimism surrounded German cinema shortly after the war. Young directors, cameramen, and film technicians, who received training creating wartime propaganda films, were eager to achieve prominence in peacetime. Major figures from the realm of live theater would try their hand at this emerging medium. Partly because of its solid organization and partly because of wide-ranging interest from various strata of society, German cinema grew at an exponential rate during the 1920s, despite the economic vicissitudes of the decade. Indeed, in 1927 Germany had produced 241 feature films – more than the rest of Europe combined and a sum rivalled by only the United States and Japan.[1]

FILM AND THEATER IN THE 1920S

What role would this young, thriving medium of silent film play in the theatrical life of the early Weimar Republic? In the first few years of the republic – a time of transition from *Hoftheater* to *Staatstheater*, from *Hofoper* to *Staatsoper*, and a time of economic and political instability – the answer was far from clear. Reduced budgets and declining ticket sales created worries for opera directors and producers alike; the steadily increasing popularity of film – which offered visual entertainment at cut-rate prices – and its potential to draw away opera audiences only added to those concerns. Would this burgeoning art form prove to be a formidable rival to opera? Would film ultimately render this venerable genre obsolete?

Berlin music critic Hans Gutman, for one, clearly believed it had, though the blame for decline lay more with outmoded musical institutions than with film itself. Recognizing a clear "breach between the public and the art of music," Gutman found that traditional cultural venues such as symphony concert or opera had ceased to be relevant to audiences. The "usual concert," according to Gutman, was outmoded because it offered its audience the same works year after year; traditional opera was obsolete because "it doles out material that has become 'old hat' to eyes that have gone to school to the cinema and [to] senses disillusioned by reality."[2] He recognized film as a positive phenomenon, a catalyst to operatic reform. Arnold Schoenberg was not nearly so charitable. In his brief essay "Gibt es eine Krise der Oper?" he recognized a genuine operatic crisis caused by film: "[Opera] can no longer take the competition of the required realism [of film, which] . . . has spoiled the eyes of the spectator: one not only sees truth and reality, rather also every appearance . . . that presents itself in a fantastic way as reality."[3] Schoenberg's comments, from 1927, were timely, for by the mid-1920s filmic elements had begun to inform German opera in various ways. But was the attraction of certain opera composers, librettists, and stage directors to film a mere gimmick, an expedient turn towards a growing popular medium, or were there broader underlying factors? Clearly many saw the potential for profit by embracing the world of film, but deeper reasons cannot be ignored.

Film, the product of art, business, and technology, reached a broader public than any other theatrical art form. That general appeal, not surprisingly, attracted those composers associated with *Neue Sachlichkeit*, composers who sought one form of *Gebrauchsmusik* that would engage a larger cultural community. Moreover, the use of film or filmic techniques represented a way in which to purge German opera of its pre-war Wagnerian legacy. Curiously, the first German opera composer who intentionally borrowed cinematic techniques in order to strip opera of its "Wagnerian musical armor" [*Wagnerische Musizierpanzer*] was none other than Richard Strauss.[4]

In composing his autobiographical *Intermezzo* (1916–23), Strauss believed he was developing a new operatic genre that "blazes a path for musical and dramatic composition" for future generations.[5] He envisioned short, open-ended scenes (which he literally called "cinematic pictures") that segu or even dissolve into orchestral interludes.[6] There are no less than thirteen scenes in this two-act opera, which premiered in Dresden (1924); some last no more than three minutes. In the ninety seconds between the first two scenes of the opera, for example, we go from a toboggan slope to a ballroom at a ski-resort inn. Other adjacent scenes take us from an attorney's office to a storm in the Prater, and then back to the composer's home. Space and time, thus, were intended to go beyond the staged scene, and Strauss relied on the symphonic interlude to make coherent the often rapid montage technique – a technique informed by film.

Through cinematic techniques Strauss successfully distances himself from Wagner, for surely a major characteristic of Wagnerian opera is its capacity to expand time. Where a mere glance in *Tristan* can be transformed into a lengthy orchestral passage, film generally aims for temporal compression, where years can become minutes in front of our eyes. Strauss may have failed to shed the Wagnerian "Musizierpanzer" in musical language and style, but his exploitation of innovative dramaturgical techniques that countered such language and style remain one of the most forward-looking and ignored aspects of *Intermezzo*.

By incorporating filmic techniques rather than film itself, however, Strauss avoids this central conflict between opera and cinema: the tension between temporal expansion and compression. How might this dichotomy be resolved if actual film footage played a role in a stage production? The first person to grapple seriously with the problem was Erwin Piscator in the early to mid 1920s. His Berlin productions made extensive use of slide and film projections that formed an integral part of his Marxist, politicized theater. More than anything else, Piscator used film to bring the outside world into the theater. In "Das Theater unserer Zeit," he observed: "When the theater visitor enters the house, the world should not sink behind him, but open up. . . . The connection between film and stage happens not out of the desire for sensationalism or shock effects, but rather with the intention to make vivid the totality of a political world picture."[7]

Piscator recognized film and spoken theater as dissimilar but complementary media; the former was denotative, the latter connotative. Film represented "epic black and white art," while theater embodied the spoken word, the "three-dimensional person."[8] Film's central goal was to thwart the audience's sense of illusion and to break down the expectations of bourgeois theater. C. D. Innes observed that in the early twenties most German critics viewed film as a realistic medium: "In the Weimar Republic, however, when moving pictures were still a novelty and the harsh lighting needed for primitive photographic equipment demanded absolute verisimilitude, the dominant impression was one of accuracy, and the primary value of the camera as far as Piscator was concerned was that it presented art with a new relationship to reality – a characteristic which was emphasized when film was used in conjunction with the artificial conventions of the stage."[9] In short, film – hiding behind an artifice of its own – exposed the artifice of live acting; it undermined subjective preoccupation with the individual on stage.

At first Piscator relied solely on slide projections, which could provide background information or captions projected over each scene. He first used such projections in connection with Alfons Paquet's *Fahnen* (Flags) of 1924. In this instance the purpose of the headline-like projections, which underscored or explained, was to offset, or undercut, an undeniable melodramatic streak in the play. A year later Piscator used film projection for the first time. In *Trotz Alledem!* (Despite all), historical events are documented from the outbreak of World War One through the deaths of Rosa Luxemburg and Karl Liebknecht: Piscator projected documentary footage on a screen behind the stage actors. Such footage played the role of running commentary, or visual footnotes, that continuously placed the individual in the appropriate socio-political context. As time went on, Piscator became more sophisticated in his integration of film and theater, sometimes projecting captions, slides, and film simultaneously, all on different screens.

His production of Ernst Toller's *Hoppla! Wir Leben* (Cheers! We're alive) in 1927 was one of his greatest such successes, and it also exemplifies how conflicting tempi in the diegetic time of film vs. theater could be manipulated to a director's advantage. *Hoppla* centers on a political prisoner sentenced to eight years of incarceration. At the beginning we see him in his padded cell; the film screen is essentially an extension of the cell's back wall. Historical events that occurred during his years of confinement are thus projected behind the prisoner and compressed into a matter of minutes: the Treaty of Versailles, the inauguration of the League of Nations, Mussolini marching on Rome, the Munich Beer-Hall Putsch, the Scopes trial, Lindbergh's solo flight across the Atlantic, the execution of Sacco and Vanzetti, and so on. Alban Berg exploited film similarly in Act II of *Lulu*, where major events during Lulu's year of imprisonment are compressed into a short silent-film montage. Film cues in the score mention her "Arrest," "Detention," "Trial," "In Prison," and the like. In *Lulu*, as in Piscator's earlier attempts, we see a fluidity of time and space in these film backdrops as we move from event to event and from place to place. Moreover, Berg's decision to make the accompanying film score a musical palindrome corresponds directly to the palindromic aspects of the layout of shots.

Piscator's productions from the early to mid-1920s represented the most innovative type of theater in Berlin, and his successes resonated throughout the Weimar Republic. Despite the strong Marxist flavor, these productions dazzled capitalists as well as communists, and his techniques galvanized a young generation of artists from various fields, not excluding opera. Strauss may have invested *Intermezzo* with undeniable innovations, but at age sixty he was unable to jettison the Wagnerian apparatus that had served him so well in the past. More substantial operatic reform would be achieved by the generation of Hindemith, Weill, and Krenek.

FILM AND OPERATIC REFORM

Krenek was one of many who believed that the greatest flaw in Wagnerian opera was the appropriation of stage action to the opera pit. Strauss merely continued the trend, and even Berg's *Wozzeck* represented more an end than a beginning. Krenek almost sounds like Piscator, or even Brecht, when he refers to Stravinsky's *L'Histoire* as a seminal stage work: "[*L'Histoire*] destroys the fictitious integrity of the stage play by exposing it, as it develops, to the critical searchlight of comment, through the agency of a 'reader' who mediates between the public and the spectacle."[10] Of course by the time of *L'Histoire* silent-film audiences had already become accustomed to a "reader" of sorts in the guise of the cinematic intertitle, which blocked the flow of the visual narrative with its blacked-out frame and white lettering commenting on the action.

Filmic intertitles resulted from the demand for greater clarity as cinematic plots became more complicated. Around 1907 some film makers and producers even experimented with the use of a narrator or lecturer who would not only explain the plot beforehand but provide commentary during the projection of the film.[11] The speaker helped to clarify the narrative and, moreover, also served a didactic purpose: he or she edified the movie-going audience. The edifying function of the narrator was seen to be especially important if, for example, the film were based on a great work of literature.

In *Die neue Oper* (1926) Kurt Weill also commented on the contemporary movement away from Wagnerism.[12] He observed a "purification process" during the years immediately following World War I, a process focussing on "absolute music" – rejecting music drama, program music, and large orchestral works. Opera would have to be discovered all over again, and that rediscovery would be the culmination of a process beginning with purely instrumental music, moving to pantomime, ballet, and ultimately opera. The two most fundamental elements of this reformed opera were a musical autonomy for the orchestra and a return to the stage – as opposed to the opera pit – as the focus for the drama. Weill's views were largely informed by the musical-dramatic theories of his teacher Busoni, but the student more successfully translated theory into practice.[13]

The opera orchestra, according to Weill, should not simply illustrate stage events but have its own formal and structural integrity.[14] His earliest explorations in music for the theater involved pantomime, for, as Kim Kowalke suggests, "in pantomime and ballet, Weill could circumvent any obligation to illustrate the dramatic events."[15] Moreover, Weill drew little distinction between music for the stage and that for silent film when addressing this problem of musical autonomy. In an interview of 1927, Weill criticized Edmund Meisel's silent film score to Walter Ruttmann's *Berlin – Die Sinfonie der Großstadt*. The weakness of the score, according to Weill, is that the music tries to illustrate everything; it uses a "melodramatic means" in a documentary idiom. Weill calls for "an objective, simultaneous *konzertante* film music, an [autonomous] creation under the influence of film and not literal illustration."[16] If we were to replace the words "film music" with "operatic music" we would have his views on modern opera in a nutshell.

But why the interest in pantomime in early twentieth-century Germany? There was no strong nineteenth-century pantomime tradition in Germany as in France or England. The cultivation of pantomime in early-Weimar Germany appears to have stemmed from two major and interrelated phenomena: expressionist theater and silent film. In Berlin, at the beginning of the century, Max Reinhardt raised the role of gesture to an unprecedented level of importance on the German stage. His focus on facial expression and body movement as central dramaturgical tools attracted, among others, Hugo von Hofmannsthal, who wrote *Elektra* (1903) with "direct regard" for Reinhardt's *Kleines Theater*. Reinhardt's 1910 production of Friedrich Freska's *Sumurûn*, based on the *Tales of the Arabian Nights*, represents a culmination in this respect, for the entire play is performed in pantomime with music by Victor Hollaender. That *Sumurûn* was viewed as such a novelty suggests how rare pure pantomime was in early twentieth-century Germany.[17]

Reinhardt's influence on expressionist theater was extensive, affecting directors and playwrights alike. One such playwright (and future Weill collaborator) was Georg Kaiser, regarded as the most prolific expressionist of the early twentieth century. The body of his work evinces a steady process of reducing language to its bare essentials, stripping away articles and pronouns, leaving only the most necessary words that suggest the essence of thought, and relying more and more on wordless gesture. From this perspective, pantomime could be seen as a logical outcome of such a process.

While Kaiser and others infused their works with aspects of pantomime, cinema was in its infancy; from the outset silent film would be informed by mimetic features from the stage. There was, indeed, a pronounced "cross-breeding" between theater and cinema during the post-war years – each medium seemed to feed off the other. Paul Bekker observed this phenomenon in 1919, criticizing cinema for employing conventions of the live stage. But he also stressed that recent theater seemed to be aping aspects of cinema: "[The fact that] the stage-poet has already enlisted the colorful material-delight in cinematic mannerisms as artistic effects in his dramaturgical technique exemplifies a phenomenon such as Kaiser. . . . It indicates a symptom . . . of an aesthetic regrouping- and exchange-process that probably operates deeper than current critics are willing to admit."[18]

The year of Bekker's criticism also witnessed the greatest example of the synthesis of film and expressionist theater: *The Cabinet of Dr. Caligari*, a work that exemplifies silent film as the ideal medium for expressionism. It is speechless, it depends entirely upon artificial lighting, it can easily distort visual reality through technical means, and its black and white images allow for stark contrasts. The literature on *Caligari* is vast, and we know that this work influenced not only film, but theater and opera staging; the term "Caligarism" spread throughout Europe shortly after the premiere. Indeed, more than a decade later, Kaiser and Weill still considered the idea of creating a musical version of *Caligari* before settling on *Der Silbersee*.

The mutual influences of screen and stage, including opera and operatic production, were far-reaching. By the mid to late twenties opera houses experimented with cinematic techniques in new works as well as pieces from the standard repertoire. Certain operas were staged in black and white, some used film projections, others employed cinematic "split-screen" effects. During the 1930–31 opera season in Darmstadt, a production of Donizetti's *Lucia di Lammermoor* even imported the intertitles of silent film.[19] Contemporary opera composers such as Weill, Krenek, Hindemith, Max Brand, and others directly or indirectly exploited aspects of cinema. An exploration of each composer's works would go well beyond the intended scope of this essay, but if we examine one composer – Kurt Weill – and three of his stage pieces (*Der Protagonist*, *Royal Palace*, and *Mahagonny Songspiel*), we can see how a composer assimilated cinematic ideas in various ways: pantomime, film projection, and epic montage techniques. All three elements formed a vital part of Weill's quest for operatic reform.

KURT WEILL: *DER PROTAGONIST, ROYAL PALACE, AND MAHAGONNY SONGSPIEL*

Der Protagonist (1925) and *Royal Palace* (1926) represent Weill's earliest operatic undertakings; both address the problem of nonverbal gesture and music's relationship to it as a central issue. In the case of *Der Protagonist*, which premiered in Dresden (1926), the nonverbal gesture is pantomime, something that had preoccupied Weill in the early to mid 1920s. Composing for pantomime (or for film), we recall, represented a way for Weill to assert musical autonomy, a way of ensuring the music's sovereign formal and structural integrity. Not surprisingly, Weill's first theatrical assay, *Die Zaubernacht* (1922), embraced pure pantomime. Based on a fairly-tale scenario by Vladimir Boritsch, *Die Zaubernacht* was commissioned by a Russian ballet troupe. Weill considered this one-act pantomime to be his first mature work, although, as children's theater, it would fail to win a broader audience. Despite *Zaubernacht*'s limited appeal, Georg Kaiser was greatly impressed, and soon he and Weill would try their hand at creating a larger-scale, three-act pantomime of their own. But, as Weill confessed, they soon grew weary of "the silence of the figures"; they ultimately realized that they "had to burst the fetters of pantomime: it had to become an opera."[20]

The final result was the one-act *Protagonist*, an opera structured around two pantomimes – one comic, the other tragic.[21] According to the stage directions, the first one is to be "performed entirely balletically and unrealistically, with exaggerated gestures, in contrast to the second pantomime later, which is to be played dramatically throughout, with vivid expression and passionate movements."[22] In the case of both pantomimes the score consists of continuous music with various gestural cues, although the comic one involves ensemble vocalizing toward the end.

The comic pantomime offers a light-hearted treatment of marital infidelity: "On the left the Wife (2nd player) turns back and entices her husband (the Protagonist) to her with languishing gestures [mm. 3–6]. Eventually the Husband comes and reluctantly accepts her caresses [mm. 12–13]. Then he gives her to understand that he must go out again [19–20]. At this the Wife becomes extremely desperate [m. 22] but finally calms down [m. 26] . . ." Soon the Wife catches her husband in the street serenading another woman sitting at a window. To keep his wife preoccupied, the Husband sends a monk up to spend time with his wife: "From here on, gradually intensifying loveplay. Opposite the Monk and the Wife are similarly occupied [mm. 167–70] . . ."

The second pantomime offers parallel events, but viewed through an expressionistic lens: "On the left the second player, as the Wife, gazes longingly into the street [mm. 3–4]: suddenly she sits up stiffly, because she thinks herself observed [mm. 7–9] – then again cautiously leans out of the window [mm. 12–14]. At once her husband (the Protagonist) appears and assails her with caresses: the Wife resists wearily [mm. 16–17]. The Husband becomes more pressing [m. 22], the Wife increasingly cold and distant [mm. 24–25]. He begins to weep; she mocks him [mm. 31–32]; he begs her on his knees; she pretends to be sleepy [mm. 34–35] . . ."

Afterwards the Husband rushes out to the street where he notices a young woman who takes pity on him, and they make love. But from her window the Husband sees a gentleman enter his wife's dwelling, where they, too, make love. Filled with rage, the Husband rushes back to his home and beats on the door. His rage becomes so pronounced that he is unable to distinguish between his character and his own personality: "This confusion is so upsetting that both players do not know how to go on with the sketch [mm. 160–61] . . ." This expressionistic turn of events continues through the end of the opera, when the Protagonist – having lost all his senses – ends up stabbing his own sister when she tells him that she soon will be married.

Though one cannot say with assurance that these pantomimes were directly influenced by silent film, one can state with confidence that "eyes that ha[d] gone to school to the cinema" did not fail to note their filmic aspects, especially in the tragic, quasi-expressionistic pantomime, where we reach the border of insanity. Hans-Werner Heister finds "Caligari-irrationalism" to be a prevailing context.[23] One critic who attended the premiere of *Der Protagonist*, in fact, expressed a certain weariness with the current emphasis on pantomime, and he squarely blamed cinema: "We have long witnessed the commercialization of mime; even longer the discovery of the film actor, of which this Protagonist reminds us a bit."[24]

Royal Palace, which premiered in Berlin (1927), crosses the border into silent film itself – as one of three surrealistic "visions." Three suitors compete for the favors of the enchanting Dejanira. The first, her husband, promises "the wealthy continent," and in a film fantasy we see her "in Nice, in a Pullman to Constantinople, at a ball, at the Russian ballet, flying to the North Pole, etc." The second ("Yesterday's Lover") offers "the heavens of our nights," and an astrological ballet ensues, capped off by an exotic off-stage vocal duet. "Tomorrow's lover" bestows nothing less than "eternal nature," and in a second fantastic choreography we go from seascape to landscape, where Orpheus himself appears with various natural creatures.

Jazz-like elements, latent in *Der Protagonist*, rise to the surface in *Royal Palace*. Sharp syncopations, evident throughout *Der Protagonist*, now take on a distinct ragtime or foxtrot flavor; the saxophone is featured for the first time in an opera of Weill. In *Royal Palace* these two elements – popular dance rhythms and jazz-like timbres – initially coalesce in the music for the film fantasy, Weill's first attempt at silent-film scoring. After the Husband exclaims, "Ich schenke dir den reichen Kontinent," we hear the anapæstic beep of an automobile horn, which punctuates a ten-bar orchestral passage (based on that rhythm) only to be interrupted by the sound of a honky-tonk piano – a clear homage to the silent-film piano player.[25] Weill would have probably indicated "Foxtrot-Tempo" in a later context, but here it is simply *Allegro un poco tenuto*. Accented by wood block, snare drum, cymbal, and trumpet, the piano soon becomes the syncopated, rhythmic background for a lyrical melody in the saxophone, a sound and a rhythm that seem to foreshadow moments in *Die Dreigroschenoper* (see Example 1.1).

Example 1.1

This film-music sequence marks Weill's first overt reference to American popular music in a stage work.

Krenek's *Jonny spielt auf*, another opera significantly informed by filmic techniques, premiered in Leipzig (1927) only a few weeks before *Royal Palace*. In reviewing both works, Paul Stefan observed that with *Jonny* "Krenek offers the magic of rapidly changing scenes, which come from film; Weill imports these [filmic elements] directly: *Royal Palace* is, in this sense, probably the first film opera."[26] But another critic, Siegfried Günther, asserted that in *Royal Palace* cinematic aspects went beyond the mere incorporation of film, and he surely had those pantomimic "visions" in mind: "Everywhere we notice attempts to construct in a series of closed pictures that have optical roundness and, as a result, are subordinate to filmic laws."[27]

The full score was never published, and both the autograph and the film sequence are lost. But the published piano-vocal score contains a wealth of orchestral indications, and it also provides visual cues for the film sequence, which exhibits a decided fluidity of time and space, though hardly along Piscatorian lines. The surrealistic *Royal Palace* film scene is anything but epic; it does not challenge fantasy, but retreats into it.[28] Thus, we come to a fundamental contradiction: on the one hand, film can be viewed as a realistic medium, able to break the illusion of theater. On the other hand, film is ultimately nothing but illusion, a series of two-dimensional still images on celluloid. This paradox, we recall, was the source of Schoenberg's criticism, which was that in film "one not only sees truth and reality, rather also every appearance . . . that presents itself in a fantastic way as reality."

This problem, pointed out by Schoenberg, may have been one reason that Brecht, whose epic-theatrical works were largely indebted to film, never exploited the actual cinematic apparatus in his staging. Brecht's fascination with low forms of entertainment, including film, is well known, and he probably relished the fact that film, unlike theater, made no attempt to hide its commodity status. From the teens onward, Brecht was intrigued by detective movies and, later, imported American gangster films, generally set in some corrupt urban setting.[29] His admiration for Eisenstein's technique of dialectical montage is well documented, as is his preference for Chaplin's less emotional, more objective and light-hearted style of social criticism in such films as *The Gold Rush*, which exposes capitalism in its most naked form. With his sure sense of timing, gesture, and humor Chaplin manages to reveal a grim human condition without Eisenstein's melodrama.

But Brecht's involvement with film went well beyond the status of spectator. He, of course, learned much about the relationship between film and theater during his period with the Piscator-Bühne, which began in 1927 – the year of *Hoppla! Wir Leben*. But even before that – in the early twenties – Brecht tried his hand at writing full-length silent-film treatments, none of which were ever produced; John Willett stresses the importance of that experience for his later career.[30] One no doubt finds the seeds of Brecht's epic theater in those film scripts. In writing a silent screenplay, Brecht had to work within a format of successive linear segments, he had to rely on gesture rather than speech, and he needed to wrestle with the problem of interpolating titles. All three elements (montage, gesture, titles) were essential to his later work, including the collaborations with Weill.[31]

Brecht's and Weill's first collaboration, the *Mahagonny Songspiel*, premiered in July 1927 at the Deutsche Kammermusik in Baden-Baden.[32] From the very opening pistol shot, it was clear that *Mahagonny* was unique among the Baden-Baden offerings; a correspondent for *Die Musik* called it the *enfant terrible* of the entire festival. The production was co-directed by Brecht and Walter Brügmann, though only Brecht's name was listed on the program. Caspar Neher designed the set as well as costumes. The extent of directorial input by each of these collaborators has not been fully sorted out, but Brecht was very likely a guiding force.[33] Critics who attended the Baden-Baden festival were certainly under that impression.[34] But the overall musical shape and structure of *Mahagonny* was the creation of Weill, who selected five poems from Brecht's *Die Hauspostille*, reordered them, and set them to music. Weill also composed a finale, for which Brecht had written additional text, as well as instrumental interludes that served as connective tissue for these various numbers. The *Songspiel* was set in a boxing ring (undoubtedly Brecht's idea) appointed with barroom furniture. Behind the boxing ring was a screen for pictorial projections by Neher and there was also a large frame ("in some prominent place on one side of the stage") to hold various titles which would be displayed throughout the production. The orchestra, to the left of the boxing ring, was in full view of the audience.

This half-hour work contains no dialogue, and there is no real plot as such, but a sense of narrative flow is attained by the use of projections, titles, and pure gestures, or "actions," as they are called in the production notes.[35] The purpose of the titles is twofold: they can either announce the title of a song or they can can serve an explanatory function – similar to silent film intertitles. Devoid of scenery, we see the imaginary Mahagonny – a city not unlike the rough Klondike town of Chaplin's *Goldrush* (which had created a sensation throughout Germany only a year before) – through the projected drawings of Neher, and they are carefully coordinated with the displaying of titles and singing of songs. But beyond these solo or ensemble songs there was a series of mimetic actions. These specified actions and gestures that were entered into the score read much like a silent film script, and Brecht surely drew from his earlier screenwriting experience.[36]

With these numerous detailed pantomimic actions, coordinated with self-contained musical numbers, Weill had finally achieved his long-desired goal of musical autonomy. He proclaimed: "[With the *Mahagonny Songspiel*] a branch of opera is evolving into a new epic form. . . . Although this form of musical stage work presupposes theatrical music from the outset, it nonetheless ultimately makes it possible to give opera an absolute-musical, even *konzertante* form [the very term Weill used in his film-music interview]. In this and other areas of new opera, it is evident that its musical development achieves a new fertilization from theater-film."[37]

Roland Barthes once described Brecht's epic theater as a series of projections, "each of which possesses a sufficient demonstrative power."[38] Barthes calls each of these projections a "pregnant moment." At the center of the pregnant moment is, of course, the social gestus: "It is a gesture, or a set of gestures (but never gesticulation), in which can be read a whole social situation."[39] In 1928, Russian film director Vsevolod I. Pudovkin stressed that a "film is not *shot*, but *built*, built up from the separate strips of celluloid that are its raw material."[40] The pregnant moment is the "shot," and – in the sense of Pudovkin – Brecht's production of *Mahagonny*, and his other epic works for that matter, are concerned with the coordination of those shots.[41]

Regardless of whether one viewed film as villain, savior, or something in between, the cinema represented a new medium to which older theatrical genres (play, opera, ballet) would unavoidably be compared. It was perhaps equally inevitable that, given German cinema's remarkable exponential growth during the Weimar Republic, film would inform – directly or indirectly – traditional theatrical media. Many who embraced cinema, especially those who sought a new post-war aesthetic, recognized film's equal emphasis on art and technology, as well as its potential to reach a larger audience. The role it played in post-World War One theatrical and operatic reform is undeniable; Weill's search for musical autonomy through the film and pantomime in *Der Protagonist* and *Royal Palace* is but one of many examples. Even the sixty-year-old Strauss recognized that film offered the alternative of montage – of rapidly changing brief scenes – that broke up Wagner's endless melody into short, scenic segments. Later on, this linear succession of wordless, gestural segments would significantly affect the development of epic theater and, ultimately, epic opera such as the *Mahagonny Songspiel*, *Die Dreigroschenoper*, and the *Aufstieg und Fall der Stadt Mahagonny*.

ACKNOWLEDGMENT

An earlier version of this paper was read at the annual meeting of the American Musicological Society in Chicago (November 1991), which included a helpful formal response by Stephen Hinton. Moreover, I am indebted to several colleagues, particularly Jane Gaines, Kim Kowalke, and Kristine Stiles, for their careful reading of the text and useful comments.

2

RETHINKING SOUND: MUSIC AND RADIO IN WEIMAR GERMANY

CHRISTOPHER HAILEY

On the subject of radio, Arnold Schoenberg cautioned in 1930 that this wonder of modern technology

accustoms the ear to an unspeakably coarse tone, and to a body of sound constituted in a soupy, blurred way, which precludes all finer differentiation. One fears, as perhaps the worst thing of all, that the attitude to such sounds will change; until now, one has taken them in, beautiful or otherwise, knowing them to represent the tone peculiar to *one* instrument, and knowing that other sounds also exist – the sounds, that is, of the instrument as it has existed until now. But as they become more and more familiar, one will adopt them as the criterion for beauty of sound, and find inferior the sound of instruments used in art.[1]

With the prescience of hindsight Schoenberg anticipated what he had had more than a decade to observe. Since the end of the First World War newer products of technology had invaded nearly every corner of cultural life and in the process had inexorably altered fundamental modes of perception and expression. Modern modes of communication and travel, from the telephone to the airplane, had revolutionized the business of art and intensified the degree and importance of artistic exchange; recording and film had forever changed the way aural and visual images were preserved and disseminated and had generated new domains of creative activity. For music the most far-reaching post-war development came with the introduction of radio, a medium whose enormous potential – as well as significant limitations – had a profound impact upon the relationship between musicians and audiences, and their currency of communication: sound.[2]

German radio service, inaugurated in October 1923, was administered by the federal postal ministry, or *Reichspost*, which supervised and regulated the technical and legal aspects of broadcasting as well as collecting and allocating the subscriber fees that provided the system's operating costs.[3] By the end of 1924 the Reichspost had licensed private firms (*Rundfunkgesellschaften*) to operate stations in the nine established broadcast zones of Berlin (Funk-Stunde), Leipzig (Mitteldeutscher Rundfunk), Munich (Bayerischer Rundfunk), Frankfurt am Main (Südwestdeutscher Rundfunk), Hamburg (Nordischer Rundfunk), Stuttgart (Süddeutscher Rundfunk), Breslau (Schlesische Funkstunde), Königsberg (Ostmarken-Rundfunk), and

Cologne (Westdeutscher Rundfunk); a tenth, the state-run Deutsche Welle (Berlin), which broadcast to the entire Reich, was added in 1926.[4] That same year a Radio Commissioner (*Rundfunkkommissar*) was appointed to administer an umbrella organization, the Reichs-Rundfunk-Gesellschaft, which coordinated regulations and activities among the various *Rundfunkgesellschaften* and with networks abroad.[5]

German radio grew quickly from a half million subscribers at the beginning of 1925 to well over three million in 1930, becoming, after Great Britain, the second largest radio market in Europe. Each of the German *Rundfunkgesellschaften* created divisions for music, literature, lectures, news and current events, and women's and children's programs to meet the entertainment, educational, and informational needs of their audience. By a judicious system of checks and balances the political and cultural content of the programming was monitored by committees made up of federal and regional representatives. Newspapers and periodicals regularly featured radio schedules and news, and over a dozen journals were devoted entirely to radio and related technologies.[6] In addition, each of the *Rundfunkgesellschaften* published its own profusely illustrated weekly guide with detailed program information, feature articles and interviews, technical news, and advertising.[7]

In his opening address to the seventh annual German radio exhibition in 1930 in Berlin, Albert Einstein praised radio as the herald of "true democracy," a disseminator of knowledge, ideas, and art to the widest possible public.[8] From the outset German radio was administered as a public trust, a technology for the people. "Radio," Einstein continued in his address, "has a unique capacity for reconciling the family of nations. Until now nations got to know one another only through the distorting mirror of the daily press. Radio acquaints them in the most immediate form and from their most attractive side."[9] The most immediately attractive of Germany's broadcast offerings were its musical programs, in which concert and popular fare were well represented. To this end radio stations programmed both recorded and live music, performed by guests or by their own in-house orchestras, choral groups, chamber music ensembles, dance bands, and jazz ensembles. By mid-decade live transmissions of concert and opera performances outside the studio were increasingly common.

While the miracle of broadcast technology dissolved political borders and brought music to regions that had never heard an orchestra, there were those who feared that radio's cultural democracy would mean the death of true art, that its haphazard and catholic repertory would substitute passive for discriminate listening and undermine and dilute musical culture. Arnold Schoenberg, for one, was convinced that radio's "boundless surfeit of music" with its "continuous tinkle, regardless of whether anyone wants to hear it or not, whether anyone can take it in, whether anyone can use it" would in the end lead to the point "where all music has been consumed, worn out."[10] But such grumbling aside, German radio

of the twenties served its large and fractured musical public with remarkable
success given those highly politicized times.

There is symbolic significance in the fact that the beginning of German radio
broadcasting coincided with the convulsive climax of the fledgling Republic's
post-war economic and political unrest. Since the armistice of 1918 rampant inflation had effectively imprisoned Germans within their borders, rendering imports
unaffordable and foreign travel impossible. By 1923 the Reichsmark had entered a
free-fall that took it from 7,525 to the dollar in January to 4,200,000,000,000 to
the dollar at the end of November. It was a year of labor unrest, demonstrations,
strikes, and protests. Political violence, which since 1918 had claimed several
hundred lives, including that of the foreign minister Walter Rathenau in June 1922,
continued to escalate. And on 9 November 1923, the fifth anniversary of the
Revolution that created the Republic, Adolf Hitler unleashed his bloody Munich
Putsch (it was the first occasion on which German radio broadcast political news).
The new Republic appeared on the verge of disintegration when drastic currency
reform, introduced in late November, brought inflation under control and inaugurated a period of relative stability. Just as currency stabilization would provide
Germany with the economic means to participate in the international prosperity
of the mid twenties, the introduction of radio epitomized the country's entry into
a technological world that was levelling the barriers erected by war and inflation.
With the abrupt measures taken to end the nightmarish cycle of inflation it
seemed as if Germany had at last made its break with the pre-war world whose
vestiges had lingered on into the early post-war years.

Music, an art form central to Germany's cultural identity, had been among the
most fiercely contested terrains of that initial post-war period. After the debilitating
dislocations of the war musical life had rebounded with remarkable resilience. In
fact, the activity was frenetic, even chaotic, and amid an overabundance of concerts
and festivals – and the abolition of censorship – new music was cultivated with
abandon. The generation that came to power in German politics, the generation
of Friedrich Ebert (1871–1925) and Gustav Stresemann (1878–1929), likewise
assumed responsibility for its musical life. It was the generation of Leo Kestenberg
(1882–1962), who as advisor to the Prussian Ministry of Culture helped reshape
the musical life of the German capital and the far-flung Prussian provinces; the
generation of critics such as Adolf Weissmann (1873–1929) and Paul Bekker
(1882–1937), who were persuasive advocates for new music in their reviews and
books; and the generation of composers such as Ferruccio Busoni (1866–1924),
Arnold Schoenberg (1874–1951), and Franz Schreker (1878–1934), who had
consolidated their mastery and now began to win their place in the repertory.

It was between this generation and the one following, that of Ernst Toch
(1887–1964), Max Butting (1888–1976), Paul Hindemith (1895–1963), and Kurt

Weill (1900–1950) – composers who had cut their teeth on Strauss and Mahler, impressionism and expressionism, and were now groping their way past their teachers – that the fissures first appeared that would become the aesthetic faultlines of the later twenties. Compare, for instance, the opening measures of Schreker's *Kammersymphonie* of 1916 (Example 2.1) with the beginning of Hindemith's *Kammermusik No. 1* of 1921 (Example 2.2). In Schreker (*Langsam, schwebend*) an ambiguous neighbor-note figure floats above a gossamer filigree of harp, celesta, harmonium, and piano in gentle, pulsing undulation; in Hindemith (*Sehr schnell und wild*) that filigree texture has become an agitated assault by strings and piano into which the flute, clarinet, cello, and harmonium plunge with aggressive vehemence. Schreker's work reduces and refines the sound of the nineteenth-century orchestra; Hindemith gives orchestral muscle to chamber music. Schreker veils and attenuates traditional symphonic form and gestures; Hindemith challenges inherited forms and syntax and, with the inclusion of a cheeky foxtrot in the last movement, upsets aesthetic hierarchies as well.

Schreker's score is music for the urban concert hall, Hindemith's an allusion to the bustling life outside; its foxtrot anticipates the shimmy, Boston, and ragtime of the composer's Opus 26 piano suite *1922*, whose first edition cover drawing shows a precarious intersection of busses, carts, electric trams, bicycles, automobiles, and harried pedestrians. Indeed, these were the very years that composers such as George Antheil and Edgard Varèse began scoring their works with artifacts of modern life ranging from whistles and sirens to bicycle bells and airplane engines. To Adolf Weissmann the energetic muscularity of the music of this unruly generation, as well as its passion for sports and technology, were an outgrowth of the experience of mechanized war and the sheer physicality of modern life.[11] The aesthetic of the machine heralded by the pre-war Futurists had become a reality: the motoric, metallic, percussive qualities of post-war music seemed to mirror life's accelerated tempo, its spirited commerce, heavy industry, mass transit systems, and swelling urban populations.[12]

As the nightmare of inflation receded the exuberant energies of this early post-war period were gradually reined in and channelled. After the revolutions of the previous two decades – the tortured confessions of pre-war expressionism and the wild experimentation that followed – there was a reaction in the arts that paralleled the neoclassical movements in France and Italy. *Neue Sachlichkeit*, first applied to painting, was a term coined to describe a broadly felt need for clarity, sobriety, and stability. Music was no longer to be a vehicle for expressing ideas and emotions but a neutral medium of sound obeying its own phenomenological laws and expressing only itself.

One is tempted to draw causal links between the political and economic stability of the mid twenties and these contemporaneous developments in aesthetic philosophy. In truth the reaction that was *Neue Sachlichkeit* was neither as abrupt

Example 2.1 Schreker: opening of *Kammersymphonie* (1916)

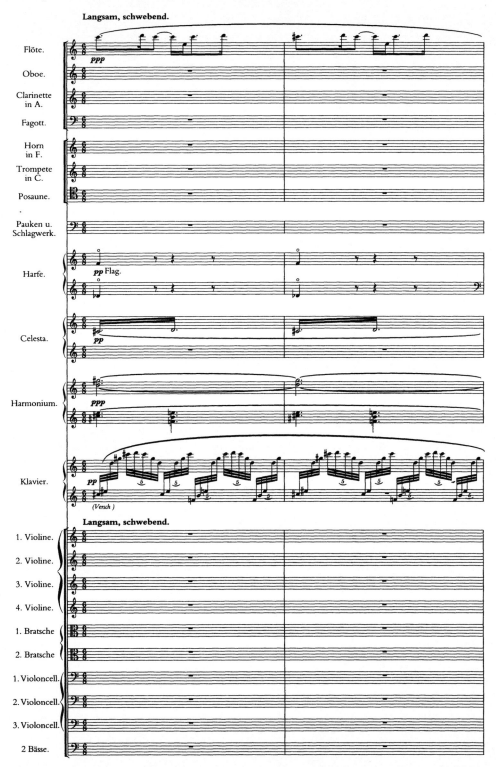

Example 2.2 Hindemith: opening of *Kammermusik No. 1* (1921)

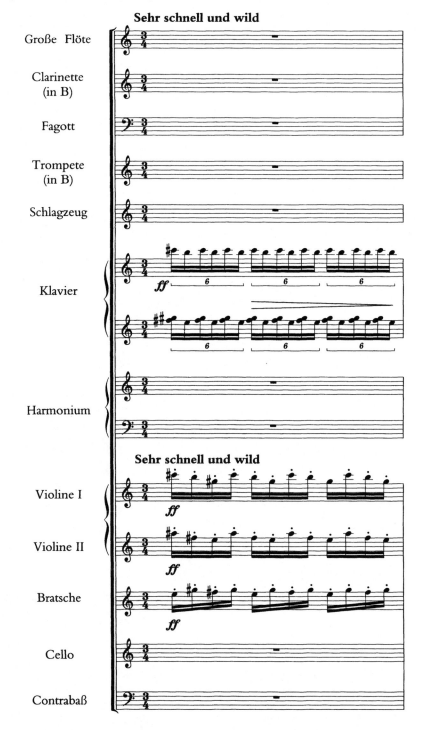

Hindemith Kammermusik No. 1, Opus 24, No. 1
© B. Schott's Söhne, Mainz, 1922, © renewed Schott & Co. Ltd, London.
All Rights Reserved. Used by permission of European American Music Distributors
Corporation, sole US and Canadian agent for Schott & Co. Ltd, London.

nor as unprepared as appearances suggest. Already in 1917 Paul Bekker had observed in movements as diverse as cubism and expressionism, in composers as different as Schoenberg and Schreker, a common search for new, medium-specific values.[13] Implicit in this longing for organic unity and purity of purpose was a critique of romanticism's aesthetic of multiplicity, of the ideal of the *Gesamtkunstwerk*. Post-war *Sachlichkeit* was less a reaction than an outgrowth and re-direction of those impulses that sought to locate and reinvigorate energies latent within the materials of each artistic discipline.[14] Thus the emotive extremes of expressionism in art gave line and color an expressive autonomy that inspired post-war formalism, just as the harmonic vocabulary of Schoenberg's post-war "structuralist" serialism was fed by the "expressionist" energies of his pre-war atonality. By the mid twenties phenomenology, not hermeneutics, was the focus of aesthetic investigation. "Form," Paul Bekker wrote in 1923, "is material taking shape according to its own *immanent* laws and serving no other purpose than the presentation of this material and this material alone."[15]

When Bekker wrote these words he was describing what he heard and saw taking shape in the music and ideas of that younger generation of Hindemith, Toch, and Weill. From the notion of *Gebrauchsmusik* to the passing fashion of the *Zeitoper*, stylistic and aesthetic choices were increasingly guided by the inquiry into music's material attributes.[16] While political and economic factors played their role in fostering this transformation, new sound technologies were a no less compelling factor. Through recording and radio Bekker and his contemporaries were being influenced in a way that affected not only *what* they heard, but *how* they heard.

Just as photography and film had radically transformed the parameters of literary and artistic theory and practice, the dramatic developments in musical aesthetics and compositional practice are scarcely explicable without the conceptual and practical stimuli provided by the technologies of sound recording and transmission. The science of mechanical reproduction was revolutionizing fundamental premises of aural perception by offering the means of fixing a reality hitherto subject only to direct experience, and exposing that experience to dispassionate and de-contextualized reexamination.[17] Recording and radio had an incalculable effect upon music, an art whose transience is one of its intrinsic qualities. From that moment in 1877 when Edison first captured the sound of his own voice, sound lost its privileged claim to the Romantic's sympathies as the ultimate metaphor for that intensity of experience which knows no recall. In obeying Faust's injunction to the moment to abide, the phonograph fatally undermined music's eloquent testimony to our impotence to arrest the decay of time.

If the phonograph redefined music's relation to time, the radio revolutionized conceptions of space. That an event could be experienced instantly and simultaneously throughout the country was a conceptual breakthrough of the first order.

Recording, in preserving an event, made that event a tangible commodity capable of preservation, transport, and recall; it objectified the musical experience and rendered it something historic and static. Radio, on the other hand, served as a mediator of the moment. By its temporal and spatial immediacy radio intensified the experience of that moment with telling consequences across the full range of musical experience.

It is in the nature of cultural history that such insights are not articulated immediately, but rather insinuate themselves by increments. In Germany, where scientists and inventors had over the preceding century made many of the key discoveries that led to modern communications technologies[18] and where the musical machines such as those described by E.T.A. Hoffmann were a central component of romantic speculation, the inroads of technology excited significant artistic and philosophical resonance, especially after 1923, the year that radio was introduced and recording shifted from an acoustic to an electric process.[19] The technology of acoustic recording had been relatively straightforward, a purely mechanical procedure, directly related to the rise and fall of a diaphragm. Electrical recording was an altogether more sophisticated process, though it did not alter the outward appearance and operation of the recording, whose messages were still capable of being decoded by purely mechanical means. The phonograph record is a tangible and conceptually straightforward storage system that demands little of the person seeking to retrieve its information (though the rituals of preserving and playing records are an important component of the experience). The radio, on the other hand, transformed tangible sound waves into invisible electrical energy that was to be transmitted by wireless signal and then converted back into wave form.[20]

Because its technology was significantly more sophisticated and the listener physically removed from the source of sound, the radio was shrouded in the kind of mystery that the phonograph lacked. If this remove from any tangible sound source would seem to have made listening to the radio more passive than playing a record, the process of radio listening was in some ways considerably more involved. After a March 1930 Berlin radio performance of Schoenberg's *Von heute auf morgen* the composer's daughter, who had heard the broadcast in Mödling near Vienna, captured something of the flavor of an evening with the radio in a letter to her father:

I am so excited about the opera that I have to write to you right away. Unfortunately we were a bit nervous when tuning in and there was a lot we did not hear very well. But what we heard was marvelous! . . . In spite of the poor transmission one had the impression it was a wonderful performance, especially toward the end. The duet was unfortunately almost inaudible; it seems to have been tuned into another frequency because of the other German station, and even though, out of sheer panic that at the last minute we might miss it, we spent the entire afternoon with booming men's choruses and brass bands, "Wacht am Rhein," etc., from the moment the opera began the signal was soft and fluctuated continuously. . . . We thought of you all day, more than ever: now he's getting dressed, now he's glad he doesn't have to wear evening dress, or should he wear evening dress after all? and were as nervous as if it were just next door. That's radio for you, for me it's one big magic box.[21]

Magic it may have been, but Gertrud Schoenberg's letter reveals that the radio technology of the 1920s often promised more than it delivered. Most stations had a limited broadcast range and all were subject to signal interference ranging from atmospheric conditions to neighboring frequencies, local electrical works, or even a passing streetcar. In the early days one listened to the radio with a headset, but by the later twenties the introduction of amplifier tubes and built-in speakers transformed listening into a social activity. Adjusting antennae and tuning in a distant station required considerable patience, ingenuity, and expertise from the dedicated "radio amateur," though good reception was often more subject to luck than skill. And even the best reception was often little compensation for the inherent defects of the medium. Alban Berg, who tuned in to that same broadcast of *Von heute auf morgen*, appears to have had a stronger signal but had to confess to Schoenberg that it had been an "incomplete experience" because, although the voices came through loud and clear, the bass instruments (unless playing *forte*) were all but inaudible.[22]

Berg's "incomplete experience" had less to do with reception than with the technical limitations of the recording microphone. In its early days radio had a particularly difficult time reproducing the upper frequencies, which include the overtones that make up the timbral characteristics differentiating the various instruments. As a result a violin often became indistinguishable from a flute. On the other end of the spectrum low instruments such as the tuba, trombone, cello, or double bass either were lost entirely or, at high volume, became muddy and unintelligible. Sometimes the fault lay in microphone placement, and many experiments in the radio studios and laboratories focussed on creating the kind of acoustic ambience to which the microphone might best respond. But even if the signal source could be amplified and transmitted without significant frequency distortion, the inadequacies of the receiving equipment remained a vexing source of distortion.[23] Thus for a variety of reasons intrinsic and extrinsic to the medium, the accurate reproduction of sound remained an elusive goal throughout the first decade of radio technology. And yet it was this collection of defects that accounted for some of radio's most significant influence in redefining conceptions of instrumental timbre, repertoire, compositional style, performance practice, concert hall acoustics, and the aesthetic premises of the concert experience itself.

One of the first effects of radio was to alter a number of traditional instrumental assumptions. The flutist Alfred Lichtenstein, a specialist in contemporary music, pointed out that the shortcomings of his instrument, which lacked both the passion of the clarinet and the chaste austerity of the oboe, were the very qualities that made it ideal for the microphone. What were expressive deficiencies in the concert hall, he wrote in a 1931 article, through radio took on the virtue of a cool, pure tone that stood out clearly against any texture.[24] Indeed, Lichtenstein argued that woodwind characteristics were in general accentuated rather than suppressed by the microphone, making radio an ideal advocate for a repertory of chamber music, which had heretofore been a stepchild of concert programming. Lichtenstein went further to envision radio as a catalyst for commissioning works for new or unusual instrumental combinations unthinkable in the concert hall; his particular passion was the saxophone quartet with harp.

Of all the musical emblems of the twenties, none had more contemporary currency than the saxophone. From the Otto Dix triptych *The Metropolis* to the cover of Krenek's *Jonny spielt auf*, the image of the saxophone seemed to appear everywhere as the symbol of the "jazz age." The composer Alexander Jemnitz noted how this instrument, virtually ignored since its invention in 1840, had suddenly become "the most popular wind instrument of our time," thanks, he wrote, "to an indefinable but no less uncontestable timbral topicality [*Klangfarben-aktualität*]."[25] Surely the saxophone's *Klangfarbenaktualität* had a good deal to do with those qualities that endeared it to the broadcast microphone, both as a solo instrument and, as Lichtenstein suggested in his article, as a connecting link between the horns and woodwinds.

Because of the microphone's finicky instrumental affinities certain repertories were ill served by broadcast. Music with full textures, a succession of dense chordal sonorities, or timbrally differentiated melodies, for instance, were a lost cause. This meant that most late nineteenth-century symphonic works were unsuitable unless substantially re-orchestrated and lightened in texture, and even the piano and chamber music of that period tended to suffer in clarity.[26] On the other hand, the microphone responded well to the classical and pre-classical repertory that so inspired the neoclassicism and *Neue Sachlichkeit* of the twenties. Not surprisingly, modern music, as Arnold Schoenberg commented in 1933, was likewise preeminently suited for broadcast because of its typically "thin" scoring.[27] Max Butting made much the same observation when he wrote that "a number of scores by our younger composers look as if they were written specifically for the radio,"[28] noting elsewhere that the radio's fundamental requirements corresponded exactly with those precepts deemed appropriate for music in general.

To Lichtenstein, Butting, and other performers and composers radio, which had no fixed repertory and an insatiable appetite for music, seemed destined to play a central role in propagating contemporary music.[29] Schoenberg, who held radio responsible for sinking concert attendance, felt the medium had a moral obligation to serve as a forum for new music. In 1933 his modest proposal was for two hours of air time a week,[30] but already by 1930 several stations (including Berlin, Frankfurt, and Königsberg) regularly exceeded that goal.[31] Indeed, radio had moved beyond cultivating a pre-existent contemporary repertory to creating one of its own. Following the fifth German radio exhibition in 1928 the Reichs-Rundfunk-Gesellschaft authorized funds for individual stations to commission works written specifically for the radio. The first to be written and broadcast (on 17 January 1929) was Franz Schreker's *Kleine Suite für Kammerorchester*, commissioned by the Schlesischer Rundfunk (Breslau). Among the commissions that followed were Josef Matthias Hauer's cantata *Vom Leben* (Königsberg); a song cycle *Vorspiel und Arie nach Danthenday*, Op. 84, by Paul Graener (Leipzig); Hindemith's *Kammermusik*, Op. 46, No. 2; Ernst Toch's *Bunte Suite für Orchester*, Op. 48; Weill's *Berliner Requiem* (Frankfurt); and Max Butting's *Sinfonietta mit Banjo* and *Heitere Musik für kleines Orchester*, Op. 38 (Berlin). Eventually dozens of composers wrote radio works during the Weimar period, but perhaps the most talked about work of the era was the *Lindberghflug* on a text by Bertolt Brecht set jointly by Hindemith and Weill and first broadcast under Hermann Scherchen in Berlin in July 1929.[32]

Another dramatic development that grew out of radio technology was early experimentation with electronic music. In 1928 the Berlin Musikhochschule, in coordination with the electronics firm Siemens & Halske, opened the *Rundfunkversuchsstelle*, an electronic music studio for electro-acoustic research. Hindemith, Max Butting, and Friedrich Trautwein (inventor of the trautonium) were among the composers and technicians who made use of the facility and produced a small body of electronic music, as well as exploring ways in which recording and radio transmission could be used for performance and pedagogy. While primitive by today's standards, these works and experiments provided conceptual stimulation for re-thinking all aspects of musical experience. They were also the focus of intense and sometimes highly politicized debates over "mechanical music," which conservatives framed as a cultural battle between traditional spiritual values and soulless materialism. Ernst Toch, among the first to experiment with mechanical instruments and artificially created recording masters, ardently defended the materiality and artistic potential of mechanical music. He spoke with fervor about a crystalline music removed from human intervention and offering "a degree of exactitude that can never be attained by human agency; the complete factualization, the complete de-personalization of performance, nothing slips in by way of pitch, meter, rhythm, tempo, or dynamics that is not fixed in the *notes*: every trace of spontaneity, of sentiment, of impulse is driven out."[33] The implications of this new musical world would not be fully realized until a generation later with the introduction of magnetic tape and computers, but Toch's radical vision of technology's influence is evident even in those domains where human agency remained operative.

Nowhere is the junction between music phenomenology and radio technology more evident than in the vocabulary associated with the efforts to create a repertory of radio music. "Sachgemäß" (appropriate), "arteigene" (characteristic), and "materialbestimmte" (materially defined) are among the adjectives that return repeatedly to describe a music so wedded to the technology of its transmission that the technology's constraints and limitations become a part of its structural and expressive content. The concept of "funkeigene Musik," or radio-specific music, was naturally predicated upon avoiding the limitations and exploiting the strengths of the medium. The organizers of the 1929 Chamber Music Festival in Baden-Baden, which was to have radio music as one of its themes, formulated guidelines that advised composers of radio compositions to employ clear structures, open textures, well-spaced chords, and restraint in the use of the horns and large percussion instruments.[34] In his 1930 article on the relationship of the creative musician to the radio Max Butting, one of the pioneers of radio music, stressed the importance of a strong rhythmic profile and intelligible phrasing, and warned of the dangers of muddy bass lines, an over-dominating treble, and the tendency of middle-range instruments to recede into a blur. Following such advice and the dictates of their own experience with radio, composers tended to favor woodwinds and high brass, to avoid massed string effects, and to use low brass with care. Such music generally placed greater emphasis on rhythm and accent, kept counterpoint simple, and refrained from overly differentiated timbral or dynamic effects.

Of the composers to receive those first radio commissions, Franz Schreker seems perhaps the most puzzling choice since his music was often criticized for its lack of thematic profile and rhythmic vigor, its lush textures and dependence upon timbral refinement. But Schreker had had years of experience in both recording and radio studios and had developed considerable expertise regarding questions of microphone placement, orchestral balance, tempo modification, and phrasing. He regularly conducted his own music on radio and despite a resistance to the medium Kurt Weill once singled out Schreker's broadcast performance of his own *Vorspiel zu einem Drama* precisely for its "fine timbral sense" (*feiner Klangsinn*).[35]

It is a testimony to Schreker's sensitivity to the medium that his *Kleine Suite* proved such a satisfying debut for the new compositional genre of *Rundfunkmusik*. What is more, it is apparent that Schreker's encounter with the microphone during the twenties played a significant role in transforming his style. A comparison of the characteristic *Schreker-Klang* of the opening of the *Vorspiel zu einem Drama* (1913; Example 2.3) and the ascetic beginning of the "Intermezzo" from *Die kleine Suite* (1928, Example 2.4) provides an optical and aural snapshot of two contrasting eras, two diverging sets of compositional premises. Both works open with chordal juxtapositions in the treble over a sensuously writhing melodic line in a lower register. The D major/B♭ minor oscillation in the upper strings, piano,

Example 2.3 Schreker: opening of *Vorspiel zu einem Drama* (1913)

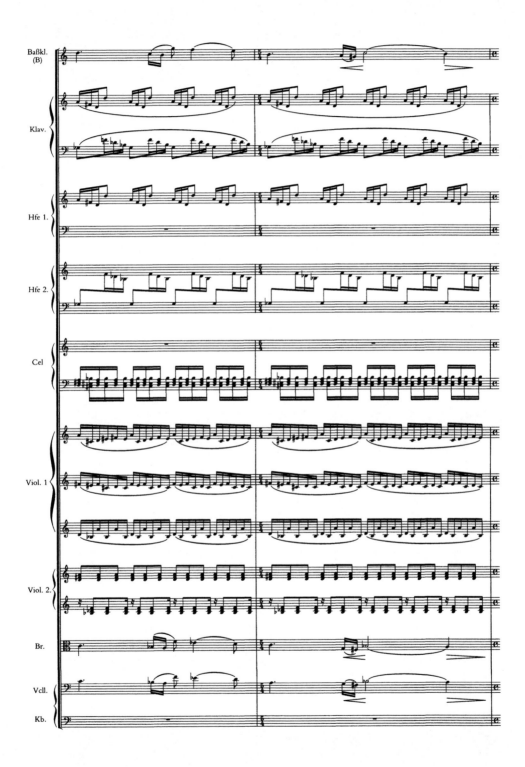

Example 2.4 Schreker: *Die kleine Suite* (1928), "Intermezzo," mm. 1–8

harps, and celesta in the opera overture furnishes a rich aural cushion for the melody in the cellos, violas, and B♭ bass clarinet. In the "Intermezzo" the same gesture has been reduced to an alternation of minor thirds a half step apart in the harps while a B♭ clarinet and saxophone in C are melodically joined in the middle register. The delicately massed orchestral sound has become a transparent web of soloists in which each new instrumental timbre (including the solo flute, horn, and upper strings in succeeding measures) is added with care.

What is striking is the frequent correspondence between compositional techniques of the new music of the twenties and the needs – and limitations – of the microphone. Ernst Krenek, though not entirely sympathetic with the goal of creating a radio-specific music, observed in 1930 that composers were beginning to treat radio's defects, its "deviations from reality" (*Abweichungen von der Wirklichkeit*), as unique properties, thus creating "a new material, which presents certain special features found nowhere else."[36] But Schreker's "Intermezzo" is far more than an accommodation to the limitations of the radio microphone; it is a creative response to a new medium, an inspired adaptation by a composer of the older generation to a dimension of musical experience that was becoming as important as the timbral qualities of orchestral instruments and the acoustic properties of the concert hall. It is telling that Schreker's other works of this period, the operas *Christophorus* (1925–27; 1928–1929) and *Der singende Teufel* (1927–28), as well as the 1927 orchestration of his 1923 Whitman cycle *Vom ewigen Leben* exhibit qualities no less characteristic of that "sound of the time" so eminently suited to radio broadcast.

Such examples of correspondence between "radio style" and general tendencies in new music led Max Butting to conclude that the experience of radio had had a direct influence upon compositional technique ("and be it only in accelerating the rejection or adoption of certain details") in such areas as rhythm, dynamics, polyphony, texture, and instrumentation.[37] Butting suggests that the elimination of horns from many contemporary scores was an example of an instrument whose sonorous properties were patently out of step with the "sound of the time." What better example of the collision of technological requisites and aesthetic preference than the disappearance of this mainstay of the romantic orchestra, so evocative of the forest and so ideally suited to the rich resonance of the opera houses and concert halls of the nineteenth century, and so alien to the dry, crystalline clarity of the radio microphone?

The radio's constrictions upon style and technique inevitably affected compositional aesthetics as well. Butting observed that the microphone, because it was less responsive to timbral finesse, encouraged composers to think in terms of abstract musical ideas freed from dependence upon "the sensuous aspects of sound" (*das Sinnliche des Klanges*).[38] The radio, he maintained, demanded "clarity, directness, and precision" (*Klarheit, Eindeutigkeit und Präzision*).[39] Hermann W. von Waltershausen likened radio to black-and-white film, in which the expressive limitations were likewise an impetus to stylization.[40] "Every art form," he continued, "has, so to speak, its black and white; this is always austerity, honesty, directness, *Sachlichkeit* in the good and true sense, this means *Sachlichkeit* with regard to the question of style. . . . Consciousness of music's black and white will have the effect of a purifying bath."[41] Butting contended that the style of radio was in essence "epic"; over the loudspeaker musical argument and narrative captured the imagination in a way static description could not.[42] Thus the aesthetic premises of the radio were fully attuned to the objective spirit of an age in which the "urgency of the matter-of-fact" (*Eindringlichkeit des Sachlichen*) had replaced grand rhetorical flourishes, and chamber music had supplanted the grandiloquence of the nineteenth-century orchestra.[43]

The orchestra and its audiences were reflected in the halls in which music was made and here, too, the microphone was abetting the erosion of old aesthetic attitudes. The resonant nineteenth-century concert hall bathed a community of listeners in ambient sound that blended even a large and variegated orchestra into a sonorous whole. The analytical microphone dissolved the ambient illusion as well as the acoustic necessity for that community. By 1930 a new generation of concert halls was being constructed on principles that stressed not resonant reverberation but clarity. While this was primarily a function of larger hall size, it also reflected shifting tastes in the experience of sound. As with the microphone, the acoustic properties of these new halls responded well to the astringent angularity of new music. What is more, these new acoustic spaces, together with the microphone, were also having a significant impact upon performance practice, as Michael Forsyth neatly explains in his illuminating study *Buildings for Music*:

> With the advance of electronic recording musicians for the first time could listen objectively to their own playing – and they did not like what they heard. Early phonograph recordings reveal prewar musicianship to be highly idiosyncratic – the charming, hurried style of Fritz Kreisler, the moan at the end of a phrase of Caruso, the mannered practice of joining the notes of a melody by extensive use of *glissando*. This expressive style of playing blended with the mellow tone of the older concert hall to produce individual performances of unparalleled excitement and charm, but when exposed in the "designed" acoustics of the hi-fi concert hall and heard at close quarters in the living room on record, prewar musical style and orchestral ensembles were frequently revealed as technically ragged and musically quaint. As the critic Desmond Shawe-Taylor has said of the Royal Festival Hall, it "tidied up London orchestral string playing overnight."[44]

To reevaluate music's space is to re-think its audience and to ask how it listens and should be addressed. One of the conundrums of radio lay in the disjunction between aural presence and visual absence. Radio dissolved the space between performer and audience and denied them a place of mutual interaction, thereby disrupting the I/thou relationship of the live performance. "The I and the universe suddenly stand face to face," was Wolfgang Martini's exalted formulation in 1925. "One cannot deny that therein resides a new grandeur. A grandeur that corresponds exactly with the grandeur one finds everywhere in the works of technology: in the dirigible, in the giant steamship, in the skyscraper, in short, everywhere. It is the grandeur of exact precision."[45] The consequences for performance practice were immediate and far-reaching, as radio announcers were the first to learn. Vilma Mönckeberg observed how ruthlessly the radio exposed the "Schausprecher," or visual speakers, "who do not work from the material of 'language,' as the sculptor works with stone, but derive their effects from other domains."[46] Accordingly Hans Mersmann, in terms remarkably similar to Butting's advice to composers, advised radio lecturers to stick to the point, avoid high-flown rhetoric and unnecessary digression, make concise transitions, and combine concentration of content with facility and intelligibility.[47]

Musicians likewise had to learn that the dramatic flourishes and physical gestures that worked so well in the concert hall were meaningless in front of the microphone. Without physical gestures and the forgiving acoustic of the concert hall all vocal imperfections were cruelly exposed, not to mention the simple fact that excessive movement in front of the microphone affected the quality of the sound.[48] Alfred Lichtenstein turned the equation around by suggesting that the radio performer, freed from the disturbances of the live performance, could at last concentrate on producing a beautiful tone and an interpretation uninfluenced by audience approval or reserve. "The substance of every musical performance," Frank Warschauer wrote in 1926, "is solely that which objectifies itself in pure sound."[49]

Many composers and performers recognized how their aesthetic sensibilities were being altered by the experience of technology. To Lichtenstein the new developments in performance technique were clear evidence of the age's "striving for objectivity,"[50] while for Wolfgang Martini, writing at a time when the headset made the ear one with the unblinking microphone, listening itself had taken on a new degree of objectivity; with time, he felt, the effects would be felt upon contemporary musical style: "Radio," he concluded, "de-sentimentalizes."[51]

It is this de-sentimentalized, sober world that Adolf Weissmann described in his *Entgötterung der Musik* of 1928. It was a "de-romanticized" world in which machines such as the airplane were shrinking the distances upon which romanticism had thrived. By obliterating the space that in the concert hall separated the artist from his audience the aural experience was intensified and focussed not on the personality of the artist but on the performance, which the clinical mercilessness of the interposed microphone laid bare to critical scrutiny. The radio performance was thus less a showcase for interpretation and personality than a vehicle for a text in which the ideal performance was the transparent mediation of that text. Performance as expressive communication (in which the multiple dimensions of the concert experience played a role) became performance as a conveyor of immanent structural tensions. The aesthetic implications for the way we listen to music are with us to this day.[52]

In 1930 Leo Kestenberg wrote of the fruitful interaction between art's longing for expression and technology's yearning for form. Art breaks into the realm of technology, he asserted, when it creates its form and expresses its content out of the very essence of the technology itself. "The first stage of this process of incorporating art [into technology] is in the naive aesthetic pleasure in the machine, in material in motion. The highest stage is reached when the technical means are subsumed, indeed disappear in artistic form."[53] The productive legacy of radio technology for the music of Weimar Germany lay in the stimulating discrepancy between what was promised and what was delivered. In its infancy radio was anything but a straightforward, transparent medium of transmission. The poor quality of early broadcasts demanded the listener's commitment and aural involvement to compensate for shortcomings of transmission, and performers, composers, and programmers had to adjust their aims to the limitations of the microphone. Radio was a "hot" medium that demanded significant technological and imaginative interaction. The medium's flaws, its technological opacity, as it were, provided not only its creative challenges but in many instances defined its conceptual potential. Beyond bringing musicians to rethink technical, interpretive, and creative premises, the radio schooled a generation in new ways of hearing, just as subsequent developments in magnetic tape, stereophonic sound, computers, and digital recording have inevitably altered the modes and strategies of aural perception of later generations. If today it seems that technology has become increasingly invisible, that the perceived discrepancy between "real" and "mechanically mediated" sound has diminished to the point of insignificance, this is not solely the function of technical advances toward increasingly faithful reproduction. As the German experience of radio in the 1920s suggests, it is also the result of a process by which the human ear has redefined its needs and expectations to accommodate a new partner in the experience of sound.

3

"OVERCOMING ROMANTICISM": ON THE MODERNIZATION OF TWENTIETH-CENTURY PERFORMANCE PRACTICE

ROBERT HILL

. . . a lady asked me to which of two existing schools of teaching I adhere, to that which makes you play in time or to that which makes you play as you feel. I had to think for a moment before I said: "Can't one feel in time?"[1]

> Artur Schnabel (1882–1951)

Three main currents dominate our musical life . . . the classical-romantic . . . the radical-modern and the retrospective-historical . . . like the radical-modern current, the retrospective-historical too wants, in its own way, to lead from the known and habitual into new worlds. . . . It appears, at all events, that we are reaching the fulfillment of the two movements whose roots lie in the Romantic. Not for nothing do we hear word of the "Overcoming of Romanticism"; on the other hand it cannot be pure chance that "objectivity" is to the utmost degree a property of medieval music. To be sure, there is a measure of exaggeration in these slogans of our time, nonetheless, they do reflect actual developmental tendencies.[2]

> Jacques Handschin (1927)

In the period immediately following the First World War, a new spirit seized the imagination of the Western mind. A profound cultural paradigm shift, one that had been gathering momentum for many decades, finally achieved critical mass. This spirit of modernism made itself felt – for better and for worse – in all areas of society. As the organization and operation of factories and businesses were streamlined in accordance with principles of efficiency, productivity increased, but so, too, did automation, unemployment, and worker disaffection. Scientific breakthroughs made science for a time seem capable of solving the problems of mankind, yet it has only emerged as a cure often more dangerous than the disease. The dark side of modernism becomes increasingly apparent only as its unfulfilled dreams assume gloomy proportions in our picture of the experience of our own century, as we witness the alienation of man from himself, his environment, his fellow man.

The alienation that accompanied modernism as it established itself seems to have gripped artists first – they are society's "canaries in the mineshaft" – then society at large. The displacement of centuries-old hierarchic social structures and the political disorientation in the aftermath of World War One left Weimar Germany, in particular, grasping for stable images of its cultural identity. The artists found what they were looking for with the Bach and Handel revivals, which satisfied the need for spiritually intact heroic national figures. The increasing emphasis on a canon of tonal works by deceased composers, and the emerging interest in historical performance practice can be seen in a similar light. We, the children of the twentieth century needed an uncorrupt authority that would confirm to us our differences from the world that had been shattered by the First World War. We assembled a rational and satisfying picture of the music and performance practice of the distant past. We scrutinized this picture with finely honed scientific tools, and pronounced it "authentic". In other words, the job of understanding the picture came to mean: fill in the blanks as they became apparent, and strip off the varnish of the nineteenth century to reveal bright, intense, highly direct, but rather unmysterious images of the past in the countenance of our modern-day performance practice.

That in so doing we remake the music of the past in our own image is a facet of the problem we could ignore as long as the modernist myth of objectivity held up. It appears, though, that humanistic disciplines are waking up to a fundamental truth recognized by physicists a good half century ago: we can never escape our own subjectivity; the act of measurement alters the thing being measured. Attempting to conceal our presence as observers, we deceive ourselves. Recently, members of the musicological community have begun to acknowledge this point of view.[3] Yet it is not enough that musicologists reflect on the intellectual integrity of their discipline. We accept the privileged status accorded scientists in our civilization. As stewards of culture, we have a responsibility to communicate our new awareness of the limits of objectivity to the classical-music community at large.

Since the 1920s, performers and music teachers have been conditioned by musicologists and critics to aspire to ideally objective readings of musical texts. That now emerges as an illusory goal. Nonetheless, the now compromised notion of scientific "progress" still informs the modern performance-practice attitude – and quite unabashedly so – in both traditionalist and historicist quarters (in the latter it partly serves commercial interests in the form of "new and improved" performance practice). Having been told for three-quarters of a century that positivist standards of detachment and objectivity are unqualifiedly valid when dealing with texts transmitting the music of the past, it should not surprise us to find that musicians lacking scholarly training all too often receive the concept of objectivity in terms of a literalist view of notation.

Since the First World War, "conscionable" standards of musicianship have come to be equated with the avoidance of "romantic" behaviors in musicianship. What began as *Neue Sachlichkeit* has consolidated itself as a rigorous dogma which for more than half a century has governed in a constraining way the artistic behavior of classical musicians. We measure competence by our skill at maintaining rational control over the executive and interpretive process. We suppress personalizing impulses that might make our interpretation appear idiosyncratic, if only with the conscious intent to streamline rehearsals and reduce the possibility of confusion in concert or recording situations. Our objectivity seems to distance us from our sense of relationship to our audience. Our best performances ever more resemble richly sensuous and brilliant surfaces that yet betray a disturbingly narcissistic component that seems little concerned with sharing a genuine spiritual quality with the listener. In this respect, modern performance practice may indeed be said to be an "authentic" reflection of our times.

Musicians of a hundred years ago, hearing a cross-section of present-day classical performances, would likely be struck by this primary difference between their performance practice and ours: the flexible treatment of time as an expressive resource, an art highly cultivated in late-romantic performance practice, has given way to an extremely circumspect – more, a restrictive – handling of this musical dimension. Our performance practice, whether classical-romantic, radical-modern, or retrospective-historicist (to paraphrase the three current main streams of classical music so presciently distinguished by Jacques Handschin; see note 2, above) assumes that a predictably regular beat is conscientiously maintained throughout a movement. Deliberate modifications of the beat other than those explicitly designated by the composer rarely go beyond a discreet ritardando at the close of a movement (to the extent this statement is a generalization, the odd exception today only proves the rule), and even this modification is increasingly dispensed with in performances of repertoire before 1800.[4] We compensate our lack of timing flexibility by a very highly developed sense of tone-color and dynamic which, however refined and polished it may be, tends to abstract and de-personalize the music-making, underscoring its "absoluteness".

The principle of strict unity of beat within a movement has been part of our understanding and experience of classical music for so many decades now, that today's musicians and listeners can hardly imagine that less than a century ago the "standard" classical repertoire was performed under significantly different assumptions. Thus a modern musician hearing an early acoustic recording or piano roll is likely to be startled by the unpredictable flow of time. Other late-romantic performance idiosyncrasies such as the relaxed alignment of voices on the beat, tolerance for note and intonation errors, and a taste for portamento as a melodic ornament, not to speak of the distorted sound quality on the recordings themselves, compound the difficulty of acclimatizing ourselves to the late-romantic performance aesthetic. The appreciation of late-romantic performance practice remains the province of "buffs", and the generally unsympathetic opinion of this performance aesthetic, formed in the 1920s and 1930s, remains, more than half a century later, firmly in place. Anti-romantic values that emerged after the First World War have, over the decades, crystallized into standards of "good" musicianship so solidly embedded in our expectations and assumptions that they are regarded as universally appropriate for the stylistically faithful rendering of musics of all periods, including the music of the late romantic period itself.

Beyond early recorded performances, a vast documentary record bears witness to the paradigm shift in performance values during the time of the First World War and the decade following. Essays, concert and recording reviews, memoirs, textbooks, and reference-work entries all mirror the change in attitude. Partisans for both the late-romantic and the modernist viewpoint engaged in polemical attacks. Actually, on most issues – espousal of fidelity to the text, eschewal of self-aggrandizing performance behavior, condemnation of expressive exaggeration – the two schools of thought differed only in degree. They differed fundamentally in their attitudes towards the acceptable range of interpretive prerogative, and very specifically in their attitudes towards modifications of tempo and agogic accent.

As is often the case with bygone debates, it is now difficult to imagine the dissonance between the old way and the new way of thinking as it was experienced by the musicians and public of the day. Obviously, some musicians of the old school must have taken liberties that were perceived by their more progressive contemporaries as a serious violation of the composer's conception of the works they were playing. Nonetheless, despite the very wide range of artists and performance traditions represented on early recordings, it is difficult to isolate specific examples of flagrantly bad taste on early recordings, once the modern listener has acclimatized his or her taste to the expressive mannerisms of the period.[5] Even an apparently obvious example of stylistic excess such as the castrato Alessandro Moreschi's rendition of the Bach-Gounod "Ave Maria", over which it is hard to suppress a giggle the first few times one hears it, begins to assume normal artistic proportions once the listener recognizes Moreschi's "heart on his sleeve" rendition as a craftsmanlike handling of a range of ornamental devices without which his audience would probably have felt deprived.[6] While Moreschi's performance may be foreign to our taste, to judge it as being perforce in bad taste is, by virtue of the cultural distance between Moreschi and his audience and ourselves, about as appropriate as making a similar value judgment regarding the performing style of the Peking Opera. Moreover, we must bear in mind that our reaction to Moreschi's performance can scarcely be separated from our perception of the piece itself, which has come to represent the quintessence of kitsch. Modernist values have thus become synonymous with "good musicianship" and they underly contemporary values of "good taste" in classical music-making. A common response of modern-day musicians hearing historical recordings, especially those made before the 1930s, is that the performance values represented reflect "bad taste". Yet if we compare our reactions to historical recordings with contemporary reviews of these same performances, it becomes apparent that what can seem outlandish to us today was often delectable to competent critics of the time. We can identify specific cases in which discriminating listeners of the time reacted positively to interpretational styles that often make modern listeners uncomfortable.[7]

Our inability to see our own standards of good taste as relative conceals the danger of a cultural chauvinism. In our revivals of extinct performance traditions we probably have been reconstructing selectively those aspects of a performance practice that suit our own values and expectations while ignoring discrepancies between our reconstructions and the evidence. Until now, the early-music scene could effectively skirt this dilemma because we could neither corroborate nor refute the products of our imagination with acoustic artifacts from earlier periods. As the historical territory claimed by the early music movement gradually comes to include music before the First World War,[8] we are increasingly confronted with acoustic artifacts that lay bare discrepancies between our own practices and those of the past. While the intellectual problem of late nineteenth-century performance practice is acquiring a distinct profile, its broader implications are being ignored, I believe because late-romantic performance style can be dismissed as being in "bad taste". Given a reception problem of this magnitude with the interpretive values of our grandparents' generation, is it far-fetched to imagine that the discrepancy between our expressive values and those of past eras is likely to be only compounded, the further back we go? It seems reasonable to assume that the more distant a period is from our own time, the less our imagination of its performing style is likely to reflect the original reliably.

We must acknowledge that standards of taste that embrace the aesthetic values of modernism are (speaking historically rather than sociologically) stylistically appropriate only for "modern" music, that is, music composed during the era in which modernist values were securely established as the dominant paradigm. For earlier repertories, we should operate under the assumption that modernist interpretive values probably seriously distort the countenance and the "message" of older repertories and consequently their effect on the listener. Thus we need to scrutinize our assumptions concerning appropriate performance-practice values for music of the past, in order to expose and to correct, for our modernist bias as far as possible.

It is to be hoped that in due course our music-making will reflect this intellectual process in terms of a relaxation of the present rigid standards of appropriate interpretive behavior. To reconstruct the sound-world of past styles of music-making without challenging the expressive values inculcated by modernism is hypocritical: we gain the moral satisfaction of the pursuit of fidelity ("authenticity") without the necessity of fundamentally modifying our point of view to adapt to the expressive character of the music we wish to play. An alternative is to admit that how music was experienced in its own time does not interest us enough to cause us to question and change our own expressive values. When musicians openly espouse the latter viewpoint, rather than hold it covertly, I welcome it as an honest, natural attitude. After all, we are products of our own time, and how we play reflects who we are. The surprisingly popular alternative of believing that listeners before the period of *Empfindsamkeit* were reacting strongly to performances that lacked externalized expressive intensity as we think of it, I reject as schematic, based ultimately on a wish for a clean-cut distinction between "subjective", "irrational" romanticism and an imagined "objective", "rational" pre-romantic performance culture.

In any case, the force of mental and physical habit is such that the standards of taste now in place will long prevail. Nonetheless, putting a historical perspective on the problem of the modernization of musical taste may help to make the requisite adjustments to our interpretive outlook easier to entertain. The way we play today directly reflects a polemical struggle that transpired three-quarters of a century ago. Although the specific dialectic of that struggle has long since lost its cultural urgency, localizing the dialectic as a historical event can help us to understand that we are making aesthetic decisions in classical-music interpretation under the power of the modernist point of view in that dialectic. Circumscribing the alleged universality of modernist values empowers us to discover the face of earlier repertories for ourselves. We should be clear: doing so will not so much recover the past as assert our own identity as individuals who are part of a post-modern culture.

The central issues separating the modernist and the pre-modernist experience of musical performance lie in two attitudes over which late-romantics and modernists of three generations ago were irreconcilable: assumptions about the nature of musical time and the acceptable extent of interpretive prerogative in the rendition of classical works. Personal experience suggests that the dimension of musical time is the decisive one, and that interpretive prerogative is cultivated by taking responsibility for the organization of time. Time is central because when the player organizes time subjectively rather than adhering to an external, regular beat, timing decisions must be genuinely intuitive. They must be improvised, even if according to some kind of schematic plan; they cannot be "reproduced". This type of improvisation is not without risk, for even the novice listener can often tell whether or not the resulting proportions are in a convincing balance. One of the advantages of choosing to adhere to an objectively regular beat is that the player is not obliged to make significant and perceptible but very delicate time-organizing decisions. In banishing the artistic manipulation of time, modernists simplified the job of interpretation enormously – akin to doing a high-wire act with the wire on the floor – and simultaneously concealed themselves from judgment for any potential lack of artistic control in this matter. Not taking liberties with time was held up as an ascetic virtue: continence.

A central theme in modernists' representations of performance ideals was a covert assumption of their moral superiority. Yet while they may have been even-keeled when defining the terms of their own aesthetic program, they often reveal an ideological vituperation – the antithesis of the aesthetic qualities of detachment and objectivity the new movement aspired to – when addressing late-romantic music-making. The proponents of romanticism present their case, by and large, in a remarkably lucid, well-balanced manner. They observe the change of attitude taking place around them and the consequences for their art with resignation.

One modernist concerned with the technical feasibility of representing musical objectivity was Hans Haaß, a composer and arranger who worked closely with the Welte-Mignon reproducing instrument company. In 1927 Haaß formulated his goals for "objective" music-making using the reproducing piano as part of an exposé in which he demonstrated that the reproducing piano itself was not absolutely free of distortion, not perfect enough to represent objectivity ideally.[9] In so doing, Haaß articulated a central modernist value, namely the abjuration of personal will:

It is often stated that mechanical music stands in the closest connection to the concepts of objectivity and detachment. I wish here to ask the question again briefly: what is objective music? In any case, the main characteristic of this music is the complete emancipation from any individuality, i.e., the exclusion of voluntary and involuntary behavior by the interpreter as well as the composer. Thus the problem of a purely *objective* music would be solved if we had compositions by which one could dispense with every dynamic gradation and every tempo-change within the piece and within the individual phrase.

A recurring theme among modernists was the notion of fidelity to the composer's intentions as reflected in the text (however, modernists largely overlooked the complications and contradictions inherent in this notion – see the remarks by Paul Bekker in the appendix below). Herbert Lichtenthal, writing in 1943, avoided open antipathy to late-romantic performance values, but he carefully confined the realm of interpretive decision-making to expressive handlings explicitly mandated in the text:[10]

I am far from denying individuality to the recreating artist, but this should not be taken as an excuse for ignorance or inequality to his task on the part of the interpreter. After satisfying the fundamental requirements of the music and carefully carrying out the intentions of the composer, there is still enough room left for the interpreter to show his individuality, his temperament, and his power of imagination. . . . But . . . it is not left to the interpreter to decide when and where a *crescendo* or a *ritardando* should be made. This has been laid down by the composer in the music. It is, however, left to the interpreter, HOW to make the *crescendo* and the *ritardando*, and it is here that he can show his individuality and the whole compass of his feeling.

Considerably more doctrinaire was the French organist Marcel Dupré, whose vision of the performer's role borders on the servile:[11]

The interpreter must never allow his own personality to appear. As soon as it penetrates, the work has been betrayed. By concealing himself sincerely before the character of the work in order to illuminate it, even more so before the personality of the composer, he serves the latter and confirms the authority of the work.

Rigorous fidelity to the text meant replacing the musicians' hitherto intuitive response to the "code" of a score with a deferential, self-effacing "reading" of the score. The abstract musical effect that resulted demanded a high degree of concentration from player and listener alike, which, in yielding as little as possible to comfortable sensuality, repaid the requisite intellectual effort, under the best circumstances, with a kind of aesthetic mortification that we may call the "bliss of denial" (in German known as "Pathos der Askese"). When the playing did not reach this height, it nonetheless possessed the virtue of a taste unsullied by individual preference. Virgil Thomson's 18 November 1940 review of Josef Lhévinne's piano-playing elegantly summarizes the result for the listener:[12]

A more satisfactory academicism can scarcely be imagined. Mr. Lhevinne's performance . . . was both a lesson and an inspiration. He made no effort to charm or to seduce or to preach or to impress. He played as if he were expounding to a graduate seminar: "This is the music, and this is the way to play it." Any authoritative execution derives as much of its excellence from what the artist does not do as from what he does. If he doesn't do anything off color at all, he is correctly said to have taste. Mr. Lhevinne's taste is authoritative as this technical method. Not one sectarian interpretation, not one personal fancy, not one stroke below the belt, not a sliver of ham, mars the universal acceptability of his readings. Everything he does is right and clear and complete. Everything he doesn't do is the whole list of all the things that mar the musical executions of lesser men. This is not to say that tenderness and poetry and personal warmth and fire are faults of musical style, though they frequently do excuse a faulty technique. I am saying that Mr. Lhevinne does not need them. They would mar his style; hence he eschews them. He eschews them because his concept of piano music is an impersonal one. It is norm-centered; it is for all musical men. Any intrusion of the executant's private soul would limit its appeal, diminish its authority. Thus it is that Mr. Lhevinne's performance is worthy of the honorable word *academic*. And if he seems to some a little distant, let us remind ourselves that remoteness is, after all, inevitable to those who inhabit Olympus.

Although late twentieth-century performance practice epitomizes modernist values, we have largely forgotten the anti-Romantic rhetoric of the 1920s. An exception is a diatribe published in 1989 by John H. Planer in *The Musical Quarterly*.[13] Planer's object of attack is the purported "sentimentality" of the Bach playing of the cellist Pablo Casals (1876–1973). He identifies sentimentality in performance with tempo and agogic modification:

In the recreative media, including absolute music, an interpretation is sentimental if it is exaggerated. Since the musical score indicates the pitches, harmonies, textures, and orchestration with relative precision, a performer can do little to change or exaggerate them. The element of music most ripe for sentimental exploitation is rhythm, particularly tempo. Sentimentalist interpretations prefer extremely slow tempos and rubato, the performer's subjective fluctuations of the pulse. While a performer can change the dynamics, phrasing, and the voicing (prominence of each part), sentimental interpretations distort the tempo the most.

For Planer, tempo modifications are a distortion that

violates a canon of restraint. For example, if a performer's rubato destroys rhythmic effects requiring a relatively regular pulse, the performer distorts the music. Admittedly, performance represents the musician's interpretation, but, to be legitimate, that interpretation must reflect the composer's intent and personality. In this sense performance carries an implicit moral obligation to recreate aurally, and thereby to perpetuate, the composer's personality.

We may see Planer's criticism of the musicality of Casals – whose musicianship was in its own time regarded as without equal – as gratuitous and anachronistic, but there is a widespread, if seldom explicitly spoken, acceptance today of the anti-romantic ideology he propounds.

In their own time, modernist attacks on late-Romantic interpretive values were directed less at the playing of specific musicians than at undesirable performance "mannerisms" in general, among which tempo and beat modification clearly occupied first place. The piano pedagogue Walter Leimer contrasted "mannered" performance with the "natural" pianism of Walter Gieseking:[14]

The naturalness of performance is particularly characteristic of Gieseking's playing. . . Meanwhile, his playing style has established itself; mannered, over-romantic performance is increasingly discredited, and a much-needed return to naturalness in music-making appears to be heralded. . . . I hope that my remarks also will help to combat mannered performance and will further the cause of playing that is true to the notes and to the sense [of the music] – simple, beautiful playing.

In a review from 25 March 1935 of a recital by Sergé Rachmaninov, Eric Blom localized objectionable liberties as those as taken by

the inferior artist who merely reproduces things that have degenerated into empty conventions, foremost among which, it must be confessed, is that artificial pianistry which is capable of making *rubato* quite as mechanical as the most rigid performance of an under-rehearsed orchestra, and a good deal more annoying for imposing false values on the hearer, whereas the opposite kind of playing merely presents him with a blank.[15]

Blom's remarks, like Johnstone's above (see note 5) offer a clue as to what at least partly motivated the retreat from subjectivism in performance practice: a significant and increasing doubt as to the "authenticity" of the feeling behind the expression. In our own time, it seems safe to say, we have a similar problem: continence itself seems to have "degenerated into an empty convention," perhaps since the concept of continence presumes the prior presence of impulses that are to be contained. The smooth-surface aesthetic of continence, imitated by young players unaware of its dependence on inner resistance or struggle, all too easily loses the inner luminescence characteristic of the playing of its finest advocates (for example Clara Haskill), leaving behind a music-making in which the discerning listener has the impression that "no one is home" – that is, the player is not making significant artistic decisions that compel one to pay attention.

As the twentieth century grew older and the late-romantic era receded farther into the past, the latter period came to be seen as a time of interpretive debauchery. What had started out as a polemic against certain kinds of perceived exaggerations in performance behavior developed into a myth of the degeneration of noble classicism into cheap vulgarity, bearing with it a moral imperative to "cleanse" the performance practice of "classicist" works in order to restore to them a purity of which they had allegedly been deprived by late-romantic distortions.[16] Repugnantly self-righteous, anti-romanticism reached a grotesque institutional extreme with the formation of a *Stilkommission* at the Akademie für Musik und darstellende Kunst Vienna in the early 1960s. Announced in the December 1962 issue of the *Österreichische Musikzeitschrift*, its name was later euphemistically sanitized to "Arbeitsgemeinschaft für musikalische Werkpraxis," but its program is clear:[17]

The new name seemed to us . . . less authoritative and doctrinaire, and to emphasize more the collective working out of interpretation guidelines, which we espouse not "by command" but out of a scientifically-based conviction. . . . The virtuoso transcription and agogic freedom of the Liszt-school have surrendered to the original version and to metrical rigor, the "Busoni-articulation" in the music of Bach, which has had catastrophic consequences on the legato-playing culture introduced in Vienna by no less a man than Beethoven, has been banished to the realm from whence it came; Chopin, [whose music was] debased by uncontrolled "Expression-Musicians" practically to the point of salon music, we have been able to recognize as a musician of classical format, orienting himself on Mozart.

The verbal imagery of the "Style Commission" report exposes a central assumption – more or less covert, depending on the speaker – underlying the modernist view of the history of performance practice: that late-romantic interpretation itself was a kind of monstrosity, an aberration in music history, a shameful descent into depths of vulgar excess. In self-congratulatory tones, the author of the report portrays a "return" to solid musical moral values, thus legitimizing modernist performance values by invoking the authority of yet another, related covert assumption: an imagined pre-romantic "classicistic" performance practice, to which modern performance practice was returning, having recovered its sense of dignity and demeanor after an extended bout of romanticism.

The virulent polemical tone of many proponents of "objectivity" stands in ironic contrast to the balanced viewpoint and subdued language of early twentieth-century advocates of late-romantic "subjective" performance values. Take for example the following remarks by Eugen Schmitz (1915) on the relationship between style and interpretive prerogative:[18]

Performance includes especially the choice of tempo and its modifications, dynamics, phrasing, tonal shading . . ., altogether all sides of inner as well as outer expression. The guidelines for a performance are to be drawn from the style character of the artwork . . . With the fulfillment of all technical requirements, the performer has addressed only the primitive basis for the deeper spiritual conception of the artwork. Here, too, the historical perspective is decisive at the outset: the artwork has to be realized in the "spirit of its time.". . . The individuality of its creator, as far as it expresses itself in the style character, must also be reflected in the performance. For example, the more subjective a composition is, the more its performance should resemble a free improvisation. . . . Insofar as the objective prerequisites for a stylistically appropriate performance are set, directly as well as indirectly by the style character of the artwork, in the actual realization, the imagination of the performing artist may to a large extent act freely. "With regard to concept," says Xavier Scharwenka [(1850–1924) a prominent pianist and teacher of the late-romantic school] correctly, "music is the most tolerant of the arts; even if certain limits must be set, nonetheless much room for the most differing individual [conceptions] remains.". . . Where the limits of caprice are, has to be decided from case to case; in general it can only be said that the style character can in no case be obliterated. Its directive significance is thus not affected by the subjective possibilities of performance.

Late-romantic artists may have played in an intensely subjective manner, but even a performer with a reputation for extremes, such as the highly successful pianist Ignace Paderewski understood intellectually the role of tempo flexibility in realizing his artistic intentions:[19]

Tempo Rubato is a potent factor in musical oratory, and every interpreter should be able to use it skillfully and judiciously, as it emphasizes the expression, introduces variety, infuses life into mechanical execution. It softens the sharpness of lines, blunts the structural angles without ruining them, because its action is not destructive; it intensifies, subtilizes, idealizes the rhythm. As stated above, it converts energy into languor, crispness into elasticity, steadiness into capriciousness. It gives music, already possessed of the metric and rhythmic accents, a third accent, emotional, individual, that which Mathis Lussy, in his excellent book on musical expression, calls *l'accent pathétique*. . . . However strong and peculiar was Mendelssohn's dislike of Tempo Rubato, we cannot recommend too unconditional a respect for the great composer's personal feeling in the matter. . . . Curiously enough, one of the most striking examples of Tempo Rubato is to be found in Mendelssohn's violin concerto, in the short *Intermezzo* leading from the *Andante* to the Finale. We well remember the playing of this by the great Joachim – in our opinion the greatest exponent of classical music; it was most distinctly *rubato*. . . . Tempo Rubato then becomes an indispensable assistant, but with it, unfortunately, appears also the danger of exaggeration. Real knowledge of different styles, a cultured musical taste, and a well-balanced sense of vivid rhythm should guard the interpreter against any abuse. Excess of freedom is often more pernicious than the severity of the law.

Artists of the time seem to have understood the practical necessity of experimenting with tempo modification in order to arrive at an intuitive balance. Adrian Boult's description of the rehearsal practices of the conductor Arthur Nikisch suggest that Nikisch made such experiments in his Leipzig rehearsals:[20]

At home in Leipzig . . . the public rehearsal on Wednesday morning . . . was filled with the musical people of Leipzig . . . [in] the fashionable subscription concert on Thursday evening, . . . seats and boxes were handed down from father to son and . . . it was very difficult to buy a single ticket. . . . [At the Wednesday morning rehearsal] various other things, notably continual exaggerations of expression and an extraordinary looseness of ensemble, were all swallowed by the complacent "musical" audience with complete equanimity . . . [but at the Thursday evening concert] I was rewarded with one of the most perfect Mozart performances I have ever heard . . . it was often amusing to note how Nikisch would finish the [Tuesday evening] private rehearsal in an hour or so, perhaps not touching a big work like the Schubert C major; how he would then blatantly rehearse the Symphony in front of his Wednesday audience, which happily drank in the absurd *rubatos* and other exaggerations; and how these things would all drop into proportion at the concert and fine performances result. . . .

Writers who appreciated late-romantic performance values in certain areas sometimes expressed modernist leanings in others, a typical case being the question of allowable tempo modifications in orchestral versus solo performance. *New York Times* critic Richard Aldrich (1863–1937), generally favorable to subjective pianism, demanded more restraint in orchestral conducting. Compare the negative tone of Aldrich's review of a concert on 6 November 1908 by the Boston Symphony Orchestra, conducted by Max Fiedler –

There is a tendency to an exaggerated modification of tempo, to retardation and acceleration and to the excessive modeling of the phrase, which destroy the repose, the continuity of line and disrupt the larger symmetry of outline without the production of deeply felt or emotional effect that is intended and is often at direct odds with the spirit of the music he is performing.

with his 21 October 1911 review of a recital by Vladimir de Pachmann, a pianist highly controversial in his own time for both his playing and his eccentric stage demeanor. Aldrich praises Pachmann's "delicate, filmy iridescent tone," which "beguiles the senses of the listener in a way that hardly any other piano playing can do," but expresses reservations about his "sticky *tempo rubato* that was probably far from Mendelssohn's idea of the rhythm and flow of his absolutely symmetrical measures, designed for absolutely symmetrical playing."[21] While responding warmly to late-romantic pianism, Aldrich also recognized both strengths and weaknesses in pianists who were developing their artistry in a modernist direction. An overriding pianistic modernism he apparently found unpalatable. In his 1 November 1908 review of a recital by Josef Lhévinne (compare with Virgil Thomson's review, above), Aldrich finds the pianist "deficient in imagination, in poetical feeling," yet possessing the virtue of having "no suggestion in his performance of personal display, of any appeal to the wonder of the unthinking," a style he found most suitable in the arrangements of works by Baroque composers.[22]

Antedating the shift from an aesthetic of tempo flexibility and interpretive prerogative to the aesthetic of modernism is a polemic from the last third of the nineteenth century, where, ironically, the labels "modernism" and "academicism" had opposite meanings to those of their later counterparts. Adherents of the highly subjective, flexible Wagnerian conducting practice regarded themselves as "modernists", whereas their opponents were lumped together as "academicists". A tendency towards classicizing the performance of music of the eighteenth century, particularly the music of J. S. Bach, gained strength from the middle of the nineteenth century.[23] By 1900, Hermann Kretzschmar found the realm of interpretive prerogative for the musician of his day to be sharply restricted compared with the rights of the eighteenth-century musician as he imagined them to have been:[24]

The difficulties with which early music confronts the modern musician go altogether back to the basic difference between the artistic position of the modern versus the early virtuoso. Today singers, performers and conductors are held to narrow boundaries in the unfolding of their gifts. They may not add any notes to those present, nor omit any; solely the treatment of accent and dynamic permit a small playing area for temperament and intelligence, allowing a greater talent to distinguish itself from the lesser. Even a freer, more individualistic handling of tempo is undertaken under the spectre of the terms "objective" and "subjective" performance.

That a witness of 1900 could experience his culture as constraining may astonish us, given that we ourselves have difficulty evaluating recordings from that time because their expressive parameters are so much more extreme than ours. Kretzschmar's feeling of constraint acquires broader significance when we note that performances by the oldest musicians to record around the turn of the century – those born in the 1820s and 1830s and educated by about 1850 (for example the pianists Carl Reinecke, b. 1824; Theodor Leschetizky, b. 1830; Camille Saint-Saëns, b. 1835; and Francis Planté, b. 1839; the violinist Joseph Joachim, b. 1834; or the singer Sir Charles Santley, b. 1834) – exhibit an expressive style in essential respects substantially more extreme than are performances by musicians born after ca. 1870.[25] Yet what is most striking about Kretzschmar's use of the improvisatory attitude of eighteenth-century interpretation as a frame of reference (Paul Bekker does as well; see the appendix following) is that he found unworthy of comment the fact that he could still view the performance practice of his day within that context, however restrictive it had become. A century later, in our day of reconstructed "authentic" performance practice, that is impossible.

Late-romantic artists witnessed the demise of their art in the face of changing values. In 1927 Eugen d'Albert lamented the loss of individuality and portended the automation of classical music:[26]

In former times one placed the most value on individuality and on spiritual depth of playing, today these things are of less and less concern. The emphasis [today] is on an immaculate, pearly style and a clean, smooth technique. We are coming closer and closer to the playing style of a Pianola [reproducing-piano], and just as everything mechanical continually makes progress, I predict we will soon have only Pianola concerts, which are already common in England and America. We will become unaccustomed to being spiritually animated by a sweating artist, and will prefer, in undisturbed placidity of spirit, to hear a perfect but inarticulate machine, producing a transitory, shallow pleasure, without any excitement. The future will certainly bring forth surprising developments in this area. We will thus become further and further removed from the intellectual and spiritual work which we all know cannot be mechanically reproduced.

Another representative of the old guard, Hans Pfitzner, felt that the literalist sensibility required to notate and perform irrational rhythms in modern music was incompatible with the intuitive feeling for the relationship between subjective rhythm and style that characterizes late romanticism. The more the "elasticity of give-and-take" is

constrained by the agogic notation style of the composition, which forces the performer to a purely technical accomplishment, to tight-rope walking in impossible time-signatures – the more the entire field of musical reproduction is reduced to a mere sports-like accomplishment. . . . [Tempo] modifications . . . are nothing but articulation of the musical oratory, [the] shaping of the musical line. . . . It is the art of performance, the realm of the performing artist. . . . [We make] interpretive assumptions such as the slowing down of the final cadence, the preparation of a new theme, certain stopping points, accommodation to word and song and countless more. We are in the process of losing all these.[27]

The prognostications of d'Albert and Pfitzner bear themselves out countless times over in "correct but dull" late twentieth-century performances.

Heinrich Boell (1942) foresaw a development in the emerging retrospective-historicist movement that likewise is fulfilled daily in much of our historicist music-making:[28]

> In no case, however, ought the happily recovered grasp of the reproduction of the original Bach-sound . . . to lead to a situation whereby the demand for an inwardly living interpretation is neglected, to be replaced by the demand for an "unromantic" objectivity. Authority for the latter is claimed by virtue of the sublime objectivity of the Bachian spirit, said to demand, like the music of the Baroque altogether, the most rigorous and detached treatment. That this is completely misguided we can learn from even the most superficial historical reflection. Already Heinrich Schütz demanded not objectivity, rather always the strongest effect possible; and the official aesthetic of Bach's time demanded first and foremost from any music, that it be moving and "expressing" (expressive, we would say today). . .

Perhaps the most insightful contemporary witness to comment on the paradigm shift in performance values was Paul Bekker (see appendix). He understood the change as a clear decline in the artistic quality of interpretation as a result of the disappearance of the improvisatory attitude in performance. Bekker included the "improvisation of interpretation" within the realm of improvisation, specifically citing the conducting styles of Richard Strauss and Arthur Nikisch. He saw the performance value of "reproduction" as resulting from false artistic values instilled by a pedantic, moralizing form of academicism, causing the decline of values based on the inherent right and ineluctible responsibility of the artist to "act on his own discretion and authority with regard to the text." Like Kretzschmar, Bekker saw the improvisation of interpretation within the context of the improvisatory performance practices of the seventeenth and eighteenth centuries.[29]

Bekker's advice to the musician to look to contemporary composition as a source for a "modern-day" improvisation style is astute. Musicians today deliver performances of contemporary music that have an instinctive and authoritative flair. They are unhesitating in their grasp of their role in "delivering" the piece to the public. Once the repertory has become "classical", however (as even neo-classical works from mid-century now have), this instinctive sense of authority seems to fade. It appears that a leap of the imagination we have yet to learn is to recreate in performance an aesthetic identity for a work such as we imagine it to have had when new (as much as we can determine, having suspended the classi-cizing assumptions of modernism). Every composition has an expressive dimension to it that felt entirely "new" to the composer at the time he was composing it.[30] Insofar as the composer was intending to explore the expressive limits of the musical language in force at the time of composition – that is, insofar as the expressive style of the work was at the "cutting edge" of what was being attempted in composition at the time – the composer was at that moment composing "avant-garde" music. For works of this nature, it is the performer's job to reconstruct for the modern public the effect of pushing the limits of an expressive style. Admittedly, this process requires a highly developed sense of style, proportion and artistic conscience that in an improvised, non-reproductive manner avoids the dangers of both safe conservatism and an equally safe stylized exaggeration. But that is the job.

Earlier I alluded to the myth of the "degeneration of classicism." I can now state the problem more forcefully: it is doubtful whether a "classicizing" performance practice of the kind invoked by modernism to lend itself authority ever existed as a mainstream before arising as a fledgling movement associated with academicism in the Romantic period.[31] It does appear that a classicizing trend in performance practice, particularly of the newly coalescing repertoire of older works in the concert repertory, emerged in the mid-nineteenth century. Classicist values gained strength, perhaps as a rallying totem for forces opposed to the direction in which Richard Wagner appeared to be taking music, and, bolstered by the success of the positivistic-philological paradigm in scholarship as well as the scientific-technological paradigm in society as a whole, became powerful enough by the 1920s to effect the banishment of the principle of interpretive prerogative that had been for centuries the dominant paradigm in performance. And, as we have seen, the intuitive and sovereign exercise of interpretive prerogative cannot be separated from the improvisatory handling of tempo and time relationships. I draw the following conclusion: a performance practice of pre-romantic literatures (going back at least to the end of the Renaissance, that is, the birth of the *secunda prattica*) *without* a fully integrated aesthetic of tempo and beat modification (one appropriate for each style as the music and the written evidence suggest), is unimaginable.[32] The artistic effect of these repertories when recreated under this new assumption remains largely a realm we have yet to discover.

One way to form a picture of a pre-romantic performance practice under the aspect of a non-modernist concept of the flow of musical time is to compare historical descriptions of those practices with early twentieth-century recordings. A risky undertaking, one might think, for it implies that our reconstructions of such practices for earlier repertories will be based on a late-romantic expression of the principles behind the practices. We must take this risk, if only because we simply have no other acoustic model to turn to. Note that in other scholarly situations requiring the filling of blanks in one historical period by analogy from related phenomena in a later period, risks of this magnitude are often taken, the more audaciously, the further removed from our time the interpretive problem lies. The very act of historicist performance practice assumes that we permit analogies between ourselves and the past. The conceptual threshold here is seeing the late-nineteenth century – habitually contrasted to rather than compared with earlier periods – as more authoritative on the matter of an improvisatory performance tradition of flexible time than is the music-making of our own day.[33]

If we compare early twentieth-century descriptions with discussions of tempo modification from the second half of the eighteenth century and first half of the nineteenth, for example those by Christian Friedrich Daniel Schubart,[34] Johann Friedrich Reichardt on the violin-playing of Franz Benda (1709–1786),[35] Reichardt on Ludwig Spohr's violin-playing (1805),[36] Carl Ludwig Junker,[37] Johann Nepomuk Hummel,[38] T. Lindsay,[39] and Carl Czerny,[40] distinct similarities emerge. The dynamic tension of temporal nuance described by late eighteenth- and early nineteenth-century writers is easily recognizable in the agogic practices on recordings from the early part of our century.

The practice of tempo modification was evidently widespread in instrumental and vocal performance well before the late-Romantic period. Indications for a tradition of tempo modification reach back at least to the emergence of the *secunda prattica* at the end of the sixteenth century. Georg Schünemann (1913) cites Cyriacus Schneegaß (1546–97), *Isagoges Musicae libri duo* (1591), chapter 11, as well as Lodovico Zacconi (1555–1627), *Prattica di musica* (1592).[41] Girolamo Frescobaldi's description of beat modification in "I Madrigali moderni" (*Toccate e partite d'intavolatura di cimbalo . . . libro primo* (1615) has a North German sacred choral counterpart in the *Musica figuralis oder Neue Unterweisung der Singe Kunst* (1618) of Daniel Friderici: "In singing, a single beat should not be sought and kept to throughout but should be regulated according to the words of the text so as to achieve decorum and convenience. Kantors who measure their beats as strictly as the clock does its minutes are thus mistaken."[42] To these can be added remarks by Thomas Mace:[43]

. . . you must Know, That, although in our First Undertakings, we ought to *strive*, for the most Exact Habit of *Time-keeping* that possibly we can attain unto, (and for severall good Reasons) yet, when we come to be *Masters*, so that we can *command all manner of Time*, at our own Pleasures; we Then *take Liberty*, (and very often, for Humour, and good Adornment-sake, in certain Places) to *Break Time*; sometimes Faster, and sometimes Slower, as we perceive the *Nature of the Thing Requires*, which often adds, much *Grace*, and *Luster*, to the Performance.

and Roger North, who includes beat flexibility as a category of ornament, one of the "graces" of music:[44]

And there is no greater grace than breaking the time in the minutes, and still holding it punctually upon the maine, to conserve the grand beat or measure. For this sprinkling of discord or error is like damask, grotesque [-work], or any unaccountable variegation of colours that renders a thing agreeable; and yet wee discerne not the distinction of parts, but onely a pretty sparkling, such as the painters observe nature hath, which art cannot altogether imitate. And a plaine sound not thus set off, is like a dull plaine colour, or as a bad coppy of a good picture, that wants the spirit and life, which a sparkling touch gives it. Thus a life and warmth in the colouring of a picture is well resembled to graces in musick, that are not the body but the soul that enlivens it, or as the animall spirits that cannot be seen or felt, but yet make that grand difference between a living and a dead corps.

A comprehensive overview of opinions on tempo and beat modification before ca. 1850 is a desideratum for this topic.

If historical evidence for a classicizing performance practice style in the period before the romantic is scanty or, as Richard Taruskin has repeatedly hinted, not to be found, then it remains to be asked: What historical basis does the classicizing style of virtually all modern performance practice have, upon which to legitimize itself? If we are classicizing out of modernist habit, is that not "Schlamperei," to paraphrase Gustav Mahler? Obviously, classicist renditions of classical repertory fill some sort of societal need, otherwise we would not be producing them. While we may find some antecedents to the emergence of nineteenth-century historicist classicism, possibly, for example, in the eighteenth-century performance practice of *prima prattica* sacred choral music, or perhaps the revival of Lully operas in late eighteenth-century France, I believe that a sober look at the historical record will show that a classicizing performance practice in the "metronomically correct," artistically constrained guise of "absolute music" such as we universally hear it today is nothing else than a fiction, an invention of our own time.[45]

This being the case, how should players engrained with interpretive reflexes under the modernist canon of classicism define their responsibility to the music of the past? Musicians will have to find their own answer to this question, which will reflect both their personality and the conditions under which they have to exercise their profession. Personal experience suggests that the search for a relatively stable yet dynamic balance in the flow of time, that is nonetheless genuinely improvised – i.e., made up as you go along – will enable players to integrate a creative treatment of musical time with their professional obligations. The Baroque specialist may want to experiment with playing flexibly within a regular but very slow beat, in common time about one beat every four seconds or so (this is one interpretation of Roger North's "breaking the time in the minutes and still holding it punctually upon the maine"). For nineteenth-century music, more appropriate seems to be a quicker lower-level beat dictated by the time signature, which is then very adaptive to subtle but distinct general tempo changes as well as to nuances of phrasing and expression. Orchestral players face the problem of per-suading colleagues and conductors to take risks which at present are neatly avoided by adherence to a work ethos that scarcely permits these issues to be openly discussed. Record producers will have to adjust their standards of competence to take account of improvisation in interpretation, learning to distinguish and support the effect of good "live" music-making. Concert and record reviewers will have to learn to view reproductive musicianship critically, and improvisatory musicianship sympathetically. The audience will have to learn to enjoy hearing familiar pieces performed in unpredictable ways. Since a broad range of individualistic musicianship at a very high level is hardly possible unless the culture is tolerant at both ends, everyone will have to put up with more music-making in "bad taste" than is now the case. For adult musicians, learning espe-cially to reintegrate the accelerando as part of their palette of expressive devices is likely to be conflict-ridden, if only because the tendency to rush is suppressed in children's classical music training as early as possible. Certainly, the time appears to be ripe for this kind of experimentation, but not every musician will find the risks worth taking. Vested interests are understandable, but we should recognize them as such, rather than invoking a convenient and comfortable classicism to legitimize essentially self-protective behavior.

Historicist performance practice, itself a child of the late-romantic period, is at a juncture defined by its own success at establishing itself as a performance paradigm and by its new claim on the repertory of the late nineteenth century. We are challenged to demonstrate intellectual responsibility in dealing with the aesthetic dilemma posed by late-romantic performance practice. It is my hope that the dissembling of modernist values as *a priori* assumptions for the performance of classical literature will enfranchise individualistic, yet intellectually and stylistically conscientious artistic behavior in the classical music-making of the next century.[46] Doing so will less recreate the past than create an opportunity for us to define a new and distinctive artistic identity divested of the expressive straitjacket of modernist classicism. In doing so we may rediscover some of the "aura" of the artworks that inspire us – to use the term so unmodernistically invoked by Walter Benjamin[47] – all the more so as that aura in classical music, in my experience, can exist only under the condition of improvised performance of the relationship between events in music. Artur Schnabel's response to the woman questioning him (insofar as he meant it sincerely) was right for his time. Today, even the condition of playing "*with* feeling *in* time" has to be reinvented, or at least explicitly recognized as such, if that is the expressive goal of the artist. Whatever his goal, the musician of today will have to modify the present preoccupation with sound-color, dynamics and articulation to include substantially more attention to timing. That the artistic faculties that regulate temporal relationships lie just

under the surface of our musicianship (such that they immediately emerge, fully
competent, when we perform contemporary compositions in improvisatory style)
suggests that the process of rediscovery of these faculties as they apply to earlier
literatures will not only be challenging, but – with some *chutzpah* – will also be fun.

APPENDIX

Paul Bekker, extracts from the essay "Improvisation und Reproduktion" (1922)

The present age occupies itself in a most intensive way with Beethoven, yet we find
lacking, whether in orchestral, chamber music, or piano performance, that sovereign
quality of creativity as we knew it in the conductor and pianist von Bülow or the violinist
and quartet-leader Joachim. . . . If such a decline is not to be attributed to a general
impoverishment of talent – and if the artistic demands of the music have not changed, yet
the attainments of the art of performing music have clearly diminished, there can be only
one explanation: namely, that the attitude the present age has towards the artworks
themselves, forces the performing artist to emphasize his physical talents at the cost of his
humanity. We have apparently lost the capacity for creative conceptualization, and the
performer thus has dispensed with the driving force through which he might transcend
from an imitative perfection to the artistic acts of the truly great personality.

The causes of this constipation of creative human transcendental power are manifold: . . .
the organization of the music business, . . . the spread of misunderstood social, unionizing
efforts. . . . The art of musical performance is, in its origins and very being, an improvisational art. It creates out of the inspiration of the moment – more than that, it is the full
and direct comprehension of a moment heightened to the most intense aliveness possible.
Actually music can only be thought of as arising in the moment of its resounding. . . . It
goes without saying that the interpretive attitude [of the Baroque musician], in which the
emphasis lay in the exercise of the performer's imagination of the moment, would not
have been bound by rigorous demands with regard to the correctness of the text.

The latter formed the basis for a transcription, the fashioning of which remained the
province of the player. . . . The last improviser in the grand manner . . . was Liszt, but
even with some later exceptional artists we still encounter the principle of a free and
individualized conception of performance. Mahler's instrumental alterations in works of
Beethoven, the impulsive conducting of Richard Strauss, given fully to the moment, the
coloristically luxuriant interpretation style of Nikisch, conceived out of an extremely
sensual feeling for sound, both exciting and saturating – all these go back to the
improvisational right of the performing artist. . . . This improvisation ideal has as its goal
to illuminate the musical work through the intimate, creative fusion of composer and
performer, as if in the moment of its first sounding, thus bringing it into harmony with
the composer's original creative impulse.

Over against this ideal, a new one arose in the second half, actually in the last third of
the nineteenth century: that of "reproduction". . . . The possibility of reproduction in the
graphic arts is at least conceivable. In music, it is not . . . one who sits at a piano in order

to realize, with the utmost fidelity and the most rigorous restraint of any input from the performer himself, a work supplied by the composer with the most detailed expressive indications – that performer will nonetheless inevitably not only mix his personality with that of the composer, he will be placing it above. What he reproduces are only notes and signs, the living breath comes from the performer himself. . . . The improviser maintains the right to act on his own discretion and authority with regard to the text, while the goal of today's reproducing artist is rather to place himself fully at the service of the composer, only following his directions in order to give a true likeness or rather reproduction of the will of the creator. This sounds both attractive and virtuous, but is in reality unrealizable . . . even the most subtle performance markings can never be more than a hint, an allusion, an approximate indication. . . . If even these primitive, elementary signs are untrustworthy, what is one then to do about those that are by nature shifting and unspecific, for example ritardando, accelerando, fermata? One has to be clear about the essential relativity, the purely subjective explicative plane of these, indeed of all expressive indications. Thus seen, there is no essential difference between the apparently pains-takingly accurate indications of Beethoven and the virtual absence of such indications in Bach – in both cases, the performer is in the final instance only left to his own resources. This further demonstrates the monstrous presumptuousness that lies behind the concept of an objectively correct, note-faithful reproduction. Presumptuousness and lack of talent, this latter in the sense of a lack of force of personality. In fact, the concept of an objectively faithful "reproduction" has its origins in one of the periods of worst taste, the time in which one formed opposition in the official nurseries of musical culture, the conservatories and academies, to the "free" performance style of Wagner, Liszt, Bülow, and Rubinstein. One's own dryness and lack of imagination were raised to a virtue and the dry notes on the page were declared sacred, because one felt unable to illuminate them, to give them new life out of the ecstasy of improvisation. To this came as support a scholarly concept of art that had been led astray to false conclusions, peaking in the doctrine of the immutable perpet-uality of historical stylistic laws, according to which the ideal of "reproduction" acquired the aspect of a mechanical copy of erstwhile performance habits – a museum object.

Now it cannot be denied that there was some positive value in the conscious emphasis of respect for the original version in light of the danger of an overgrowth of arrangements, specifically with regard to its educational value. The limitation of subjective arbitrariness, the thwarting of the caprice of mood that reduces the musical-text to the inconsequential object of personal vanity, the constraint of subordination to a set of given, immutable directives – initially these were an estimable moment of thoughtfulness, of respect for the demands of a greater authority. They became dubious only when they staked a claim for exclusive canonical validity, when they were raised to the level of the highest law for performing art. This sham objectivity [*Sachlichkeit des Scheines*] meant in fact the dimin-ishing of decisive values of personality in favor of an imaginary ideal of objectivity, the mechanization of the methods and goals of performing art, the subversion of concepts of quality, the advancement of mediocrity, the insinuation of artistic immorality and a suspicion of the extraordinary. The luxuriantly flourishing conservatory business, with its goal of the mass production of average talents corresponded to this course of development, and the external economic and social conditions gave it the necessary anchoring in the real world. Thus all the factors mentioned above contributed to the inhibition of independent personalities in the performing arts.

The artist, by virtue of his artistic nature dependent on the outer world, no longer received from it the motivation for a humane, individual unfolding of his talent; rather, he saw himself ever more reduced to the level of a mechanical functionary. Many of our best talents, with excellent predisposition to a true and great virtuosity, have been thus turned into that fatal sort of "good musician." Creative imagination has seen its authority yielded to objective science, and a chaste boredom has been raised to the highest virtue. [All that can be done to oppose this] . . . is to prevent an inherently dependent natural force from being led astray by a false artistic ideology. Just this however is to be found in today's ruling paradigm of objective reproduction. The latter is a philistine self-deception and, in the realm of music, preposterous. To be sure, we cannot return to the free improvisation of the classical and early romantic period. . . . The problem of performing art in our day lies in moving from a pedantic concept of reproduction to an objectively founded and nonetheless personally unhampered improvisation. This may sound purely theoretical, and yet already much is won if we dare to declare and hold fast to the concept of improvisation as actually the highest and only true artistic exercise. The way towards this goal will be the easier to find, the more the performing artist occupies himself with the creative art of his own time. Out of the latter, not out of the historical sciences, stem the laws of performance style, also for older music. And in it we can find a style of modern improvisation; the power to regenerate the personality can only be found in the courage to turn in this direction.

4

LEHRSTÜCK: AN AESTHETICS OF PERFORMANCE

STEPHEN HINTON

INTRODUCTION

"This 'Lehrstück' should become a fully-fledged work of art, not a parergon."

The words are Kurt Weill's, from an interview published in April 1930, two months before the première of his "school opera" *Der Jasager*. In the same interview he described himself as a "simple musician", for whom "the simple style is no problem, the simple works . . . no mere *parerga* [*Nebenwerke*], but *chefs-d'œuvre* [*Hauptwerke*]."[1] And in 1935, newly arrived in America, he was to call *Der Jasager* his most important work to date.[2] Yet there is no denying an element of special pleading, expressed in the pre-première interview with characteristically feigned modesty. Making a school opera a *Hauptwerk* rather than a *Nebenwerk* meant nothing less than inverting traditional priorities – priorities that might account for stylistic simplicity in terms of some aesthetic concession or sacrifice on the composer's part.

Weill was not alone in his views, despite the apparent need to plead his case. The first performance of *Der Jasager* was originally planned for a festival of new music at which it and similar compositions took center stage. (The reasons for its withdrawal will be discussed below.) The plan of the festival was symptomatic: for a brief period, which coincides with the zenith of cultural activity in the Weimar Republic before the abrupt and tragic demise of that era, the genre of music theater known as "Lehrstück" became the focus of interest for a number of Germany's leading musicians and writers. Although the field of Brecht studies, whose literature is legion, has had much to say on the Lehrstück, little has been written either about its origins or about its broader relevance to Weimar culture.[3] The present investigation aims to redress the balance by dealing with five related issues: 1) the etymology of the term; 2) the inception of the Brecht-Hindemith piece itself entitled *Lehrstück*; 3) the aesthetic trends that characterize the second half of the Weimar Republic; 4) the emergence of the Lehrstück as a new type of musical theater; and 5) the musical implications of the genre for the composers involved.

ETYMOLOGY

"Lehrstück" (literally, teaching piece) can denote anything of didactic import. The Grimms' *Wörterbuch* defines the compound tautologically by dismantling it: "Stück einer Lehre": that is, "a piece of a teaching or doctrine."[4] More recent dictionaries restrict their definitions to a type of theater; some mention Bertolt Brecht; and they all ignore the earlier history of the concept, which predates Brecht by several centuries.[5] For the development of Brechtian theater, the first part of the compound, "Lehr-", is crucial. For understanding the etymology of "Lehrstück" however, it is the second part, "-stück", that requires special attention.

Applied to theater pieces, the term "Lehrstück" is best translated as "learning play". Brecht generally preferred to call all his stage works *Stücke* (literally, pieces), eschewing the traditional term *Schauspiel* and its various subcategories – *Lustspiel* (or *Komödie*), *Trauerspiel* (or *Tragödie*), etc. – and he styled himself a *Stückeschreiber* rather than a *Dramatiker* (the latter label hardly apt for a practitioner and theorist of "epic theater"). Since many of his *Stücke* have a strong didactic (or "Lehr-") component, however, the subcategory "Lehrstück" might seem to border on the tautological.[6] Aren't the majority of his *Stücke* in one way or another intended as Lehrstücke?

This latter question has given rise to a considerable amount of critical commentary in the secondary literature on Brecht. How do the Lehrstücke proper relate to the remainder of his stage works?[7] Yet it is precisely that literature's almost exclusive focus on Brecht that has perpetuated a rather myopic understanding of the Lehrstück, precluding a more comprehensive account of its history. In most studies the term first appears in 1929, as it were out of thin air, with the Hindemith-Brecht piece entitled *Lehrstück*, which subsequently serves as a generic designation for a number of didactic pieces, including some by writers and composers not directly associated with the Brecht camp.

The Grimms' dictionary traces the compound "Lehrstück" back to the seventeenth century. In both religious and secular contexts, it meant "lesson" in the sense of an illustration of a general truth.[8] That meaning is still preserved today, usually in the sense of a lesson or moral to be derived from specific historical situations. When it is applied to a piece of fiction, "cautionary tale" might be the best English equivalent.[9] "Lehrstück" is also encountered as a synonym for "Lehrsatz" in the sense of "theorem" or "dogma", as in "das . . . aristotelische Lehrstück von der Seele als Form des Körpers" (the Aristotelian dogma of the soul as the form of the body).[10] But there is a precise technical meaning which is documented neither by the Grimms (the relevant volume of whose dictionary was compiled in 1885) nor by any other German-language dictionary, but which is familiar in theology, both Protestant and Catholic. Here the word "Lehrstück" has less to do with theater than with catechistic instruction.[11]

Although the word Lehrstück did not become part of established catechistic terminology until the early twentieth century, with the introduction of the so-called *Lehrstück-Katechismus*, it originated in the teachings of Luther, whose own *Small Catechism* (*Kleiner Katechismus*) of 1529 represents one of the earliest attempts to codify oral religious instruction, particularly for children. Luther's work also provided the prototype for all future catechisms. According to the general meaning of the term detailed above, the entire catechism may count as a Lehrstück: it is "a piece of a teaching or doctrine" in that it sets forth the tenets of the Christian faith.[12] But to apply the term in this colloquial way is to deny, first, the special sense of "-stück" and, second, the form of the catechism known as *Lehrstück-Katechismus*, whose involved history has a special relevance to the emergence of secular theatrical Lehrstücke in the late 1920s.

Luther divided his *Kleiner Katechismus* into five parts (later six), which he called *Hauptstücke* or "main elements". They are 1) the Decalogue; 2) the Apostles' Creed; 3) the Lord's Prayer; 4) the Baptism; 5) Holy Communion. *Hauptstück* used in this sense commonly signifies a central premise or argument, as in the *Hauptstücke* or "principal sections" of a philosophical or instructional tract; or it can merely describe the sections themselves.[13] But *Hauptstücke* in this theological context can also have the more specific meaning of the *capita religionis christianae*: the principles of Christian faith. Each section of the catechism constitutes a principal dogma, especially the first three *Hauptstücke*. (The term "article" is reserved for the elements of the tripartite Creed.) As Luther wrote in his *German Mass* of 1526, "What we need first of all is a plain, good Catechism."

For such instruction I know no better form than those three parts which have been preserved in the Christian Church from the beginning – the Ten Commandments, the Creed, and the Lord's Prayer – which contain, in a brief summary, nearly all that a Christian ought to know.[14]

The educational nature of Luther's Catechism – his mission to inculcate the *Hauptstücke* of Christian faith in the face of ignorance and incompetence[15] – is quite obvious in its construction in terms of questions and answers. This expressly didactic part, known as the *Fragestück*, was further expanded by subsequent authors, especially for the purposes of instructing confirmands.[16]

So much for *Hauptstück* and *Fragestück*. What about "Lehrstück"? The spirit, if not the letter, of the concept comes from Luther himself. When the German Union of the Evangelical Church (*Evangelische Kirche der Union* or EKU) in 1953 proposed a revision of the Protestant Catechism, they removed what they called the "Lehrstück vom Amt der Schlüssel und von der Beichte."[17] This section, originally absent from the 1529 text, was interpolated by Luther in his 1531 revised edition between the fourth and fifth *Hauptstücke*, though not initially under the heading "Amt der Schlüssel," as in later inauthentic editions, but simply as "Wie man die Einfältigen soll lehren beichten" (How plain people are to be taught to confess). Here, then, is the specific theological sense of "Lehrstück": a didactically motivated supplement to the *Hauptstücke* of the Catechism.

But Luther did not use the term. In fact, it was not coined in a catechistic context until the middle of the nineteenth century, when it was used to challenge the methods of instruction enshrined in the *Fragestücke*. In general, the history of catechistic teachings reflects an involved discourse on questions of form and content – that is, it reflects attempts to find adequate means for imparting central truths, and an acceptable balance between upholding Christian belief, in its integrity, and subjecting that belief to rational pedagogic processes informed by the Enlightenment.[18] The envisaged audience was also an important factor, and it was to play a crucial role in the emergence of the *Lehrstück-Katechismus*. Whereas Luther's *Small Catechism* was compiled expressly for the instruction of children, its Roman Catholic counterpart, the *Catechismus Romanus*, published in 1566, was commissioned by the Council of Trent expressly for adults.

The mid-nineteenth century brought a critical development with John H. Newman's work, which sought to consolidate the disciplines of theology and science. Both of these, Newman thought, could be founded on the same episte-mological premises. "If religion," he wrote, "is consequent upon *reason* and for *all* men, there must be reasons producible for the rational conviction of every individual."[19] For Newman, that meant inductive, as opposed to deductive, method. The general should be derived from the particular, not vice versa.[20]

Newman's ideas soon found advocates on the Continent, for example Gustav Mey (1822–77), who similarly sought to combine scholastic methods derived from Aristotle with biblical catechetics. It was Mey, according to the theologian Franz Michel Willam, who first introduced the term Lehrstück in connection with these reforms.[21] Mey's Lehrstücke, for example in his *Vollständige Katechesen für die unterste Klasse der katholischen Volksschule*, are designed as organically constructed lessons for use in schools.[22] As such, they represent a Catholic attempt to formulate catechistic teachings expressly for children, from the Lutheran perspective once scorned by the Catholic Church.

But it was not until the early twentieth century that Mey's innovations bore fruit in catechisms proper. The first so-called *Lehrstück-Katechismus* was Heinrich Stieglitz's *Größeres Religionsbüchlein*, published in Kempten in 1916. Stieglitz, a Catholic teacher (and also a reviser of Mey's work), replaced the traditional *Fragestücke* with a continuous narrative text in a lively and uncomplicated language, including illustrations from biblical legends. Stieglitz applied what was termed the "Munich Method" (also referred to as the "psychological method"): an approach to catechistic teaching developed by reformists in Munich, Stieglitz among them, stressing the didactic importance of interaction between teacher and pupil. This, then, is the precise theological sense of Lehrstück: an instructional unit related to the catechism, presented in a language accessible to children, and based on inductive rather than deductive principles. Writing in 1905, E. Christian Achelis stated "the principle of providing a religious grounding for all Christian morality and the goal of enabling students to become morally autonomous are inalienable."[23] It is to the spirit of such autonomy that the religious Lehrstück owed its emergence – and to which the later secular one also aspired.

LEHRSTÜCK (BRECHT-HINDEMITH)

At its première at the Baden-Baden Festival on 28 July 1929, the Brecht-Hindemith piece entitled *Lehrstück* caused a scandal.[24] The critic of the *Badische Volkszeitung*, Elsa Bauer, called it "a subjugation that made a mockery of all the laws of aesthetics and morality."[25] Sensationally offensive to the sensibilities of the audience, according to reports, was the second of two "investigations" into the question of "whether one man will help another". The scene involves three giant clowns. The first and second clowns answer this question by attending in a gruesome way to the bodily ailments of the third, called Herr Schmidt: they amputate his limbs, one by one, and then unscrew his head. Conclusion: Man *does* "help" man! According to reports, one member of the première audience even fainted. The rest of the piece concerns a crashed pilot, as it were a refugee from the Brecht-Weill-Hindemith collaboration *Der Lindberghflug*, also given its première at the Baden-Baden festival.[26]

   Lehrstück is divided into seven parts: 1) "Report of the flight"; 2) "Investigation: whether man helps man"; 3) "The chorus addresses the crashed one"; 4) "Looking at death" (film); 5) "Teaching"; 6) "Second investigation: whether man helps man" (scene for clowns); 7) "Examination". The story of the crashed pilot is of course a parable, especially in view of the existentialist exhortation from the speaker in the chorus after the first "Investigation": "If you want to overcome death, then you will overcome it when you actively acquiesce to [*einverstanden seid mit*] death." When Brecht revised the text of *Lehrstück* he gave it the new title *Das Badener Lehrstück vom Einverständnis*. As will be seen, the word *Einverständnis* (active consent) becomes a key term in the Lehrstücke on several levels.

   In *Lehrstück* the crashed pilot is reduced, as the chorus declaims at the end, to "his smallest denominator": "now he knows that no one dies when he dies." That is the sober conclusion, from which performers and audience alike are left to draw their own moral. What does *Lehrstück* mean? The most comprehensive discussion to date, that by Reiner Steinweg, considers the possibilities of "mysticism, substitute religion or parody."[27] By rejecting all three of these possibilities, Steinweg seeks to defend Brecht against the attacks of his Marxist critics such as Ernst Schumacher, who criticized the piece's "ideological nebulosity [*ideologische Unklarheit*]."[28] Instead, Steinweg interprets the piece as "philosophy", posited for discussion by the participants in the sense of Brecht's later theory of the genre "Lehrstück". He also asserts that "Brecht apparently coined the term *Lehrstück* while writing [the first version of] the text."[29] Yet there are several reasons to believe that Brecht was not only aware of the theological associations of his title, but also that those associations inform the significance of the work. For all its connections with the philosophy of the later Lehrstücke, *Lehrstück* relates to the theological tradition of *Lehrstück-Katechismus* in an openly provocative way.

Brecht's pervasive use of theological motives in his work is well known. Several studies have already documented his use of the Bible; "You will laugh," he himself said in an interview in *Die Dame* in 1928 about the "strongest influence" on his work: "the Bible."[30] His religious background was mixed: his mother was a Protestant, his father a Catholic. At the Augsburg *Realgymnasium* he received religious education as a Protestant, although the school also offered classes for Catholics and Jews. During his nine years there, the first four included intensive study of the Catechism.[31] Consequently, his knowledge of the formulations of Lutheran doctrine must have been exhaustive. It is fairly safe to assume, therefore, that the title *Lehrstück* was intended to have religious echoes similar to those of his poetry collection *Hauspostille* (House Breviary; derived from the Latin *post illa verba texta*); this is named after books of biblical exegesis, of which Luther's collection of that name also serves as a model.

The ultimate test is the works themselves: both the diction and structure of *Lehrstück* are redolent of catechistic teachings, not just in the interrogative style but also in the inductive method of investigation: only after concrete demonstration are any generalities formulated. Against such a background, of course, the content of the piece is ultimately blasphemous. Sacred means (underscored by Hindemith's sparse polyphonic choral style) serve highly profane ends. The "-stück" of *Lehrstück* professes an article of anti-faith.

Whereas the relationship between *Lehrstück* and its religious source is quite apparent – substantially intended as provocative negation – any overall didactic aim behind the piece seems at best unclear. The confusion is reflected in the collaborators' published theoretical statements. Hindemith said one thing; Brecht said several things, some agreeing with Hindemith's aims, others in flat contradiction of them. Open dissension ensued over Hindemith's preface to the piano vocal score of *Lehrstück*, published in October 1929, three months after the Baden-Baden première. Hindemith concentrated on purely musical matters, such as in his description of the work's adaptability:

Since the Lehrstück has the sole purpose of engaging all those present in the work's execution and does not, in the first instance, aim to create particular impressions as a musical and poetic utterance, the form of the piece is, if possible, to be adapted as required. The order given in the score is therefore more a suggestion than a set of instructions. Cuts, additions, and reorderings are possible.[32]

Brecht took exception to Hindemith's preface, describing his instructions as based on "a misunderstanding":

Even if one expected . . . that certain formal congruencies of an intellectual nature came about on a musical basis, it would never be possible for such an artificial and shallow harmony, even for a few minutes, to create on a broad and vital basis a counterbalance to the collective formations which pull apart the people of our times with a completely different force.[33]

Brecht wrote these words for the preface to his revised *Badener Lehrstück vom Einverständnis*. However, he was prepared to shoulder the burden of responsibility:

Mainly to blame for this misunderstanding is my own willingness to subject to purely experimental purposes as unfinished and misleading a text as the version of *Lehrstück* performed in Baden-Baden. Consequently, the only didactic purpose that could be served was a musical one of a purely formal nature.[34]

Had Hindemith really misunderstood Brecht's text? The evidence suggests not. Brecht's *mea culpa* for the "misunderstanding" in the preface to his revised version serves, as it were, as a smoke screen. In 1928/29, for example, he could still maintain that "it is not necessary that action [*Handeln*]" – by which he meant making music – "be directed towards useful ends."

Music [as] *feeling aloud* (whereby it does not matter whether there is singing or whether the "animal that makes tools" uses instruments) lends the feeling of the individual, insofar as it wishes to become general, a general form and is thus the organization of people on the basis of the organization of tones.[35]

Moreover, accompanying the performance at Baden-Baden was a huge placard which bore the motto of the proceedings: "Besser als Musik hören, ist Musik machen" (making music is better than listening to it). And projected on the wall during the previous day's performance of *Der Lindberghflug* (except for the final sentence) was a text, purportedly by Brecht, which corroborated that motto:

Following the principle "the state should be rich, man should be poor," the state should be duty-bound to be capable of much, man allowed to be capable of the little he can – the state should, concerning music, produce everything that demands special study, special apparatus and special skills, but the individual should learn everything that is necessary for pleasure. For pleasure in music, it is necessary that no distraction is possible. Freely-associating

feelings occasioned by music, certain thoughts without consequence, such as those
thought while listening to music, exhaustion which easily sets in while just listening to
music, are distractions from music and reduce the pleasure in music. In order to avoid
these distractions, the thinking person takes part in music, thus following the principle
"action is better than feeling" by following a score of the music and humming the missing
parts or following the music with his eyes or singing loudly in unison with others. In this
way the state delivers incomplete music but the individual makes it complete.[36]

Like the textual backdrop to *Der Lindberghflug*, the motto on display during *Lehrstück*
the following day proclaimed that its original purpose, apart from its shocking
"alienation" of religious pedagogy, was largely of a musical nature (it was after all
given its première at a music festival) and that Hindemith's preface accurately
reflects that purpose. The *Frankfurter Zeitung* (21 May 1930) specified the piece's
objective, praising *Lehrstück* as an example of a new "community music . . . in
ideal rapprochement with the youth singing movement." Brecht's 1930 version
changed all that: rather than resolving any "misunderstanding", Brecht sought
completely to radicalize the content of the original, calling for political action and
change, augmenting its structure, and substantially reducing its musical portion.
His chief motivation behind the revision, as with his 1931 reworking of *Die
Dreigroschenoper*, appears to have been one of "de-musicalization", effectively
suppressing the work's musical origins and revising its ideological function in line
with his more recent ideas about didactic theatre.[37]

AESTHETIC TRENDS

The fact remains that *Lehrstück*, despite its later "de-musicalization" by Brecht,
owed much to trends in music pedagogy and that those trends, while epitomized
by the work of Germany's youth-music movement (*musikalische Jugendbewegung*),
had also taken hold of that country's cultural *avant garde*. The positive notices of
Lehrstück readily acknowledged this fact. Heinrich Strobel, Hindemith's first
biographer, called *Lehrstück* "nothing but the creative realization of the music-
pedagogical idea," by which he was referring to the totality of pedagogical reforms
that characterized the epoch.[38] Casting a yet wider net was the report on the Baden-
Baden festival written for the *Zeitschrift für Musik* by Karl Laux. Laux's article is
worth quoting extensively, not because it is exceptional, but because it offers a
succinct rehearsal of ideas that many musicians and critics were airing at the time.
Laux begins by describing "the situation":

We are living in a new age. Our image of music has also changed. What comprised a
city's musical life twenty years ago? Symphony concerts, choral concerts, recitals. People
attended because they wished to delight in the performances of others, but also because it

was the thing to do to have been there. People attended, at least physically. How far they participated spiritually could not be ascertained. They could indifferently allow a symphony to wash over them or they could experience it inwardly, as a storm over one's soul, a struggle with intellectual forces. This was a matter for the individual. Concerts were more or less an affair of great passivity.

That has now changed. Just as the audience's sociological mix has changed – the working masses rising upward, wishing to participate in cultural activities – so the internal structure has also changed. People no longer sit in subscription seats. They sit together in rows wishing to form a community. Moreover, this community is no longer content with just listening. They want to make music themselves. Inner involvement is thus guaranteed. *Activity of the community* replaces passivity of the individual.

It is something new, but it also existed before.

Heinrich Besseler, in his essay "Basic issues of musical listening," juxtaposed *practical Gebrauchsmusik* with *autonomous concert music*.[39] The latter contrasts with Being as "in some way self-contained"; with the former the emphasis is "wholly on the active execution of the music." Such execution is "essentially bound up with practical behavior, with prayer, avowal of beliefs, work, recreation in dance and community, entering into a mythical or magical constellation: it always comes about as ornament or intensification, as a specifically 'musical' manifestation of such behaviour."

Such *Gebrauchsmusik* – that is the word that everyone is using – has (according to Besseler) always existed: in dancing, work songs, communal singing, anthems, liturgical music, in the mythic and the magic, in vocal intensification during the narration of fairy tales, lullabies, and incantations.

The youth-music movement as well as the younger generation of composers wishes to rejuvenate such *Gebrauchsmusik*. They no longer want concerts that release listeners *from* life but music-making that redeems the listener *in* life. In the summer of 1927 people decided to act collectively. The yearly *Deutsche Kammermusik Baden-Baden* was to coincide with the annual meeting of the youth movement. They wanted "to support amateur music in every form."

In 1929 three such *utility forms* of contemporary music were to be discussed in Baden-Baden.[40]

Laux then goes on to report on the "sensation" of *Lehrstück* under the rubric "music for amateurs"; the other categories are "music for radio," including *Der Lindberghflug*, and "music for film." By invoking Besseler, Laux places *Lehrstück* in a context that had been a controversial talking-point ever since Besseler's lecture was published in 1926.[41] Although Besseler's theory of *Gebrauchsmusik* had begun as methodological reflections on the study of early music, it soon expanded into a critique of contemporary music, culminating in emphatic support for the youth movement.[42] And his theory's relevance was again stressed when, in 1930, the left-liberal journal *Musik und Gesellschaft* published an abridged version of Besseler's essay in its first issue as a kind of aesthetic manifesto.

"LEHRSTÜCK" AS A NEW TYPE OF MUSIC THEATER

Following Besseler's essay in the next issue of *Musik und Gesellschaft* were two articles, the first entitled "Lehrstück," by Hilmar Trede and Hans Boettcher, the second, "Lehrstück und Theater," by Gerhart Scherler, *Dramaturg* in Oldenburg. The authors dealt, however, not merely with one piece but with a whole collection of pieces, several of which had been written for – though not necessarily performed at – Neue Musik Berlin 1930, the successor to the 1929 Baden-Baden festival. Within the space of a year, "Lehrstück" had become the designation for a thriving genre of musical theater. "I see therein," Scherler wrote, "a new and great movement, capable of radically changing the whole condition and kind of our contemporary theater." The pieces specifically referred to in the articles are: *Lehrstück, Der Jasager, Das Wasser* (Ernst Toch and Alfred Döblin), *Der neue Hiob* (Hermann Reutter and Robert Seitz), *Wir bauen eine Stadt* (Hindemith and Seitz). Stravinsky's *Oedipus Rex* is also discussed as an "anticipation of what the 'Lehrstück' . . . can achieve." The journal *Melos* followed developments with comparable interest. By 1931 it could offer a brief "history of the 'Lehrstück'" in an article entitled "Lehrstück und Schuloper" by Siegfried Günther. Further pieces mentioned by Günther are: *Das Eisenbahnspiel* (Paul Dessau), *Das schwarze Schaf* (Paul Höffer), *Cress ertrinkt* (Wolfgang Fortner), *Jobsiade* (Theodor Jacobi and Robert Seitz) and *Der Reisekamerad* (Hans Joachim Moser).

The most frequently performed and discussed of these pieces was, without doubt, *Der Jasager*, a "school opera" (*Schuloper*) in two acts after the Japanese Noh play *Taniko* and first performed in Berlin at the Zentralinstitut für Erziehung und Unterricht on 23 June 1930.[43] Although the festival Neue Musik Berlin 1930 had commissioned the work, Brecht and Weill withdrew it. The text of the Lehrstück *Die Maßnahme*, which Brecht had submitted for scrutiny to the festival's committee (Eisler not yet having composed the music), was rejected on "purely artistic grounds." But not only Eisler and Brecht, but also Weill, sensed that there were other reasons for the rejection of the work, namely its political content.[44] *Der Jasager*'s withdrawal was intended as a protest against the inferred politics of the committee's decision.

Weill himself associated three aims with his school opera, all of them musical: "a schooling for composers or a generation of composers, in order to place the genre of 'opera' on new foundations"; "a schooling in operatic presentation" requiring "simplicity and naturalness"; and the placing of music "at the service of institutions" such as schools, "rather than its being created as an end in itself."[45] Yet there is no denying that the didactic content justifying the designation "Lehrstück" is also highly political, as the intense debates that *Der Jasager* occasioned testify.

The piece's gestation began with Elisabeth Hauptmann's translation of the fifteenth-century Noh play *Taniko*. (Her source, Arthur Waley's English version, is itself a free rendering of the Japanese original.) Although Brecht uses about ninety percent of Hauptmann's translation, he departs from it in one significant respect by introducing the concept of *Einverständnis*, which the chorus extols at the beginning of each act. The Boy, who has joined an expedition across the mountains in order to fetch medicine for his ailing mother, demonstrates *Einverständnis* in his willingness to act in the interests of the community, even to the point of sacrificing his own life, an action which becomes "necessary" when he himself falls ill. Therein lies the difference: whereas his suicide in the oriental original represents unquestioning obedience to convention, the new version attempts a demythologization, with the boy being allowed to make his own rational, autonomous decision. (An obvious parallel can be drawn with the innovations of the *Lehrstück-Katechismus*: tradition and custom are subjected to inductive scrutiny.)

Celebrating *Der Jasager's* success, *Melos* reported in 1931 how arguments about the piece went on "for weeks on end, not just within the school community but in all musically interested circles. For the first time the Critic, a man of fine musical sensibilities, is now unconditionally committed to new music. The musically indifferent have suddenly been awakened. Outsiders, not just the parents of performers, enter the battle over new music. Centers of resistance include: the Nationalists, the Wagner Youth (led at our institute by a philologist) and the orthodox wing of the church (because of the unChristian thought)."[46] Nonetheless, a number of critics appeared to misconstrue the authors' intended message: some on the right, for example, even greeted what they saw as endorsement of their conservative Christian principles, while others on the left interpreted the piece as lending support to authoritarian and reactionary tendencies, despite the authors' clear intentions to the contrary.[47]

Der Jasager even provoked a direct creative response, albeit a negative one. Hans Joachim Moser conceived his "Schuloper" *Der Reisekamerad*, mentioned above, expressly as a corrective (*per oppositionem*) to the Weill-Brecht work.[48] Freely based on Hans Christian Andersen's fairy tale, Moser's academically eclectic piece stresses the "good deed" of the individual over the notion of his or her subjugation to the collective moral preached by Brecht. Apart from his response to the success of *Der Jasager*, Moser no doubt had in mind Brecht's more recent "Lehrstücke" as well, such as *Die Maßnahme* and *Die Ausnahme und die Regel*, both of which placed the issue of *Einverständnis* in a party-political context. As the composer Hanns Eisler reportedly described *Die Maßnahme*: "It is a political seminar of a special kind on questions of the party's strategy and tactics. . . . The Lehrstück is not intended for concert use. It is only a means of pedagogical work with students of Marxist schools and proletarian collectives."[49]

Brecht was just one of many artists who were finding overtly political outlets for their art. To that extent the furore over *Die Maßnahme* was wholly symptomatic. Criticism of the traditional social apparatus of music-making, both concert and opera, was widespread, just as the organic community (*Gemeinschaft*) was favored in opposition to the inorganic, anonymous society (*Gesellschaft*). Such opposition was to be heard on both sides of the political spectrum. The call for *Gebrauchskunst* was similarly widespread and similarly unrestricted to any one political stripe. In dispute were the nature of the "use" being proposed and the type of community which the new "utility" art should serve. By way of making its voice distinct the left replaced the neutral notion of *Gebrauchswert* (use value) with the ideologically more colored criterion of *Kampfwert* (the value of didactic art in the service of a specific political struggle). Traditional aesthetic values had to yield to the requirements of agitprop.[50]

The development of the Lehrstück can be seen to reflect the general course of Weimar culture whereby the simple opposition to cultural institutions characteristic of the early and middle years of the Republic (often involving parodistic iconoclasm) gives way to the grounding of counter-cultures. Thus the parodic alienation of the Christian catechism in *Lehrstück* was transformed into the serious secular catechetics of *Der Jasager*. But like the Republic itself, the movement that produced Lehrstücke was only short-lived. Although strongly influenced by the *Schulmusikbewegung*, those Lehrstücke were principally produced by an experimental *avant garde*; they owed their inception directly to the music festivals for which they were written; and, as is exemplified by *Der Jasager*, they relied for their further dissemination on the willingness of pedagogical institutions to collude in the experiment. When the National Socialists came to power the musicians associated with the new music festivals largely fell out of favor. With their works being branded as "degenerate", most of them left Germany.[51] But if Lehrstücke necessarily ceased, their influence did not. Ingredients of the Lehrstücke – the involvement of the audience, the cast of types rather than individuals, the use of a chorus, judicial scenes in which the chorus acts as intermediary, the central theme of the relationship of the individual to the community – a theme played out by the performers, who themselves form a microcosmic community – have been identified in the so-called "Thingspiele" of the Nazi period prior to 1937, in particular the ritualistic stage spectacles of Eberhard Wolfgang Möller.[52]

THE MUSICAL IMPLICATIONS OF THE LEHRSTÜCK

Although the Lehrstück owed much to the burgeoning amateur music movement of the 1920s, one might readily assume that its implications for the composers of new music were aesthetic rather than specifically musical, especially in view of the apparent concessions that amateur music necessitated – not just stylistic and technical simplicity but also adaptability in matters such as instrumentation. Yet the cases of two of the most prominent composers who contributed to the "Lehrstück" movement, Hindemith and Weill, illustrate that such an assumption is far from the truth. As Weill said in the interview cited above, *Der Jasager* should be considered central to his output: a *chef-d'œuvre*, not a mere *parergon*. For him, as for Hindemith, amateur music not only corresponded with his personal philosophy of music but also determined how he would compose. And for Hindemith, the experience was to affect his music theory as well.

In his stage works prior to *Der Jasager* Weill utilized modern dance music to powerful dramatic effect. In the full-length opera *Aufstieg und Fall der Stadt Mahagonny* (begun in July 1927 and completed in October 1929, three months after *Der Jasager*) he oscillates between two stylistic extremes: his so-called "song style" (inaugurated in the earlier *Mahagonny Songspiel* and refined in *Happy End*) at one extreme and a more austere "neo-classical" idiom at the other. The two styles serve a symbolic purpose. Within the opera, the latter style seems to signify unadulterated nature, while the former represents the corruption of nature through civilization. Hence the hurricane at the end of Act I is an academic fugue, while the earlier "Alabama Song" is the nearest Weill gets to the idiom of commercially popular music. Similarly, the celebrated "Cranes Duet," also written in the "neoclassical" idiom and a late addition to the opera, creates an enclave in the midst of social corruption. Jim and Jenny step outside the world of commercial sex to sing a poetic love duet. Commenting on the "stylistic transformation" in his work Weill described this later style as "a perfectly pure, thoroughly responsible style," adding "I presume that it will endure longer than most of what is being produced nowadays."[53] *Der Jasager* seems to consolidate this development. As Weill said in the above-quoted interview, "the rhythms are no longer expressly dance rhythms, but have been transformed, 'digested' [*verdaut*]." The simplicity and restraint, a function of the Lehrstück, go hand in hand with the urge towards a new classicality (to use Busoni's expression). Moreover, in a work which debates the question of individual responsibility (devoid of the selfish recklessness of *Mahagonny*) Weill cultivates his own musical embodiment of such responsibility, a kind of musico-dramatic *prima prattica*.[54] The influence of *Der Jasager* is perhaps most strongly felt in Weill's next full-scale opera, *Die Bürgschaft* (1932–33), with its terse parabolic plot, neoclassical musical textures, and moralizing chorus. Yet while such stylistic and dramaturgical traits imbue *Die Bürgschaft*, it cannot really be called a Lehrstück. The generic tradition certainly persists, however, in Weill's "folk opera" *Down in the Valley* (1945–48) and, to a certain extent, in the various pageants he wrote for causes such as the American war effort.[55]

With Hindemith, the connection between pedagogy and composition is still more far-reaching. For him, too, the new simplicity prompted by writing for amateurs also affected what traditional musicology terms his "personal style".[56] Writing about the musical language of *Lehrstück*, Heinrich Strobel identified a "strength and monumentality" as opposed to the earlier "broad playing-away [*breites Ausmusizieren*]" which he felt "often endangers Hindemith's operas."[57] In other words, *Lehrstück* signals a shift in Hindemith's approach to composition, and it is a shift that continues to make itself felt in the immediately succeeding instrumental works. It is through these works – for example, the Symphony *Mathis der Maler* (1934) – that Hindemith made his later reputation. The connection between pedagogy and composition is intensified in Hindemith's case in as much as he based the music theory published as *Unterweisung im Tonsatz* (*Craft of Musical Composition*) on his own musical language. The very mobility and flexibility required by *Lehrstück* and other amateur pieces, as I have demonstrated elsewhere, generate the type of harmonies and part-writing that become the cornerstones of Hindemith's theory.[58]

CONCLUSION

In an attempt systematically to distinguish between Brecht's "Lehrstücke" and his other "Stücke", Reiner Steinweg has posited a much-discussed axiom or *Basisregel*. This suggests that Lehrstücke are different from other theatrical pieces by their being conceived primarily for the players themselves. Steinweg drew his axiom from Brecht's last written observation on the genre: "This designation [Lehrstück] is only valid for pieces that are instructive for the *performers*. They do not require an audience."[59] The rule emphasizes less the didactic content of the works than the mere fact of active participation. In defining our involvement in an aesthetic act, the rule is phenomenological. As such, in circumscribing an aesthetics of performance, it reflects a pervasive trend in Weimar culture.

The present investigation has also identified a connection between the innovations of the theatrical Lehrstück and those of its religious predecessor that goes beyond mere etymology. Just as the early twentieth-century Catholic Catechism sought to further an active comprehension and interpretation of Christian creed, so the creators of the secular Lehrstück hoped to break down traditional barriers between composers, performers, and audience in the dissemination of music. The inductive–deductive dichotomy addressed by theologians such as Heinrich Stieglitz thus has a precise analogy in the active–passive debates that characterize 1920s musical aesthetics. To that extent, the Lehrstück represents a remarkable example of the secularization of religious thought. The connection is encapsulated in an *aperçu* made by a reviewer of *Die Maßnahme*, albeit with a significance beyond the intended one (which was to draw a parallel between Brecht's work and the religious dramas of the Baroque). "It is remarkable and it is important," wrote Julius Bab, "that after Catholicism communism is now developing a 'Lehrstück'."[60] That the development of this type of music theater eventually came to grief on a platform of ideological disputes is utterly in keeping with the political Republic whose spirit the "Lehrstück" embodies perhaps more than any other artistic genre.

5

SINGING BRECHT VERSUS BRECHT SINGING:PERFORMANCE IN THEORY AND PRACTICE

KIM H. KOWALKE

During the last hour we spoke about the transformation of opera into music drama, and I explained the concept of the *Gesamtkunstwerk*. So that nobody has any excuses, I'll write on the blackboard once more the names of

Richard Wagner

Richard Strauss

Now we come to a new chapter. You'll remember that I read to you from the Wagner texts. They always dealt with gods and heroes and curious concepts like forest murmur, magic fire, knights of the Grail, etc., which you found rather strange. Then there were some difficult thought processes, which you were unable to follow, and also certain things that you could not yet comprehend and which are as yet none of your business. None of this was of much interest to you. . . .

I have just played you excerpts from the music by Wagner and his followers. You have seen for yourselves that there are so many notes in this music, I could not even reach them all. You would have liked now and then to join in singing the tune, but this proved impossible. You also noticed that this music made you feel sleepy or drunk, as alcohol or other drugs might have done. But you don't want to go to sleep. You want to hear music you can comprehend without special explanation, music you can readily absorb and sing with relative ease. . . . Nowadays there are matters of greater interest to all, and if music cannot be placed in the service of society as a whole, it forfeits its right to exist in today's world.

WRITE THIS DOWN!: Music is no longer a matter of the few.[1]

Thus Kurt Weill began his response on Christmas Day 1928 to the *Berliner Tageblatt*'s request of prominent artists (including Otto Klemperer, Heinrich Mann, and Annette Kolb) to explain their work, as if to "a class of intelligent urban twelve-year-olds who read newspapers, interested themselves in current events, and had a keen appetite for information."[2] Apparently not immune himself to *Dreigroschen*-fever, a lightheaded Weill brazenly pitched his and Bertolt Brecht's own brand of epic theater with this ill-considered ploy, parodying a tyrannical Prussian schoolmaster's lesson. The soon to be widely-quoted article concluded:

The theatrical movement that most explicitly meets the artistic demands of our time was founded by Bertolt Brecht – open parenthesis: Bertolt Brecht, the originator of epic drama – close parenthesis. Weill has recognized that this movement offers the musician a wealth of new, surprising tasks. Brecht and Weill have examined the question of the proper role of music in the theater. They have come to the realization that music should not advance or underscore the action on stage, that it fulfills its genuine function only when it interrupts the action at appropriate moments. Make a note of the most important result of Weill's work to date, the concept of the "gestic character of music," which we'll study in detail next year when those of you who intend to become professional critics will have left us.

STAND UP! We will now sing no. 16:

Der Mensch lebt durch den Kopf, der Kopf reicht ihm nicht aus, ver -
such' es nur, von dei - nem Kopf lebt höch - stens ei - ne Laus.

[Man lives by his wits / but wits will not suffice / Inspect his head to find his wits / and all you'll find is lice.][3]

As his closing polemical plug, Weill had chosen the "verse" from the first strophe of Peachum's "Das Lied von der Unzulänglichkeit menschlichen Strebens" (The song of the insufficiency of human endeavor) from *Die Dreigroschenoper*, since September a runaway hit at the Theater am Schiffbauerdamm in Berlin. The following spring, that same strophic ballad was one of the first "vocals" from the show to be recorded and commercially released. The singer on that recording was Brecht himself. The companion piece on the reverse of the shellac 78 was the song's motivic retrograde, the "Moritat vom Mackie Messer," the other sixteen-bar strophic ballad from *Die Dreigroschenoper* suited to Brecht's vocal capabilities.[4] Definitely not beautiful, yet charismatic and unforgettable in effect, Brecht's rendition resembled those of the barrel-organ accompanied *Bänkelsänger* he had witnessed in his youth at the Augsburg fairs.[5] His razor-sharp enunciation slices the text's syntax to reveal new strata of sense, while the rattler-rolled rs roil the otherwise almost stoic surface of his nasal, coarse tone. These two *Balladen* are the only available recordings of Brecht singing.

That is regrettable if only because eyewitnesses to his mesmerizing live performances – whether in theater, cabaret, or brothel – concur in their accounts of a magnetism (not to mention an entourage) of a magnitude that we now expect only of rock stars.[6] And when he stopped singing in public himself, performance became no less important. Recognizing that the "text" of music-theater is fully assembled and experienced only in performance, Brecht adhered to the "inflexible rule that the proof of the pudding is in the eating."[7] The adjective "Brechtian," therefore, early on came to denote not only his idiosyncratic contributions to playwriting, poetry, language, and dramaturgical theory but also – and perhaps more so – to performance practice: modes and techniques of acting, directing, lighting, and singing. He claimed "to be thinking always of actual delivery," how his authorial voice would be mediated by the performer for the spectator.[8] Many of the tangled theoretical commentaries that he drafted before 1935 address problems of performance; they were intended as retrospective correctives to what he perceived as failed practice. Yet that practice remains a surer guide to understanding his work in the theater than its fragmentary and frequently self-contradictory *ex post facto* theory.[9]

Brecht asserted that in *both* theory and practice it was music that "made possible something which we had long since ceased to take for granted, namely the 'poetic theater'."[10] Music provided the means by which Brecht could reclaim and refunction the presentational mode of address, long a standard convention in most forms of music-theater but discarded by modern drama after the "fourth wall" had been dismantled by naturalism and realism. His relationship to music, therefore, was as essential as it was complex. Although little interested in musical repertoire or issues extraneous to his own work for the theater, ironically Brecht first gained widespread recognition through the musical settings of his works: opera librettos, plays with music, a ballet, dramatic cantatas, an oratorio, musical films, even commercial jingles. By 1931, music critic Hans Mersmann could even proclaim: "New music in Germany has found its poet. This poet is Bertolt Brecht."[11] Of his nearly fifty completed dramatic works, only one lacks music. More than 600 of his 1500+ poems reference musical genres in both title and structure; intended as songs, most were set as such during his lifetime. Subsequently, despite copyright disincentives, there have been well over a thousand additional settings, including many by major composers. Music is a pillar so central to many of his theoretical constructs and as a parameter so determinant for the shape, diction, and delivery of his texts that Brecht's legacy cannot be fully understood or properly assessed without reference to it.[12] Confidence in his own musicality allowed him to influence settings of his works, to critique compositions by the less independent of his collaborators, and even to offer them his own melodies, of which almost 100 have survived. The remarkably small number of multiple settings of Brecht's poems during his lifetime attests to the authority commanded by those composed in direct collaboration with him. Today the songs are not infrequently still credited as Brecht's rather than the composers'. Not even Goethe overshadowed the musicians who set his texts during his lifetime so overwhelmingly. Unfortunately the attendant assumption that composers who worked closely

with him were transmitting Brecht's own readings of his poems has limited much
commentary to decidedly uncritical application of Brechtian theory, often in
dogmatic demonstrations of the fulfilment of its propositions rather than in
genuine critical examination.[13]

While very much under the spell of Frank Wedekind's cabaret models, Brecht's
first poetic impulses manifested themselves in "songs to the guitar, sketching out
verses at the same time as the music" and primitively notating them with his own
ecphonetic symbols.[14] Many of these early poems were intended to be sung either
in private to a small group of friends or in informal public settings, hence their
colloquial turns of phrase and casual appropriation of traditional forms. The songs
didn't really exist as independent texts *per se*, because the author's, composer's,
performer's, and protagonist's personas all coalesced into a single voice – Brecht's.
Carl Zuckmayer described that voice as "raw and trenchant, sometimes crude as a
ballad singer's, with an unmistakable Augsburg accent, sometimes almost beautiful, soaring without any vibrato, each syllable, each semitone being quite clear
and distinct."[15]

Prior to 1925 Brecht himself handled the music for all productions of his plays.
Each of them included several songs in which his musical voice was only a
minimal extension of the poetic one. Some are *contrafacta*, wherein one or more
pre-existent melodies are stripped of their original lyrics to allow a new text to
engage in provocative dialogue with the images associated with the too-familiar
music, "putting quotation marks, as it were, around a lot that was cheap, exaggerated, unreal."[16] More numerous are strophic ballads with neutral accompaniments
and primitive, recitative-like original melodies that insured textual preeminence.
At their most successful they reified Brecht's goal: "They must be cold, plastic,
unflinching, and, like tough nutshells when they get caught in his dentures, knock
out a few of the listener's teeth."[17] Brecht's earliest critical champion Herbert
Ihering wrote of *Trommeln in der Nacht* that one really felt "the whip-driven
rhythms of his sentences" only when Brecht sang and accompanied himself on the
guitar. In response audiences "whistled, yelled, howled, and applauded"; they were
anything but cool, rational, or "distanced."[18] Yet Brecht admitted that in these
first plays "music functioned in a fairly conventional way. There was usually some
naturalistic pretext for each musical piece":[19] in his earliest, quasi-autobiographical
play, for example, the drunken nihilist poet Baal sings four of Brecht's songs in a
seedy nightclub.

But Brecht came to realize that what Hanns Eisler would later call his "colossal
musicality without technique" would be inadequate to address music's role in the
non-Aristotelian, "dialectic" drama he was beginning to formulate.[20] Unable to
write both libretto and score as Wagner had done, after 1924 Brecht regularly
recruited or was recruited by professional composers, to whom he tried to harness

his own musical intuitions and aspirations. The first of these musical associates, Franz S. Bruinier (1905–28), apparently didn't assist much beyond such practical tasks as re-notating, arranging, and orchestrating some of Brecht's songs.[21] Dead from tuberculosis at age twenty-three, Brunier was followed briefly by Erwin Piscator's house composer, Edmund Meisel (1894–1930), who arranged the "Mann ist Mann Song" for the poet himself to sing in the Berlin Radio's 1927 production that brought him to Weill's critical attention.[22] When Weill and Brecht met shortly thereafter, they immediately explored the possibility of writing an opera together, then collaborated on a half dozen other large-scale projects during the four years of the rise and fall of plans and prospects for *Mahagonny*. Brecht's briefer association with Paul Hindemith was more rancorous and less productive, yielding only the Weill-Hindemith version of *Der Lindberghflug* and its sequel, the *Lehrstück*, both dating from 1929.[23]

Only in 1930, after setting himself the task of extracting an economically-determined aesthetic system from the conditions of the class struggle, did Brecht find an ideal musical colleague in Hanns Eisler, who more than matched Brecht's new commitment to art for ideology's sake. What Ernst Bloch labelled the "radical monotony" of Eisler's post-Schoenberg music made it the ideal counterpart within their didactic pieces to Brecht's unrhymed, irregular verse. If Brecht, as Carl Friedrich Zelter had characterized Goethe, "had a melody of his own hovering in his mind," then Eisler qualified as the playwright's Zelter, his musical alter-ego:

I feel your compositions are absolutely at one with my poems: the music simply lifts them up to the heights like gas inflates a balloon. With other composers I first have to take note of how they've treated the song, what they've made of it.[24]

Although Eisler had independently set several of Brecht's texts earlier, their full-scale partnership commenced with *Die Maßnahme*; it would span nearly three decades. During this period Brecht would formulate and reformulate his theories on the proper nature and function of music within the epic model in a series of prescriptions to which Eisler's music (for their collaborative works) conforms more closely than any others'.[25] But during the fifteen years of exile when Brecht produced most of his finest plays, he rarely collaborated with composers to create entire musico-dramatic works, as he had in the previous decade. Rather, music played only a minor role, as the dramatist maintained full control by calling in musicians only for certain numbers – after the script had been completed. Among these lesser figures were the Finnish composer/conductor Simon Parmet (1897–1969), Franz Lehár's musical executor Paul Burkhard (1911–77), the Swiss composer Huldreich Georg Früh (1903–45), and most prolifically Paul Dessau (1894–1979), Brecht's principal composer at the Berliner Ensemble.[26] During the last eight years of Brecht's life collaborations with Carl Orff and Gottfried von

Einem aborted prematurely, while that with Rudolf Wagner-Régeny (1903–69) yielded only two scores. None achieved the *Mitarbeiter* status Brecht reserved for only Weill and Eisler, who had not only supplied music but also actually contributed to the texts of their collaborative works. At the time they began working with Brecht, both of the composers had already rejected the aesthetic assumptions and hierarchies that modernism had inherited and left largely unaltered. By 1925, each was in Berlin seeking in his own way to transcend the self-preoccupation, subjectivity, and ultimate isolation of the new music and to forge new contacts with mass culture and mass audiences for socially-engaged musical art.

Although Brecht considered Eisler's settings to be "the tests of his poems, what productions were to his plays," he credited Weill with "first providing what [he] had needed for the stage."[27] The four years of their nearly continuous collaboration were transitional for Brecht; he concentrated on Marxist studies begun in 1926, published his first collection of poetry, and completed only dramatic works in which music was essential rather than incidental. In these pieces of socially-engaged music-theater the montage techniques that have become fixed in public consciousness as "Brechtian" were developed and the dramaturgical foundations of "epic" drama laid. The four cornerstones of that new theater comprised an unsentimental, repertorial, *sachlich* mode of presentation; development of new didactic genres for production outside the state-subsidized system; adaptation of cinematic techniques; and radical separation of the elements. With the latter Brecht tried to avoid the detested muddle of the Wagnerian *Gesamtkunstwerk*, where the various constituents are fused and consequently degraded. He hoped to bypass what he called "the great struggle for supremacy among words, music, and production – which always brings up the question 'which is the pretext for what?': is the music the pretext for the events on the stage, or are these the pretext for the music?".[28]

That question was especially bothersome to Brecht on the localized level, within the hybrid genre central to "epic" dramaturgy, namely the German *Song* – the new genre which Marc Blitzstein characterized in 1930 as "an outlandish mixture of German beer-drinking ditty and American ballad."[29] On the one hand, music's importance within the epic model required collaboration with professional composers. On the other, Brecht thought they would probably insist on "music having its own meaning" and resist his control over its composition and performance. Subscribing to a firm but unarticulated aesthetic belief that music is indeed capable of communicating its own non-verbal content, Brecht was suspicious of all "autonomous" music, particularly those attributes associated with the nineteenth-century tradition of *espressivo*, including the opulence of operatically-trained voices and the narcotic sensuality of string-dominated orchestration:

A single glance at the audiences who attend concerts is enough to show how impossible it is to make any political or philosophical use of music that produces such effects. We see entire rows of human beings transported into a peculiar state of intoxication, wholly passive, self-absorbed, and according to all appearances, doped. Their gapes and stares signal that these people are irresolutely, helplessly at the mercy of unchecked emotional urges. . . . Such music has nothing but purely culinary ambitions left. It seduces the listener into an enervating, because unproductive, act of enjoyment.[30]

He was well aware that poetry had seldom been able to withstand treatment by "serious music [that] stubbornly clings to lyricism and cultivates expression for its own sake."[31] Brecht distrusted musicians in general, he said, because they tended to view texts as "series of words that are there to give them the opportunity to enjoy themselves."[32] Because music tends to stimulate the listener so seductively and potently, as though without mediation, he feared that his poems would become mere material for their music and be embraced without critical reflection.[33] Consequently his own voice, no longer present as the performer's, would be appropriated by the composer's.[34] He intuited what Edward T. Cone would explicitly formulate: "In most encounters between poetry and music, poetry can become the more powerful of the two only by the intentional acquiescence or the unintentional incompetence of the composer."[35] To change this, Brecht eventually tried to posit a new paradigm, one that challenged what he feared was fundamental to the very nature of music. If it were to escape both its formalism and emotional entanglements, music would have to be turned inside out and become "Misuk," the term he invented in the 1950s for the radical refunctioning of both composition and performance that he required. Not even Eisler, who shared so many of Brecht's other values, however, could endorse so restricted a definition:

Brecht's rejection of certain sorts of music was so extreme that he invented another variety of music-making, which he called "*Misuk*.". . . For a musician it is difficult to describe *Misuk*. Above all it is not decadent and formalist, but extremely close to the people. It recalls, perhaps, the singing of working women in a back courtyard on Sunday afternoons.[36]

The ultimately unreconcilable contradiction between Brecht's absolute need for and fundamental suspicion of "cultivated" music would, in the end, limit his impact on both music theory and performance practice.

Weill recognized Brecht's dilemma and in 1929 confided to a friend his strategy for dealing with it:

Music has more impact than words. Brecht knows it and he knows that I know. But we never talk about it. If it came out in the open, we couldn't work with each other any more. Brecht asks for complete submission. He doesn't get it from me, but he knows that I'm good and that I understand him artistically, so he pretends that I'm utterly under his spell. I don't have to do anything to create that impression. He does it all himself.[37]

Brecht indeed later claimed that he "had whistled things for Weill bar by bar and above all performed them for him."[38] This familiar account of Brecht's ventriloquism (and the single-handed rescue of his "dummy" from Schrekerian "atonal psychological operas") has been obliquely substantiated by a frequently cited essay published under Lotte Lenya's name but written by her second husband, George Davis: "Sometimes Brecht impressed on Kurt his own ideas for a song, picking out chords on his guitar. Kurt noted these ideas with his grave little smile and invariably said yes, he would try to work them in." The original typescript includes another sentence suppressed in publication: "Naturally they were forgotten at once."[39] Except on two or three celebrated occasions, Weill proved an unwilling mouthpiece for Brecht's melodies. He was as aggressive as the poet when it came to defending his territory. In a recently rediscovered interview from 1934, when the interviewer commented on the dominant role Brecht had played in their collaboration, Weill answered him sharply:

It almost sounds as if you think Brecht wrote my music. I've often been amazed at hearing this view. Like most erroneous opinions, it comes out of nowhere. . . . Brecht is one of modern Germany's greatest literary talents; but being a great poet doesn't necessarily mean he's also a good composer. . . . Brecht is a genius, but for the music in our joint works, I alone am responsible.[40]

What permitted poet and composer to pursue common goals, while gradually realizing that aesthetic and sociological premises were insufficiently shared, was the mediating concept of *Gestus*, a term introduced in print by Weill in his hypothetical lecture to twelve-year-olds.[41] Within the dramaturgy of a music-theater that strove to illuminate social relationships between characters rather than internal psychological states, Weill and Brecht both conceived *Gestus* as a means of making manifest on stage the behavior and attitudes of human beings toward one another.[42] They agreed that music was indispensable in communicating the fundamental *Gestus* of a theatrical situation. A new "gestic" language, combining dramatic, lyric, and epic modes of poetry, would require a "gestic" music in which musical autonomy and expressivity would yield before dramatic and socio-political purposes. In their respective prescriptive essays, Weill and Brecht borrowed terminology and exchanged examples as each groped toward a working definition of both *Gestus* and *gestische Musik* based on his own reading of their evolving practice.

For Brecht, *Gestus* was but one of several strategies for "epicization" of interpretation, presentation, and reception of his dramatic works. The inconsistencies of terminology, definition, and usage in his various writings betray an underlying conflict and growing tension between the dramaturgical function and ideological impact that Brecht envisioned for *Gestus*. Sometimes he demanded that the fundamental *Gestus* of a scene prescribe a certain attitude or behavior for the *performer*;

elsewhere he asserted that "the theater would benefit greatly if musicians were able to produce music which would have a more or less exactly foreseeable effect on the *spectator* [italics mine]."[43] Although Brecht progressively referred to *Gestus* in less behaviorist and more Marxist terms (characters' social relationships must be presented as determined by economic and political factors), initially it seems to have served primarily as a means to reserve space within the song for his own poetic voice/persona and to dictate readings of his texts by both composer and performer. It is, therefore, not accidental that the concept emerged only after he had stopped writing and publicly singing his own songs, when he himself could no longer entirely control the reading of his poems.

By fixing the rhythm, stress, pitch, timbre, pauses, phrasing, dynamics, tempos, and intonation of his poetry in a musical setting, Brecht hoped that he could make his works virtually performer-proof and insure a "drug-free" effect on their audiences. He was far from isolated in his quest; it is not merely coincidental that Stravinsky, at precisely the same time, was attempting to "safeguard his work by establishing the manner in which it ought to be played" on a series of definitive recordings for Columbia initiated in 1929. In his *Autobiography*, Stravinsky lamented the project's failure: "Is it not amazing that in our times, when a sure means, which is accessible to all, has been found of learning exactly how the author demands his work to be executed, there should still be those who will not take any notice of such means, but persist in inserting concoctions of their own vintage?"[44] Sound recordings alone, of course, could not proscribe authentic performance *practice* for Brecht's theatrical works; he hoped the *theory* of *Gestus* could.

Although Weill's theoretical formulations were equally convoluted and undeveloped, the practical significance of the concept was very different for him. He described *Gestus* almost exclusively as a technical tool of the composer, with historical precedents in the music of Bach, Mozart, Beethoven, Offenbach, and Bizet. He assumed that *Gestus* would enable music to regain predominant position in the structure of musical theater works, "right down to the execution of the smallest details." *Gestus* could free music from its traditional parallelism to the text, as well as its descriptive and psychological functions, thereby granting wider melodic, formal, and harmonic latitude. "The specific work of the composer occurs when he utilizes the means of musical expression to establish contact between the text and what it is trying to express."[45] In other words, the composer thought that gestic music could articulate that which the text does not make explicit and thereby provide a subtext ready-made for the performer. The resulting "play" between the music and the lyric could convey complicated layers of meaning and contradictory attitudes of overlapping personas. Competition among these various internal voices would reach its greatest intensity at the point where duality, ambiguity, and paradox emerge as stylistic hallmarks.

When Brecht wrote that "Weill's music for [the opera *Mahagonny*] is not purely gestic," he called attention to discrepancies in both theory and practice in their respective gestic formulas.[46] In light of such concurrently evolving parallel constructs as *Verfremdung*, Brecht probably found music gestic where it most distanced itself from the text by means of parody or irony. But having asserted the primacy of music and its independence from the text, Weill could only reject Brecht's definition as too restrictive: "Any bias in the presentation of [*Mahagonny*] toward the ironic or the grotesque is emphatically to be discouraged."[47] Perhaps the dissonance of their non-unison voices is best observed in the example Weill himself chose to illustrate *gestische Musik*: the "Alabama Song," a key number in both the *Songspiel* and the full-length opera. Brecht and Weill's first collaborative effort, the *Songspiel*, appropriated from Brecht's *Hauspostille* the five exotic pieces of *Amerikanismus* entitled "Mahagonny-Gesänge," for which he had already sketched rudimentary tunes "out of necessity," according to Weill's essay, "of making the *Gestus* clear." Because Elisabeth Hauptmann had a hand in its primitive, pop-song English of the poem, we know that Brecht wrote the text of the "Alabama Song" after November 1924, when he first met the former English teacher. Brecht's tune, which was issued in slightly different variants in the privately published *Taschenpostille* (1926) (Example 5.1) and *Hauspostille* (Propyläen-Verlag, 1927), predates 21 November 1925, when Bruinier completed a textless, strophic

Example 5.1 Brecht's melody as it appeared in the *Taschenpostille*

Alabama Song

Oh, lead us the way to the next whis-ky-bar,— oh, don't ask why,—

oh, don't ask why,— for we must find the next whis-ky-bar, for if we don't find

the next whis-ky-bar, I tell you, I tell you, I tell you we must die!

Oh! moon of A-la-ba-ma, we now must say good-

bye, we've lost our good old mam-ma and must have whis-ky, oh! you know why.

piano realization of the melody (Example 5.2).[48] Whatever its shortcomings from a purely musical point of view – even Bruinier had found it necessary to modify portions of the childlike melody in order to make its chain of descending minor thirds conform to syntactical structures of diatonic tonal music – Brecht did indeed set forth a *Gestus*: short, plodding phrases in the verse, breathless and monotonous, cramped into the span of a minor third in the mid-range of the voice, with no syllable sustained much beyond a sighed half note; a refrain of no more musical interest, but one that expands its range phrase by phrase until it spans a ninth. Weill analyzed Brecht's music in some detail and asserted: "A basic *Gestus* has been fixed rhythmically in the most primitive form, while the melody adheres to the totally personal and inimitable manner of singing with which Brecht performs his songs. . . . One sees that this is nothing more than a notation of the speech-rhythm and completely useless as music." This is more than just a professional composer summarily dismissing the efforts of an amateur: it is a musician reasserting the primacy of his art.

Example 5.2 Bruinier's setting of Brecht's melody (1925)

When Weill reordered the "Mahagonny-Gesänge" for the *Songspiel*, he separated the two English lyrics, breaking up a poetic dyad (the sensual Alabama moon vs sacred Benares sun) to effect a strict alternation of German and English up to the added new Finale. Weill scored the opening fox-trot "Auf nach Mahagonny" for four men in close harmony, a sonority invoking both *Singverein* and barbershop. With the textual trope on the refrain of the "Jungfernkranz" chorus from *Der Freischütz*, the listener expects the four hunters of pleasure to croon to the beautiful green moon of their longing for the "Spiel und Tanz, Glück und Liebesfreude" of Weber's verse; instead they anticipate eating, drinking, gambling, and whoring in Mahagonny, with plenty of cold green cash in their pockets to pay for their vices. While the women in *Der Freischütz* discover a funeral wreath in place of a bridal bouquet, the men of Mahagonny find death not life, for the *Songspiel* is a *Totentanz*. Weill changed the first line of Brecht's refrain from "Schöner, grüner Mond von Mahagonny" to "von Alabama" – presumably to make explicit its new pairing with the "Alabama Song" that directly follows. The pursuit of money corrupts even the moon; no longer the romantic symbol of the unattainable, in the "Alabama Song" it points the two whores toward "the next whisky bar" and "next little dollar."

In his *Songspiel* version for two sopranos, Weill treated Brecht's melody as a pre-compositional framework; he preserved its opening pitches nearly verbatim, but as world-weary *Sprechstimme*. Weill altered the rhythm to accommodate the natural accents of the text and to avoid Brecht's awkward placement of an extra eighth note at "I tell you." (Weill seems to have known English better than Brecht at the time.) (Example 5.3.) By the fifth measure chromaticism has stolen into the melody, and Brecht's bland modality is left far behind. The fifth-generated sonorities of the accompaniment are presented in Bartokian garb of secondal dissonances. But the real contrast is in the refrain, where Weill claimed that "the same basic *Gestus* has been established, only here it has actually been 'composed' with the freer means of the musician." (See Example 5.4.) Although it too spans a ninth, Weill's major-mode refrain unfolds in broad melodic sweeps, which yearn for that which has been lost no less than Lenya's famous gesture of palm upturned toward the moon. Its recurrent whole notes suspended across barlines not only emphasize the exoticism of rhyming "moon of Alabama" with "good old mamma" but also liberate the vocal persona from the incessant rhythmic drive of the accompaniment so that it can communicate things not explicit in the text. In Theodor W. Adorno's words, "The 'Alabama Song' is altogether unique among the pieces in *Mahagonny*, and in no other song does the music suggest the primal power of remembering long forgotten snatches of baleful melodies, whose mindless repetition in the introduction seems to be recalling them from the realm of madness."[49] Having thus established the *Grundgestus* in the first strophe, Weill had freer rein in successive strophic varations for purely musical elaboration and

Example 5.3 Weill's "Aabama Song" from *Mahagonny* (1927)

Example 5.4 Weill's refrain

expansion. In the refrain of the final strophe of the *Songspiel* setting, for example, Jessie and Bessie sing in canon – imitation that can still be read as the characters' rather than the composer's. In the analogous spot in the version for Jenny and the six whores in the opera, Weill allows himself the "coloratura embellishment" characterized as "suitable gestic lingering" in his essay.[50] Brecht couldn't possibly agree; such musical delights would tantalize listeners into traditional culinary consumption.

After the tumultuous impact of the *Songspiel* in Baden-Baden, and as Brecht and Weill worked on the full-scale opera, they experimented with other recipes for hybrid forms of musical theater and tested them in performance: the plays-with-music *Die Dreigroschenoper* and *Happy End*; the didactic cantata *Der Lindberghflug*; and the school opera *Der Jasager*. But the enthusiasm with which audiences of the late 1920s digested these offerings left the impression that Adorno, who had defended the works against their popular success, was almost alone in reacting along the lines that Brecht now claimed to have intended.[51] By the time *Aufstieg und Fall der Stadt Mahagonny* arrived in Berlin late in 1931, after productions in several provincial opera houses, an ad hoc company of actors, operetta singers, and cabaret artists, some of whom were also working with Piscator, had gathered around Brecht: Peter Lorre, Oskar Homolka, Carola Neher, Helene Weigel, Ernst Busch, Kurt Gerron, Harald Paulsen, Theo Lingen, Kate Kühl, and, of course, Lotte Lenya.[52] *Die Dreigroschenoper*'s sensational popularity had propelled many members of that loose collective into the recording studio: the songs appeared on more than forty discs with twenty different labels.[53] A large selection of these shellac recordings have now been re-released, so we can still hear many of Brecht's vicarious voices. Most were indeed actors first, with razor-edged diction, but almost all of them could also really sing; the theatrical system required such versatility, and customary training of actors had nurtured it. Paulsen, for example, took over Tauber's roles in Lehár, and Weill chose Busch for the Heldentenor role in *Der Silbersee*. Carola Neher and the young Lenya, both soprano songbirds, competed neck and neck for recordings of the *Dreigroschenoper* songs. But Lenya monopolized the "Alabama Song"; she was the only vocalist known to have recorded it during Weill's lifetime. It had been her audition song for Brecht, had stunned the audience in Baden-Baden, and then had become almost emblematic of the entity Brecht-Weill. As described by Ernst Bloch, her voice then was "sweet, high, light, dangerous, cool, with the radiance of the crescent moon." Her 1932 performance – with members of the Berlin cast covering some of Jenny's vocally formidable passages – is as close as we can come to sampling the original pudding, a bit of *echt* Brechtian performance practice.

Although it had been cast largely with singing actors rather than opera singers (necessitating certain cuts and simplifications) and accompanied by a reduced orchestra under Alexander von Zemlinsky, even this production was not pleasing to Brecht's acquired "dialectical materialist" taste. He bemoaned that "all is washed out by the music." During rehearsals, in a scene worthy of *Capriccio*, Brecht publicly denounced Weill as a phoney Richard Strauss. Separating the ingredients and fixing the *Gestus* had failed to settle the "great struggle for supremacy" between text and music or to eliminate the lively competition among the multiple voices. Brecht's dissatisfaction with the results of his collaboration with Weill is most vividly demonstrated by the fact that he either repudiated or unilaterally revised each of their theatrical works, eventually republishing all but one of them in literary versions incompatible with Weill's music.[54] In two cases Brecht paralleled these revisions with commentary reinterpreting or correcting, from his maturing Marxist perspective, the "misunderstandings" engendered by the originals. In his and Peter Suhrkamp's lengthy notes to *Mahagonny* published in 1930, Brecht acknowledged that in the eating, the opera had turned out to be "culinary through and through." *Mahagonny* had demonstrated that opera could not be reformed; it must be replaced:

The opera *Mahagonny* was written three years ago, in 1927 [*recte* 1927–30]. In subsequent works attempts were made to emphasize the didactic more and more at the expense of the culinary element. And so to develop the means of pleasure into an object of instruction, and to convert certain institutions from places of entertainment into organs of mass communication.[55]

If Brecht's notes to *Mahagonny* set forth theoretically an aesthetic and political agenda for epic theater that the opera itself had failed to address, much less accomplish, the notes to *Die Dreigroschenoper* were intended as a corrective to the performance practice that had accounted for its unexpected success, which Brecht (and his Marxist critics) now viewed as "mistaken."[56] The revisions to the text and the new notes reflect what he would have liked the play to be, in light of the dire post-première changes in political and economic circumstances and Brecht's subsequent experiments with didactic modes of music-theater. They evince the shift in emphasis from dramaturgical structures to ideological stance as Brecht attempted to refunction the work. Informing subsequent readings of the play with tropes on the original seemed his best bet for bringing out a clear socio-political message absent or diffused in the text of the "comic literary operetta" (then still being staged around the world), which the communist periodical *Rote Fahne* had dismissed as an "entertaining mishmash without a trace of modern social or political satire."[57]

Brecht's *Dreigroschenoper*-notes were intended to be corrective rather than descriptive in yet another sense: several sections are barely camouflaged attempts to privilege future readings of the piece capable of reversing text-music relationships inherent in the original. If the text had lost round one in the struggle for supremacy,

Brecht was not inclined to concede the bout. He would simply change strategies: the composer's need not be the last nor necessarily the decisive reading of a poetic text. An audience's reading will be based to a large degree on that of the director and performers, who give empirical voice to the personas of poet, composer, and dramatic characters and modulate those with their own. Thus, in the section of the *Dreigroschen*-notes entitled "About the singing of the songs," Brecht admonishes actors not "to follow the melody blindly." "There's a way of speaking against the music which can be very effective just because of an obstinate matter-of-factness, independent of and incorruptible by the music and rhythm." He also stipulates that "the actor must not only sing but show a man singing."[58]

In these three suggestive sentences Brecht set forth the underpinnings of what thereafter would be taken at face value to be the essence of authentic "Brechtian" performance practice. By calling for uncultivated voices that have avoided training in classical technique and by reminding his actors that they need not sing all the time, the aesthetic distraction of the "voice-object" is minimized, and the scope of the performer's (and consequently also the composer's) voice restricted. Leaving the melody "unsung" at crucial moments simultaneously muffles the composer's and mutes the character's virtual voice to allow the poetic persona to be heard without competition, clearly enunciating the text while the singing voice retreats.[59] The composer is banished to the orchestral pit, but Brecht offers him compensation for loss of his voice. Invoking the "lyrisches Ich," in German literary criticism a construct roughly analogous to "persona," Brecht suggests that

In the orchestra, no matter how small, lies your chance as a musician. You have had to relinquish the melody to the non-musician, the actor. What can you expect from them? Your orchestra is your troupe, your gang, your constant. True, it has to supply supports for the aforementioned non-musicians; otherwise he will collapse, but every instrument that you can wrestle free from this duty is won for you, for the music, sir! . . . Instruments don't speak per "I" but rather per "he" and "she." What forces you to share the feeling of the "I" on stage? Where are your own feelings? You are entitled to adopt your own position to the song's theme. Even the support you give can serve other arguments![60]

Requiring that the actor "not only sing but show a man singing" can be read as a parallel effort to insure that the poetic persona also shares the stage with the protagonist. Brecht distances the performer from the performed and differentiates the presence of the character from that of the performer. With characteristic dialectics, Brecht requires the actor to depict his character's reality and yet stand outside it observing as an eyewitness: "The singer becomes a reporter, whose private feelings must remain a private affair."[61] The poet thereby forges an alliance with the performer, who then stands in for him as narrator and commentator, displacing the protagonist as author of the words being sung. Thus even a solo performance is a type of montage, a combination of mimetic immediacy and diegetic distancing, a composite of dissected realities. Although intended to seem "naïve" to an audience, it is anything but simple for the performer, who must demonstrate awareness of his own presence in the performance. When used sparingly for narrative passages of speech-like declamation by singing actors consciously holding additional vocal resources in reserve, and not out of necessity, "theory" proved itself effective in practice in the best recorded performances of songs by Lenya, Neher, and Busch.

But in the wake of posthumous interpreters of Brecht, ranging from the composers Cerha, Henze, and Berio to singers as diverse as Dagmar Krause, Teresa Stratas, and Sting, "Brechtian" has now come to mean something very different from what would have been recognized as such in performances of the Weimar period. A "performance tradition" based on theory post-dating the works in question, with precepts from a later period of Brecht's career misapplied to works from an earlier, is now routinely invoked as a standard for the entire Brecht canon and, because of his paradigmatic stature, beyond. That fact has important ramifications for the performance and critical perception of a wide repertory of music from the Weimar period. Whereas "Brechtian" originally denoted an unsentimental, "cool," repertorial, *sachlich*, but nonetheless musically accurate manner of presentation, closely allied to the matter-of-fact directness of popular singers and cabaret artists, it has now been extended – by privileging theory over the musical demands of the works themselves – to repertoire, most notably *Aufstieg und Fall der Stadt Mahagonny*, inherently incompatible with such an approach. The common practice of transposing songs down to actresses' speaking registers produces the now *de rigueur* Brechtian bark. High notes are frequently replaced or rendered as *Sprechstimme,* musical subtleties ignored, the youthful vulnerability that once balanced textual toughness lost. Rearranging scores for smaller ensembles has eliminated much of the play among personas and has inhibited music's counterpoint to the lyric; the text may seem to win, but the song certainly loses. The poet is diminished as much as the composer, for Brecht's inimitable voice is never truer, more telling, or more powerful than when competing for cohabitation with worthy music sung by performers capable of meeting the particular challenges it presents.

An extreme case in point, but an important historical milestone and precedent for posthumous performance practice, is "Das kleine Mahagonny," the Berliner Ensemble's 1963 adaptation of the *Mahagonny* opera. Rewritten according to theories that undermine the structure and content of the original, the resulting sixty-minute "*aggressiv*" play-with-songs was intended by Brecht's official widow, Helene Weigel, as an antidote to contemporaneous productions in opera houses. As performed by a company of actors and a *Dreigroschen*-band in an uncredited arrangement, the composer's voice is no longer recognizable as his own.

Responsibility for the presumed ideological failings of the original has been shifted posthumously from the playwright to the composer; Brecht's intentions for the work, sabotaged in Weill's opera, have thereby finally been fulfilled.[62] Such practice still reverberates, and its cumulative effect is nowhere more obvious than in the progressive decline of the theater company Brecht founded. The Berliner Ensemble has paradoxically demonstrated many parallels with Bayreuth, its ideological and aesthetic antipode. Not least among them is the loss or suppression of the founder's contradictory impulses and ideas and the powerful heirs' substitution of an orthodoxy (mistakenly) derived from the master's theory rather than practice:

If theory were not of such secondary importance, nor so much a mere retrospective, superfluous celebration of his talent, then his work would undoubtedly have become as untenable as the theory has. Nobody would ever have taken the theory seriously even for a minute if it were not for the work which seems to be giving evidence of it for as long as one sits in the theater – a work which, in the end, though, gives evidence only of itself.[63]

Thomas Mann's remarks about Wagner apply as aptly to Brecht. And Brecht surely would have agreed: we know that his rehearsals consistently pitted Brecht the director against Brecht the playwright and Brecht the theorist. "'How could anyone write such Dreck?' he would ask rhetorically." Everything remained provisional, a *Versuch*, subject to change, in light of new ideas or changed circumstances, in practice:

At the first run-though of *Baal* . . . the leading actress, Margarete Anton, fainted and was carried off. Brecht remained unmoved by all these carryings-on, but after Anton recovered from her faint he did publicly inquire about the color of her underwear saying that he had been thinking about the question for three days, wondering whether she was wearing a pink rather than a sky-blue slip. She lifted her skirt coquettishly and said, "grey," to which Brecht is supposed to have replied, "Grey, friend, is all theory."[64]

If, with that admonition, we return now to our opening scene of Brecht singing "Der Mensch lebt durch den Kopf," we can envision him, in Eisler's words, "striving for reason, even in music." But for maximum dialectical dynamic and theatrical effect, that performance must be juxtaposed with another, a prologue, set in the privacy of Brecht's Augsburg apartment. There, in his living room, with an audience of a few friends, he liked to conduct – without an orchestra or singers but otherwise fully equipped with a baton, a music stand, and a well-worn *Partitur* of *Tristan und Isolde*.[65]

ACKNOWLEDGMENTS

Earlier versions of this essay were read at "German Literature and Music: An Aesthetic Fusion," University of Houston (2–4 March 1989) and the Annual Meeting of the American Musicological Society, Chicago (6–10 November 1991). I am indebted to several colleagues for their helpful comments, especially Professor Stephen Hinton's formal response in Chicago. Documents of Kurt Weill are quoted with the permission of the Kurt Weill Foundation for Music. Brecht's and Bruinier's settings of the "Alabama Song" are reprinted courtesy of the Bertolt-Brecht-Archiv. Weill's "Alabama Song" is used by eprmission of European American Music Corp.

6

GERMAN MUSICOLOGY AND EARLY MUSIC PERFORMANCE, 1918–1933

PAMELA M. POTTER

The emergence of amateur performance organizations in Weimar Germany in all socio-economic groups comprised a powerful reaction against the nineteenth-century soloist cult. Within the workers' movement alone, the Deutsche Arbeitersängerbund experienced an increase in membership of nearly a quarter of a million in 1920 to nearly half a million in 1928.[1] Bourgeois and right-wing amateur groups appeared as well, in the form of male choirs, mixed choirs, amateur orchestras, and chamber groups. The large number of journals and newsletters begun between 1918 and 1933 is a testimony to the seriousness of amateur performers. This period saw the first issues of music periodicals dedicated to music education, folk music, and amateur music-making. Even though many did not outlive their first issue, the burgeoning of publishing activity represents a heightened concern with the cultivation of music for and by the public (see the appendix to this chapter).

With the increase in amateurs' participation came a demand for repertoire that was within their technical reach. Critics attacked the art music of the nineteenth and earlier twentieth centuries for alienating music from the public and straying from the roots of folk culture, but their complaints also reflected the purely practical need to supply the growing number of amateur groups with new performance repertoire. The burden of providing performable pieces fell on the shoulders of not only composers but also publishers and editors. Folk music offered one solution to the problem, and from the turn of the century the German government and private organizations initiated large-scale projects for collecting, editing, and publishing folk songs.[2] But this was a slow and arduous process, requiring field research, transcription, and arranging, and folk music alone could not furnish enough variety to suit the tastes of the wide range of new groups.

Another rich source for performance repertoire was early music, which, unlike folk music, had been a focus of scholarship for many years. German musicologists had invested much of their energy over the preceding decades in the rediscovery of early music, and the vast amount of material already accumulated yielded a rich source of "new" and less challenging repertoire that could be edited for performance editions. Scholars drew attention to newly discovered works of long-forgotten German masters, exposed the community to the fruits of their labors by facilitating performances, and secured government funding for the continuation of such large editing projects as the *Denkmäler deutscher Tonkunst*. The demand for performance repertoire in the post-war period provided an opportunity for German musicology to turn its scholarly activities into a practical enterprise as well as to avert the potential crisis of budget cuts for editing projects and musicology departments.

SOCIO-ECONOMIC CLIMATE AFTER WORLD WAR I

The First World War had devastating effects on German musicology. Travel restrictions and a shortage of research funds greatly curtailed the progress of music scholarship, which had flourished before the war, and the dissolution of the International Music Society in 1914 not only put an end to one of the field's most important journals, the *Sammelbände der Internationalen Musikgesellschaft,* but also stopped the flow of international scholarly exchange. Toward the end of the war, musicologists used their negative experiences of wartime alienation from the international community to establish a new, exclusively German scholarly society, the Deutsche Musikgesellschaft, and a national research institute in Bückeburg dedicated to the history of German music, with their respective journals, the *Zeitschrift für Musikwissenschaft* and the *Archiv für Musikwissenschaft*.[3]

The prospects of peacetime encouraged German scholars to expand the field by setting up new musicology departments throughout the German university system, and several universities appointed full professors in musicology between 1915 and 1932.[4] But the short-lived promises of prosperity soon met with harsh economic realities: the costs of war, the period of inflation, and the job shortage problem caused by the return from the front of unemployed musicologists. The November Revolution of 1918 posed an additional obstacle to the revival of music scholarship after the war. The new government was inclined to reassess all intellectual activity not just for its budgetary feasibility but also for its contribution to the well-being of the community in all social strata. Weimar authorities demanded that all government-subsidized enterprises be of direct service to the masses and undertook a far-reaching plan to democratize the education system, a plan which included expanding more practical research areas in universities in an effort to bring higher education closer to the needs of the nation.[5]

The success of newly established musicology departments depended on a system that would guarantee the future growth of the field as a humanities discipline, but the unexpected reductions imposed by the new government and the change of philosophy in higher-education policy stunted their growth, and musicological scholarship paid a heavy price. The effects of cutbacks were most devastating in Prussia and Saxony, where two of the oldest and most famous musicology departments in these provinces, those in Berlin and Leipzig, suffered severe setbacks in their scholarly activities despite their reputations. The Leipzig faculty had maintained high standards of scholarship under the direction of Hugo Riemann, Hermann Abert, and Theodor Kroyer, but Kroyer's departure in 1932 gave the authorities in Saxony the opportunity to save money by terminating his senior position and replacing him with the junior colleague Helmut Schultz, a move which outraged the entire scholarly community.[6] Economic difficulties also took their toll on the Berlin faculty in 1931 when professors experienced a series of salary reductions as a result of emergency measures that siphoned funds from higher education.[7] The following year, the musicology faculty had to exercise its own budget cuts by reducing the service of two of its most active scholars, Johannes Wolf and Hans Joachim Moser.[8]

One reason for the new plight of musicology was the fact that by 1918 scholars were hard-pressed to demonstrate the accessibility of their work to the new government or to anyone outside the field, with the possible exception of the middle-class concert-goer. Despite Hermann Kretzschmar's warnings in 1903 that musicology should always maintain close ties to practicing musicians and composers,[9] the trend toward detailed study of the past in the intervening years had led the field astray from his goals. Musicology found its place in the university rather than the conservatory, identifying itself as a humanities discipline in a league with art history, classics, and other philological fields and allowing scholars to retreat from community service and become alienated from musical life.

Some musicologists recognized the problem and were quick to denounce the acquired elitism of their discipline. In 1925 Arnold Schering publicly criticized the growing gulf between contemporary musical scholarship and composition, the result largely of musicology's tendency to bury itself in the remote past, and insisted that musicology reach an understanding with musicians and composers.[10] Others chose to seek points of contact outside the musical realm, emphasizing the public service potential of music scholarship. The initiation of a new political order inspired an interest among musicologists in music policy and recommendations to create new institutions. Hans Mersmann asked the state to implement a conscious and systematic public education (*Volkserziehung*) by setting up programs to cultivate folk music, to organize public concerts in urban centers and smaller towns and villages, and to provide lectures and workshops in music appreciation.[11] Egon Wellesz offered similar suggestions, proposing that the state appoint committees to organize and promote concerts for workers and that the state be responsible for making music a part of everyday life through education.[12] Other musicologists tried to form an alliance with private music instructors and composers by articulating the need for the state to protect these groups with quality control measures, minimum instruction-fee regulations, and copyright guarantees.[13]

Musicologists rallied under the banner of *Volkserziehung* as a potential inroad to public recognition. Johannes Wolf lauded *Volkserziehung* as musicology's "noblest task" in his contribution to the Festschrift honoring Kretzschmar's seventieth birthday in 1918[14] and spread his message beyond the scholarly community by reprinting his essay in the more popular *Allgemeine Musikzeitung*.[15] Several scholars followed suit and began to demonstrate a heightened interest in music education, music policy, and amateur music-making, but their newness to these areas resulted in varying degrees of success. They treated music education as an area in which to offer learned suggestions based on historical knowledge, but their attempts rarely went beyond the theoretical realm. In 1927 Georg Schünemann published a history of German music education,[16] Ernst Bücken edited a handbook for music educators,[17] and Hans Joachim Moser and Hans Albrecht offered practical suggestions for regulating music in elementary schools and private instruction.[18] In practice, however, attempts to reach out to the masses were sometimes only half-hearted, revealing the social gulf that lay between academy and factory. Moser, for one, complained bitterly of the low honoraria he received in the service of "Bildung zum Volke" and of the frustrations of putting his proletarian audiences to sleep with his scholarly lectures.[19]

While these adventurous scholars explored new areas of potential practical application and validation, other musicologists continued to pursue their interests in familiar territory. Their perseverance in rooting out early music sources and producing scholarly editions paid off as musicologists and directors of amateur groups recognized their common purpose. The results of detailed research accumulated over the years yielded a rich source of repertoire that lay within the performance means of amateur groups. This repertoire could easily be selected, adapted to the modern availability of instruments and musical expertise, and presented to the amateur market in the form of performance editions.

EARLY MUSIC PERFORMANCE EDITIONS

The *Denkmäler deutscher Tonkunst* (*DDT*) had been in operation since 1889, and its early history paralleled that of its Austrian counterpart, the *Denkmäler der Tonkunst in Österreich* (*DTÖ*). Both were conceived when their publishers made appeals for government subvention by presenting to the respective monarchs editions of music written by members of the royal families (an edition of Frederick the Great's compositions for flute was a forerunner of the *DDT*, and the two-volume "Kaiserwerke" preceded the *DTÖ*). In both cases this tactic succeeded in drawing attention to the need for preserving musical "treasures" in published editions, and the Prussian and Austrian officials supported the ventures not only for their "patriotic and artistic goal" but also because of prearranged guaranteed subscriptions.[20]

After the First World War, low morale created a need to redefine German identity and rebuild national pride, and musicologists responded by promoting studies and musical activities in purely German areas. Especially in border districts such as Cologne, the "needs" of the community included reinforcing German culture in order to stave off the "threats" of foreign culture, and authorities placed great value on "the strengthening of German musicological aspirations in the Rhineland" and provided state funding for "musicological cultural activities (public lectures, observation of foreign propaganda)."[21]

The desire to develop a German national identity in musicology was most pronounced in early music projects, such as those of the Music Research Institute in Bückeburg, founded in 1917 to provide cataloguing, bibliographic, and publication services to the musicological community and focussing primarily on German music. Director Max Seiffert described the institute's broader practical aims as fulfilling duties to the Fatherland by educating German youth to distinguish between good and bad, between noble art and "shallow pseudo art of the changing times" through a "living union of music practice and science," not only through acquaintance with the great masters but also through the rediscovery of local heroes or *Kleinmeister*.[22]

In the economic and political climate of Weimar, however, symbolic importance for national identity was not enough of an attribute to secure scarce government funds for early music editions. The *DDT* was forced to suspend its publication in 1919, following thirty years of uninterrupted activity that yielded nearly sixty volumes of works by German masters.[23] The *DDT* also had to face competition at this time from an increased number of editions of early music intended for performance. Some series, such as *Collegium musicum* (edited by Hugo Riemann from 1903 to 1911), had already been initiated at the turn of the century, and the period following the inflation saw the emergence of important new multi-volume performance editions: *Das Chorwerk,* edited by Friedrich Blume (1929); *Nägels Musik-Archiv* (1927); *Kammersonaten* (1928); *Organum,* edited by Max Seiffert (1924); *Das Chorbuch des Musikanten,* edited by Fritz Jöde (1927); and *Musikalische Formen in historischen Reihen,* edited by H. Martens (1930).

The *DDT* could resume publication only after undergoing significant changes that reflected a desire to justify the project to the government and to meet the demands of performance needs. At a meeting attended by both Prussian ministry representatives and musicologists in the fall of 1924, participants agreed forthwith to remove the critical commentary from the edition and publish it in a separate volume and to render editions of older works that would be "performance-ready."[24] Thus the *DDT* revived its suspended activities but adopted a new design that would make its volumes more practical and less intimidating. It is hard to imagine that the publication of two separate volumes for each edition was a money-saving measure. Rather, it is more likely that those involved hoped to extend sales to the general public and demonstrate a willingness to accommodate public education and amateur performance.

The preparation of performance-ready editions of early music that downplayed the scholarly interests of the editors was a concession to the public that helped to sustain the enterprise, but it was not a direction that found favor among all scholars. In a speech delivered to the International Musicology Society, Theodor Kroyer angrily criticized the necessity to justify musicological activity to the public. He complained that although the detailed *Denkmäler* work may have appeared "incomprehensible and useless for the people's community" and less important than technology and material sciences, the power of music to bring salvation or misfortune justified even the most minute details of musicological scholarship. It was the duty of musicologists to detect potential dangers in the power of music and to guide humanity out of its current confusion. He concluded "that even musicology has a part in the obligatory common task of all university sciences to raise humanity from the present dissipation to a unified, whole life. State and municipality have given us this workshop – we too work for the state and the *Volk*!"[25]

The Weimar period also witnessed an increased interest in regional history and an accompanying output of independent regional *Denkmäler* editions. The emergence of these editions reflects in part a disillusionment with the *DDT* as a false representation of "pan-German" music. Under Kretzschmar's direction, the *DDT* had endured the criticism that too many volumes concentrated on the Saxony-Thuringia region, apparently because of Kretzschmar's "enthusiasm for the 'competence of the Saxon-Thuringian cantors,'" to the point where two thirds of its output centered on the area between Eisenach and Dresden, to the exclusion of many other regions.[26] In addition, at the 1925 Leipzig meeting of the Deutsche Musikgesellschaft, Hermann Abert's opening address and the two sessions entitled "Musikalische Landeskunde" emphasized that local research of regional music history should become a major focus for future musicological endeavors.[27] This summons soon prompted the initiation of such editorial projects as the *Denkmäler der Musik in Pommern* (1930),[28] and the *Denkmäler der Tonkunst in Württemberg* (1933),[29] as well as organizations such as the Verein zur Pflege Pommerscher Musik (1930),[30] the Arbeitsgemeinschaft für rheinische Musikgeschichte (1933), the Arbeitsgemeinschaft zur Pflege und Forschung thüringischer Musik (1933),[31] and a chapter of the Deutsche Musikgesellschaft in Frankfurt am Main (1924), which pledged to de-emphasize the scientific side of the scholarly society and promote interdisciplinary research on local history.[32]

There were many pragmatic arguments in favor of a regional approach. Musicologists could not only limit their studies to manageable proportions and a minimum of travel but could also take advantage of local funding.[33] In his 1932 article "Organisationsfragen der Musikwissenschaft," Hans Engel noted that even in bad economic times, one could always count on support from cities, counties and communities. Exploiting "local patriotism" would also solve the problem of publicizing the field of musicology to the public at large by bringing the musicologists working in small-town libraries and archives in contact with other library patrons and the local media.[34] Thus musicologists could make their work more accessible, cultivate contacts with scholars in other disciplines who were also working on a particular region, publicize their editions of music of native *Kleinmeister*, and above all open themselves up to the possibility of financial support from local authorities.

MUSICOLOGY'S ROLE IN EARLY MUSIC PERFORMANCE

The production of early-music performance editions alone was not enough to endear the musicologist to the community at large. It was incumbent upon the musicology professor to publicize his findings and those of his colleagues through actual performance. In smaller cities, the musicology department was frequently asked to provide for the musical needs of the community, and the collegium musicum often played a central role in cultural life. The collegium served the special function of finding a common ground between musicology departments and the community while promoting early music, sometimes with a regional flavor. Scholars could exhaust local resources to unearth and edit works of lesser-known composers and arrange collegium performances of these local *Kleinmeister*, thereby reinforcing the cooperation with local authorities and bolstering feelings of regional pride. The collegium was also a vehicle for public relations beyond the confines of the community and served to spread the reputation of musicology departments and their work to other communities.[35]

Giving priority to a collegium served the best interests of any musicology department. As early as 1915 the Leipzig faculty stressed the importance of the collegium director when the university considered appointing Arnold Schering as assistant professor, calling attention to his direction of collegium performances in "strict historical style."[36] Before appointing Abert in 1919, the Leipzig selection committee again focussed on collegium activities as a point in Abert's favor, since the collegium in Leipzig had come to be considered "customary and necessary."[37] Direction of the collegium was then reserved for full professor rank starting with Kroyer (appointed in October 1923), whose activities as collegium director were cited not only for their own "scholarly and educational value" but also for their "unmistakable favorable effects on wider circles."[38] Even the Bückeburg Institute, although primarily intended as a research center, originally planned to include a collegium as one of its divisions, and in the first academic year of the musicology department in Bonn (founded in 1919), director Ludwig Schiedermair could report on the department's successful historical performances of early operas and church music, "which received notice far beyond Bonn."[39]

The cultivation of a viable collegium served the multiple functions of contributing to the cultural life of the community, serving as a public-relations vehicle beyond the community, and creating an automatic market for early music editions. Nonetheless scholars looked beyond the collegium for other markets not under their direct control, namely the widespread activities of the youth movement (Jugendmusikbewegung) and the growing interest in informal music-making (Hausmusik). Since these two spheres lay beyond the boundaries of the academic community, musicologists had to make a special effort to appeal to them.

The Jugendmusikbewegung not only attracted the attention of musicologists as a market for editions but also invited their direct involvement. The movement drew many of its ideas from the writings of Ernst Kurth, scholars such as Moser and Karl Hasse got caught up in some of its more controversial issues,[40] and Joseph Müller-Blattau, Walther Lipphardt, Hans Mersmann and Wilhelm Ehmann were noted for their active participation in the movement.[41] As the Jugendmusikbewegung grew, more musicologists began to take part in conferences, performances, retreats, and publications. In 1926 the program of the Hochschulewoche der Musikantengilde featured lectures by Friedrich Blume, Hans Mersmann, Wilibald Gurlitt, and Hans Joachim Moser;[42] in 1927, Moser, Gurlitt and Heinrich Besseler gave lectures and performances at the national retreat for group leaders in Lichtenthal; and Moser participated in three more of such events in 1929.[43] Prominent scholars also dedicated some of their scholarship to the movement, either in an editorial capacity (Hans Mersmann served as co-editor of Das Neue Werk, a collection of contemporary works, along with Paul Hindemith and the founder of the movement, Fritz Jöde,[44] and Moser and Müller-Blattau served on the editorial board of the periodical Die Singgemeinde[45]) or with essays on early music performance practice for the movement's journals.

The non-musicologist leaders of the Jugendmusikbewegung were as keen on promoting early music as were the musicologists who made themselves visible in the movement. These leaders recognized the importance of Gregorian chant[46] and madrigals[47] for their purposes and promoted the revival of secular song stretching back five centuries.[48] They acknowledged the important position of J.S. Bach as a model for their ideas, particularly in his role as Thomaskantor,[49] and they helped organize a Heinrich Schütz festival in 1929.[50] In their concern for issues of performance practice of both instrumental and choral works,[51] they promoted the revival of such early instruments as the recorder, the viola da gamba, and the harpsichord, and encouraged the employment of alternative instruments that could be used for music otherwise considered obsolete, such as the guitar as a substitute for the lute.[52]

The revival of *Hausmusik* was an equally fortunate development for musicologists promoting early music and gave the field unprecedented public recognition. Musicologists could fall back on a long legacy of accomplishments and invoke names of predecessors such as Hugo Riemann to illustrate musicology's pioneering contributions to *Hausmusik* through editions of early music.[53] On the occasion of Hugo Riemann's seventieth birthday in 1918 Rudolf Steglich lauded Riemann as a model musicologist sensitive to the musical needs of the general public in his scholarly editions, pointing out how Riemann's edition of Binchois included a German translation of the French text in order to make it more accessible for the German-speaking public.[54]

Hausmusik was one of the few areas of musical activity that actually thrived in the unfavorable economic conditions of the Weimar Republic. *Hausmusik* was recognized early on for its potential to help the German economy: in 1919 Eugen Schmitz recommended economic measures to encourage *Hausmusik*, suggesting that cheaper instruments, such as the guitar and the clavichord, be mass produced to replace the more expensive lute and piano, and that the state circumvent the paper shortage by driving up the prices of "useless" entertainment music and keeping the prices of art music at a minimum.[55] The 1929 Depression, while severely reducing normal concert attendance, created a situation in which entertainment had to be sought more at home, thus the demands for *Hausmusik* rose.[56] In 1932, Schünemann reiterated the need to encourage *Hausmusik*, not only because of its historic demonstration of German musical superiority, but also because of its benefits for the music and publishing industries.[57] Well into the early years of Hitler's Reich, the *Hausmusik* enterprise continued to attract attention for its potential to boost the economy by providing markets for instrument manufacturers, music publishers and retailers, and private music instructors.[58]

Hausmusik placed musicology in the unusual position of meeting both the economic and ideological needs of Weimar musical life, since its revival conformed with a socialist perception of the history of music. Historians noted a marked decline in *Hausmusik* in the late nineteenth century that coincided with a bourgeois admiration for virtuosi. They attributed its recent rebirth, demonstrated by increased participation in amateur groups and the early music revival, to the growing awareness of the needs of the masses for musical expression.[59] Early music played a significant role in the *Hausmusik* festivals of the Weimar years,[60] and music historians' depiction of *Hausmusik* as a pre-bourgeois phenomenon was in harmony with the ideals of the state.[61]

THE LEGACY OF THE EARLY-MUSIC REVIVAL AFTER WEIMAR

The capacity to supply early music editions to a growing market of amateur musicians in the 1920s succeeded in bridging the gap between musicology and the general public and gave musicologists the opportunity they needed to rationalize their research to the pragmatists of the age, despite the anti-intellectual tendencies of the German government. Following on the heels of the Weimar university reforms came Nazi policies that completely restructured the university hierarchy, changed the requirements for appointment, and set out to break up established "schools" by transferring faculty members from one university to another on a moment's notice.[62] The Nazi government's preference for science and technology did not eliminate the need for non-practical fields, but humanities and theoretical social sciences were encouraged or ignored based on their potential usefulness for propagandistic or ideological aims. Once determined as useful, a university curriculum could then be completely revised and monitored for fulfilling its functions for the state.[63]

The Nazi government further undermined the authority of musicology departments through a conscientious effort to concentrate musicological research outside the university by reviving the dying Bückeburg Institute. In 1935, under the direct supervision of Nazi education minister Bernhard Rust, the institute moved to Berlin, was renamed "Staatliches Institut für deutsche Musikforschung," and was reorganized to take over previously independent enterprises, including all *Denkmäler* operations, both national and regional.[64] This huge *Denkmäler* operation became known as the *Erbe deutscher Musik* and consisted of two separate series, the *Reichsdenkmal* and the *Landschaftsdenkmal*. The change of title from "Denkmäler" (monuments) to "Erbe" (heritage) suggested a fundamental break with the old tradition: the new series would produce musical editions not for the purpose of exhibiting them as museum pieces but for the purpose of reviving the music of the past in editions that lent themselves well to practical use for live performances. Heinrich Besseler, heading the Musikdenkmäler committee in the new institute, explained this change in title and emphasized the new task of German musicology in the "völkischer Lebensraum" to preserve the German musical heritage as a "living acquisition."[65] The goal of the new series was to reach the "people's community" (*Volksgemeinschaft*) by standardizing the format of the editions to meet both scholarly requirements and the needs of amateur musicians. Forthcoming editions would eliminate archaic clefs, provide translations for Latin and Italian texts and full realizations of figured basses, and – perhaps an unforeseen sacrifice on the side of scholarship – shorten the introductions and critical commentaries.[66]

Contributions to early music performance survived as the mainstay of musicological activity beyond the demise of the Weimar Republic. After the

Nazis came to power, musicologists portrayed the production of critical editions as their main activity and drew attention to their predecessors who prepared early music editions in an undying spirit of service to the *Volksgemeinschaft*. Hans Engel's 1939 summary of musicology's accomplishments, "Die Leistungen der deutschen Musikwissenschaft," published for a general readership in the journal *Geistige Arbeit*, introduced the field by giving a detailed account of *Denkmälerausgaben* and *Gesamtausgaben* activities and reporting that "the Third Reich has recognized the necessity of promoting and compiling musical *Denkmal* editions."[67] Rudolf Gerber, in his article "Die Aufgaben der Musikwissenschaft im Dritten Reich," also featured the *Denkmäler* as musicology's highest duty to society, imploring musicologists to heed the call of the nation and make the fruits of their scholarship accessible to the public.[68] When Friedrich Blume contributed the chapter on musicology to a Festschrift in honor of Hitler's fiftieth birthday, he chose to focus almost exclusively on the activity in *Denkmal* editions and *Gesamtausgaben*. Blume opened his contribution with the following remarks:

German musicology has the task of protecting one of the noblest commodities of German culture. Music has always been the most vital and most characteristic expression of the German spirit. The German *Volk* has set up for itself and for its fate in music a "victory boulevard" of the greatest monuments [Denkmäler]. With this fact, the direction of music research is predetermined and is to be taken seriously along with its duties to the *Volk* and to the state. The heritage of German music dictates its commission.[69]

The editing of *Denkmäler* and *Gesamtausgaben* had served as musicology's closest link to the outside world and remained one of the few musicological enterprises that the state had consistently been willing to finance. The early music revival, and especially its contribution to *Hausmusik*, was the most important feather in musicology's cap in the post-war period and was the source of much public praise for scholarly work. Early music came to play such a significant role that some critics lauded musicologists for unearthing works that could easily be adapted for modern performance[70] while others saw it as a threat to the development of a newer repertoire. Such critics also praised musicology for providing the abundance of early music suitable for private amateur performance but interpreted their success as revealing a dearth of equally worthwhile *Hausmusik* by contemporary composers.[71] By the late 1930s, the huge output of editions of early music had become so prominent that the activity was once again blamed as well as applauded.[72] Critics blamed the trend for influencing musical performance and composition to the extent that contemporary composers moved toward archaism in their works, and they urged musicologists not to allow musicians to "get lost in the past."[73]

Needless to say, these criticisms indicate that musicology had not faded into oblivion, as might have been expected given the utilitarian focus of the Weimar period and the anti-intellectual atmosphere of the Third Reich. To the contrary, musicologists had exploited their editorial expertise acquired over several decades to cater to a performance market eager to rediscover technically non-demanding music of the past. The publication of early-music performance editions was one of the few saving graces of an otherwise isolated discipline and helped to sustain musicology throughout Germany's economic, political, and ideological upheavals between the two World Wars.

APPENDIX

List of new music periodicals dedicated to amateur performance and music education, 1918–1932

I.   Music education, musical life, and *Jugendmusikbewegung*

Das deutsche Musikblatt: Zeitschrift für Musikpflege und Unterrichtswesen
Die Musikantengilde: Blätter der Erneuerung aus dem Geiste der Jugend
Hellerauer Blätter für Rhythmus und Erziehung
Mitteilungen des Bode-Bundes für Körpererziehung
Die Musikerziehung
Musikblätter für die "Deutsche Jugend"
Jahrbuch für Musik- und Gesang-Unterricht
Musik im Volk, Schule und Kirche
Zeitschrift für Schulmusik
Musikalische Jugend

II.   Musical life and the cultivation of German music

Musik im Leben: Eine Zeitschrift der Volkserneuerung
Das Taghorn: Schlesische Monatshefte für deutsche Musikpflege
Die Musikwiedergabe und deren verwandte Gebiete: Zeitschrift für die Reform des gesamten Musikwesens
Musik und Gesellschaft: Arbeitsblätter für soziale Musikpflege und Musikpolitik
Lied und Volk
Musikalische Volksbildung

III.   Folk music, amateur groups, and *Hausmusik*

Die Laute: Monatsschrift zur Pflege des deutschen Liedes und guter Hausmusik
Die Gitarre: Zeitschrift zur Pflege des Gitarren- und Lautenspiels und der Hausmusik
Lauten-Almanach: Ein Jahr- und Handbuch für alle Lauten- und Gitarrenspieler
Muse des Saitenspiels: Fach- und Werbe-Monatsschrift für Zither-, Gitarren- und Schossgeigenspiel
Münchner Zither-Zeitung: Fachblatt für Zitherspiel
Die Volksmusik
Die Zupfmusik

Der Lautenspieler
Schallkiste: Illustrierte Zeitschrift für Hausmusik
Bundeszeitung des Deutschen Mandolinen- und Gitarrenspieler-Bundes
Jahrbuch für Volksliedforschung
Der Blockflötenspiegel: Arbeitsblatt zur Belebung historischer Instrumente in der Jugend- und Hausmusik
Collegium Musicum

IV.   Choral singing

Der Merker
Saar-Sänger-Bund
Der Kreis: Arbeits- und Mitteilungsblatt für Singkreise
Die Singgemeinde
Mitteilungen des Gesangsvereins Breslauer Lehrer
Sänger-Echo
Sängerzeitung für das Chorwesen Kurhessen, Waldeck, Mitteldeutschland
Der Chormeister
Hessischer Musik- und Sänger-Freund
Hessische Sängerwarte
Mitteldeutsche Sängerzeitung
Nachrichtenblatt (Berliner Lehrer-Gesangverein)
Der Bayerische Sänger
Der Elbgau-Sänger
Fränkischer Sängerzeitung
Jahrbuch des Deutschen Sängerbundes
Sängerbundes-Zeitung für Schleswig-Holstein, Hamburg und Mecklenburg
Ora (Kieler Oratorien-Verein)
Rhein- und Ruhr-Sänger-Zeitung
Deutscher Sang
Der deutsche Chorgesang
Neue bayerische Sänger-Zeitung
Sängerbundes-Zeitung
Sängerzeitung des Gaues XVI. Mittelschlesischer Sängerbund
Die Musikpflege
Sächsische Sängerbundes-Zeitung

V.   Male choirs (*Männerchöre*)

Deutsches Lied
Mitteilungen des Erkschen Männergesangvereins
Spitzerscher Männergesangverein
Mitteilungen (Leipziger Männerchor)
Vereins-Bote des Männer-Gesangvereins "Schalk"
Der Burgbote
Vereinsblatt des Männerchors Concordia
Bund der Männerchöre
Der Männerchor: Zeitschrift zur Erforschung des Wesens und der Geschichte des Männerchors

7

JAZZ RECEPTION IN WEIMAR GERMANY: IN SEARCH OF A SHIMMY FIGURE

J. BRADFORD ROBINSON

As in America, though without benefit of an advocate as authoritative as F. Scott Fitzgerald, who actually coined the term, the Twenties have gone down in German cultural history as the "Jazz Age." So domineering is our picture of bare-kneed flappers dancing the shimmy with tuxedoed lounge lizards in post-war Berlin, a city caught in a frenzy of sexual excess and political thuggery, that few have bothered to ask those mundane questions so obvious to social historians: Who actually consumed this music, and in what amounts? Where did Germany's jazz originate? How was it imported, learnt, and disseminated? The meagre statistics that have emerged in answer to these questions are sobering. Germany's Jazz Age, it seems, was restricted to a small segment of the urban middle class; legitimate American jazz[1] was known only to a tiny subculture of aficionados, none of them in positions of influence; record issues and radio audiences were ludicrously small by today's standards; working-class young people continued as before to spend their leisure time reading penny dreadfuls or playing cards at home with their parents, while Germans in the towns and countryside, who then as now made up the bulk of the population, had little inkling of the nature of this music and still less desire to consume it.[2] The Jazz Age, it seems, was a creation not of German society but of the Weimar media. The music, dance forms, and cultural epiphenomena that bore this label captured the imagination of German journalists and intelligentsia to such an extent as to elevate jazz, a music entirely foreign to German traditions and ethos, to the level of what was called by one of its champions a *Zeitfrage* – an "issue of our times."[3]

German art composers could hardly help but respond to a music so massively represented in the media, whether their response was negative (Schoenberg), enthusiastic (Krenek), playful (Hindemith), socio-critical (Weill), or simply opportunistic (Eugen d'Albert). Few composers could or wished to maintain the lofty detachment of an Anton Webern or Ivan Vishnegradsky, least of all when their works were meant to engage with those institutions of Weimar society where music was actually performed. But to what aspects of jazz and jazz performance did these composers respond? How did they acquire their knowledge of jazz? Did they learn from listening to live performances, or to studio recordings, or from other sources altogether? Above all, what sort of music constituted jazz in the minds of German art composers, dance-band musicians, and publicists? To answer these questions we shall begin by narrowing our focus to one of the institutions of Weimar's musical culture most strongly affected by the jazz craze: the opera house.

I

From Helsinki to Zagreb, from New York to Odessa, not to mention dozens of stages in Weimar Germany itself, Ernst Krenek's *Jonny spielt auf* was granted a box-office success comparable only to the great cinema hits of D. W. Griffith and Charlie Chaplin. Assuming a conservative estimate of one thousand spectators at any of its nearly five hundred performances from 1926 to 1929, we arrive at a total of half a million listeners, a figure exceeding by a factor of fifty the retail sales of the greatest hit recordings of the day. In purely quantitative terms, then, Krenek was as much a part of the German Jazz Age as Paul Whiteman or Al Jolson, and far more so than Armstrong or Ellington. For many Germans Krenek's assimilation of jazz, especially in *Jonny's Blues*, the opera's "hit single", was authoritative and definitive. To understand the nature of this assimilation let us narrow our focus still further.

Jonny's anxiously awaited first entrance occurs 573 bars into the score. At this point the music radically changes character and we hear, announcing the appearance of the work's title-hero, the rhythm in Example 7.1 played on a *Holztrommel*, or woodblock, with punctuation from the bass drum:[4]

Example 7.1 Ernst Krenek: *Jonny spielt auf*, piano-vocal score, mm. 573ff

Our focus has now narrowed down to a single rhythm, divested of melody, timbre, and other features associated with jazz. Yet this figure, played behind the stage and isolated from the rest of the orchestra, is obviously meant to be immediately recognizable as jazz. It is the first clear indication in the work of a jazz ambience and introduces a character who, together with his female namesake Yvonne, will embody a jazz milieu and morality for the rest of the work. The figure is immediately expanded to form the rhythmic basis of Jonny's first number – a *Shimmy*, we are told in the score – taken at a breakneck "gramophone tempo" by an invisible jazz band (see Example 7.2).

Example 7.2 Ernst Krenek: *Jonny spielt auf*, piano-vocal score, mm. 611ff

At this point, as latter-day observers, we might be inclined to agree with the critic of the New York première who acidly remarked of Krenek's work that "the supposedly American features . . . are about as American as a *Konditorei* on the *Kurfürstendamm*".[5] This figure has little to do with 1920s jazz as we know it today. We listen in vain to the work of Jelly Roll Morton or King Oliver, Sidney Bechet or Louis Armstrong, for a percussion figure remotely like it.[6] Not even the pseudo-jazz of Paul Whiteman, the *soi-disant* King of Jazz, can offer us a starting point to explain Jonny's shimmy. Yet this inconspicuous figure is more interesting than might seem at first glance. We will now trace Jonny's woodblock figure through the music of the Weimar period. It will lead us through many levels of musical life and performance in Germany – from opera to popular songwriting and humble dance-band music, from radio and the sheet-music trade to the greatest art composers of the day – touching on several levels of culture and yet showing points of intersection between them. At times we will abandon the figure to discuss points that stand in need of greater illumination. But in the end we shall return to it, perhaps having overturned a number of received opinions about jazz reception and jazz performance in Weimar Germany.

II

Let us remain at the level at which we entered: at the opera house. The Jonny figure, as it happens, is by no means specific to Krenek's opera. Indeed, we discover it in a good many of the "jazz operas" or related stage works that have left such an indelible imprint on our popular image of Weimar music. One place to look for it is in the works of the many young composers who closed ranks behind Krenek and Weill to form the new anti-expressionist idiom of the late 1920s. Among these was the Polish-born composer Karol Rathaus (1895–1954). Known today primarily for his superior work as a teacher at Queen's College in New York, Rathaus was at the time a venturesome writer of *Zeitopern* and had just been accepted into the Universal catalogue. His ballet-pantomime *Der letzte Pierrot* (1926, perf. 1927), as the Schoenbergian allusion of its title implies, is a study in the demise of expressionism. At the work's climax Pierrot is forced to dance a *pas de deux* with a flapper and finds himself unequal to the eroticism of the situation, symbolized by an onstage jazz band of the sort already familiar from *Jonny spielt auf* and soon to become de rigueur in Weimar opera from Eugen d'Albert to Max Brand. We have no trouble recognizing the rhythmic figure, which, as in *Jonny*, announces a scene change to a jazz milieu (see Example 7.3).[7]

Example 7.3 Karol Rathaus: *Der letzte Pierrot*, piano score, p. 30

Another of these composers was Wilhelm Grosz (1894–1939), a musician whose career and aesthetic outlook parallel those of Kurt Weill in several important respects. Where Weill collaborated with Bertolt Brecht, Grosz worked with the playwright and early cinematic theorist Béla Balázs to produce, among other works, a joint ballet-pantomime *Baby in der Bar* (1927). Here Balázs, indulging in a penchant for Freudian depth psychology already apparent in his librettos for Béla Bartók,[8] has a proletarian woman abandon her newborn infant in an upper-class cocktail lounge. In a demonstration of infant sexuality, the Baby then proceeds to seduce the customers to the strains of blues, tango, and foxtrot. At the work's climax, the hapless head waiter succumbs to a "shimmy" (Example 7.4), whose rhythm has already been announced thematically at the opening of the score (Example 7.5):[9]

Example 7.4 Wilhelm Grosz: *Baby in der Bar*, piano score

Example 7.5 Wilhelm Grosz: *Baby in der Bar*, piano score

Once again the Jonny figure is unmistakable – and once again it occurs at a dramaturgically critical juncture. As in the Krenek and Rathaus examples, it is the contrast between atonal expressionism and the jazz of the *grand monde* that forms the motor of the work. The same figure is found in the opening pages of Grosz/Balázs's lightweight parody of the silent film industry, *Achtung, Aufnahme!* (1930), announcing the work's commitment to a jazz ambience. Here, too, it is given the puzzling label "shimmy" (see Example 7.6).[10]

Example 7.6 Wilhelm Grosz: *Achtung, Aufnahme!* piano score

But we needn't confine ourselves to the compositional second rank to find other examples of the same figure. One of the earliest scenes conceived for Kurt Weill's *Aufstieg und Fall der Stadt Mahagonny*, Jimmy Mahoney's nocturnal soliloquy before his trial and execution (No. 17), originated in the lost opera *Na und?* of 1926. (This is, perhaps, one reason why it stands out musically and "culinarily" from the rest of the score.)[11] As in Krenek's work, Jimmy is introduced by a solo percussion instrument, this time not by a woodblock but by a tom-tom or, as it was known in the jazz parlance of the time, a Chinese drum. At a fraction of Krenek's tempo we hear the same rhythmic motif that introduced Jonny (see Example 7.7).[12]

Example 7.7 Kurt Weill: *Aufstieg und Fall der Stadt Mahagonny*, p. 251

Once again the motif is elaborated to form the rhythmic basis of the entire number, whether in its original 4/4 or expanded to 6/4 in the refrain (see Example 7.8).

Example 7.8 Kurt Weill: *Aufstieg und Fall der Stadt Mahagonny*, p. 251

Weill, then, was aware of this jazz figure and used it at a crucial moment in the dramaturgy of one of his major stage works.[13] Nor need we look far to find other examples of it in his music. The well-known "Lied der Seeräuber-Jenny," or at least the jazz section of it as opposed to its Judeo-Slavic refrain, is unthinkable without it (see Example 7.9).[14]

Example 7.9 *Brecht Liederbuch*, ed. Fritz Henneberg, p. 56

These examples – and others could easily be found – will suffice to show that our figure was not unique to Krenek's *Jonny*, but was a key element in the *Kunstjazz* of the 1920s.[15] As inconspicuous as it may seem, it was in fact central to the musical thought of those Weimar composers who adapted what they considered to be jazz for their stage works. It was set aside for crucial moments in the drama, heralding the entrance of a jazz backdrop, precipitating a turning point in the hero's fortunes, or standing out by being placed in the spotlight of an onstage jazz combo. Yet this does not help explain its provenance. Why would Krenek attach this rhythm to a specifically American character, Jonny, as though it were as self-evidently American as the ragtime syncopations that greet the California miners in Puccini's *Fanciulla del West*? Why was it termed a "shimmy" when we know from countless examples in popular music, beginning with "I wish I could shimmy like my sister Kate," that it bears little if any relation to the historical American shimmy of the 1920s? And where, outside of German opera scores, should we begin to look for it in order to establish its jazz pedigree? These questions should be borne in mind as we probe more deeply into German jazz reception of the 1920s.

III

Two misconceptions haunt all discussions of the impact of jazz on the musicians of Weimar Germany. One is that the music they confronted was legitimate jazz; the other, that it was specifically American. Neither was the case, and yet much research has followed these false premises in order to establish that Weimar composers listened enthusiastically to Sam Wooding's or Claude Hopkins' live appearances in 1925–26, lauded the performances of Sidney Bechet and Tommy Ladnier, and avidly absorbed the classic recordings of legitimate black-American jazz. In fact, the Wooding and Hopkins performances, though effectively reported in the German media (thanks mainly to the cult of Josephine Baker), were primarily socio-cultural rather than musical events: Bechet and Ladnier remained anonymous backup musicians,[16] and legitimate black-American jazz, as apart from its diluted commercial imitations, was unknown in Germany as a concept until 1930.[17] The rare and isolated appearances of legitimate jazz in Weimar culture were overwhelmed by the great mass of commercial syncopated dance music, especially Germany's home-grown product. Weill's much-quoted words of 1926 in praise of black-American improvised jazz have to be seen in their context: a critique of radio dance music, followed by words of almost equally high praise for the "genuine jazz" of Ernö Rapée (a Hungaro-American who led the stage band at Radio City Music Hall in New York) and the popular German bandleaders Julian Fuhs, Bernhard Etté and Marek Weber.[18] Krenek's documented enthusiasm for the Chocolate Kiddies must be seen against his later remarks on the sources of his jazz borrowings: "Real jazz was unknown in Europe. We gave the name jazz to anything that came out of America."[19] Only in his American exile, then, and not with the Chocolate Kiddies, did he confront "real jazz." Just as Krenek's quintessential jazz musician Jonny can, with equal ease, sing a spiritual, a work song, a popular dance tune, or a snatch of Stephen Foster, jazz to Weimar Germany was an all-embracing cultural label attached to any music from the American side of the Atlantic, or indeed to anything new and exciting, whether this be the "jazz time" of American automobiles or "Maori jazz from New Zealand." Weimar composers inherited a concept of jazz vastly more inclusive than our own. Jonny's banjo and the cinema-like automobile chase of Act 2, the live jazz broadcast on radio and Jonny's uninhibited love life: all were props from the same arsenal of Americanesque effects which bore the label "jazz".[20]

For the purposes of this essay, however, we shall limit our focus to the assimilation of musical techniques and try to fit them into the evolution of Germany's post-war commercial music. It is important to bear in mind that both Weill and Krenek formed their basic notions of jazz music in the early 1920s, at a time when no American jazz musicians had yet visited central Europe, and indeed when no or negligibly few American recordings were available. Krenek's jazz scores can be traced from the early "Foxtrott" in his *Suite*, Op. 13a (1922; published 1923), and more importantly from the superior predecessor to *Jonny*, his comic opera *Der Sprung über den Schatten*, which was composed in 1922–23 at the peak of Germany's hyperinflation. Weill, too, had dabbled in modern dance forms long before his purportedly first essays in jazz assimilation, *Der neue Orpheus* (1925, perf. 1927) and *Royal Palace* (1926). The Weill-Lenya Research Center at Yale University preserves sketches and fragments of exercises in dance idioms, some of them worked out to a high level of contrapuntal and motivic intricacy.[21] All of them, according to David Drew,[22] date from the early 1920s. Let us put these surprisingly early dates into the context of Weimar Germany's popular music industry.

Germany's reception of American jazz and commercial dance music differed from France's or England's in several major respects. The effects of the post-war blockade, the unwillingness of allied companies to reestablish economic ties with a pariah nation, and particularly the effects of the hyperinflation, which still could be felt long after the introduction of the Reichsmark in October 1923, effectively isolated Germany culturally from the rest of western Europe. The number of American recordings imported into Germany was negligible, and in the early 1920s virtually nil.[23] Even those American jazz musicians such as Harry Pilcer, Louis Mitchell, or Arthur Briggs (not to mention Sidney Bechet), who settled in England or France, avoided Germany until the late 1920s for the simple reason that its money was worthless. The mass media, rightly regarded today as the most important vehicles for the dissemination of legitimate jazz, were non-existent or underdeveloped. The matrix-exchange program, which accounted for the bulk of the import of American jazz and dance recordings, had yet to be introduced (it was not fully underway in Germany until 1927); the first radio stations were only established in 1923–24; the only medium that could carry on the process of international cultural exchange, the printing industry, was limited by its nature to commercial music rather than an improvised art such as jazz. Yet the German urban middle classes, perhaps more so than in any other European country, were seized by a jazz fever in the early 1920s that reached the proportions of a psycho-social phenomenon. What was the music that fed this mania and gave Hindemith, Krenek, and Weill their initial and formative impressions of jazz?

The music, as might be expected, was German, not American. German commercial musicians invented their own brand of jazz, based on a certain amount of lore regarding the fabled music from America, and grafted it onto their own tradition of salon dance music and the café music of the *Stehgeiger*, which could at least boast a heritage of improvisation in the untutored "gypsy" music that had so impressed Liszt almost a century earlier. It is no accident that almost all of the celebrated German jazz bandleaders were violinists with Hungaro-Slavic names such as Marek Weber, Ernö Geiger, Barnabas von Gécay, or Dajos Béla; and for the same reason it is no accident that Krenek's Jonny "strikes up" with a violin rather than the banjo and saxophone that he also carried about in his luggage. To the mass public of Weimar Germany, a jazz musician was typically a *Stehgeiger*, and no amount of polemicizing by jazz adherents or purists was able to change this fact.[24]

What about the recording industry? Horst Lange's exhaustive discography of jazz on German 78 shellac recordings[25] creates a false impression unless we take the trouble to examine the order numbers and establish the unstated facts, so essential to reception history, of when these recordings appeared and in what numbers. Despite the impressive number of titles by major American jazz figures apparently available on German 78-rpm discs, only a tiny fraction of them actually appeared in Germany during the 1920s. Armstrong's Hot Five and Hot Seven recordings largely remained unissued until the late 1930s during the German "Swing craze" (a little-known and seemingly self-contradictory phenomenon), by which time Armstrong had developed a commercial following even in Nazi Germany.[26] The Red Hot Peppers recordings of Jelly Roll Morton appeared even later, when the tireless Horst Lange discovered the matrices unissued and forgotten in a Berlin warehouse after World War II. The only Morton title to appear in Weimar Germany was *The Chant* (1926).[27] None of the titles of the Original Dixieland Jazz Band or the 1922–23 recordings of the New Orleans Rhythm Kings, so essential to the proliferation of early jazz in England and America, was issued in Germany. Small wonder, then, that these names and virtually all others from the world of legitimate American jazz fail to occur among the millions of words published on "jazz" by the hyperactive Weimar press.[28]

The reason for this was quite simple. The matrix-exchange program, worked out at high corporate levels by the German and American recording monopolies,[29] followed a simple policy of bartering German classical recordings for American dance music. The actual matrices chosen for exchange excluded *a priori* the so-called "race records" on which most legitimate jazz of the time was released. Even a well-informed Parisian jazz expert such as Hugues Panassié, with his "shelves and shelves of records," was entirely unaware of the great black jazz artists until enlightened in 1929 by a visiting white American clarinettist who explained to him the American system of segregated record catalogues.[30] Weimar Germany, being still more isolated from American sources than France, was even less *au fait* with American developments. Instead, the matrix-exchange program fed its unsuspecting public a jazz fare made up largely of sweet white dance bands such as Guy Lombardo, Paul Specht, and above all the two giants of Weimar's jazz reception, Vincent Lopez and Paul Whiteman. It was this music, once the matrix-exchange program began in earnest around 1926, that nurtured Weimar Germany's image of jazz, that provided models for its own commercial musicians, and that dominated the catalogues of its recording companies.[31] It should therefore come as no surprise to learn that some leading German jazz writers (including Theodor Adorno and even Lange himself) energetically fought what they considered the "myth of black jazz." Jazz, for Weimar Germany, was a white dance music based on but entirely superseding some colorful black musical traditions. Black musicians, in Adorno's immortal words, merely contributed the "coloristic effect of their skin" to a white man's art.[32]

Even those few legitimate jazz recordings that did enter the German market did so in numbers that would be considered negligible by the standards of today's commercial music industry. A German jazz record was first issued in a run of 500 copies.[33] Not until this stock had been depleted, as very seldom happened, was the work reissued. Only major hits by Paul Whiteman, Al Jolson, or the now-forgotten banjo virtuoso Harry Reser could expect larger press runs, namely of about 10,000 copies. Mass culture, though structured roughly as we know it today, was in its infancy, and it is highly likely that many more Weimar Germans heard the music of Krenek's *Jonny*, and especially "Jonny's Blues," than ever heard a note of legitimate American jazz.

Nor did this situation change with the introduction of radio in the mid-1920s. German radio stations had three options in their transmission of jazz: broadcasts by their own radio dance orchestras, live broadcasts from dance halls and jazz locales, and the broadcasting of gramophone recordings. With remarkable unanimity they settled for the first option, decking out their standard radio dance orchestras with jazz titles and producing that music which occasioned Kurt Weill's excoriating review of 1926 (see note 18).[34] Broadcasts from dance halls, pioneered in Switzerland from luxury hotels, were less frequent (yet frequent enough that Krenek could draw on this cliché for the climax of *Jonny*).[35] But given the paucity of American musicians in Weimar Germany the result was a further massive reinforcement of the German jazz surrogate. As for recordings, it was not possible to broadcast them until the late 1920s, after the introduction of the electrostatic cartridge had led to the production of discs of broadcast quality. By this time, however, Weimar Germany's image of jazz and American dance music was already fixed, and radio programmers, intent on satisfying the existing expectations of a mass public rather than forming new ones, simply aired standard German dance fare by Julian Fuhs and Dajos Béla, or hit tunes by Friedrich Holländer and Nico Dostal, all under the name of jazz. A study of the weekly program guides issued by several major German broadcasters during the decade reveals that of 12,500 jazz titles known to have been broadcast, only three were by Ellington and none was by Armstrong.[36]

Surprisingly, the greatest turnover by far in commercial music was made neither by the gramophone industry, which, as already mentioned, had tiny pressings by today's standards, nor by the radio networks, which were already public institutions dependent on government funding, but by the sheet-music trade. There were several reasons for this. First, the system of musical copyright was based on printed music, giving music publishers control of royalties. Second, and immediately germane to the present study, Weimar's commercial musicians, trained in conservatories and experienced in the printed salon and march music of the Wilhelmine period, had no tradition of or aptitude for improvisation. The natural instinct of a German musician interested in acquiring a knowledge of jazz was to turn to the printed page, whether this be the latest dance hit from Berlin or the leading guide on pseudo-improvised instrumental breaks. We will later see that this was also the natural instinct of art composers.

IV

A fascinating and amusing first-person account of the early days of jazz in Weimar Germany has survived in an obscure source, a weekly trade magazine published in Düsseldorf whose lengthy title – *Der Artist: Zentral-Organ der Zirkus, Varieté-Bühnen, reisenden Kapellen und Ensembles* [The Acrobat: central organ for circuses, variety stages, travelling bands and ensembles] – reveals its origins in nineteenth-century vaudeville and music hall. In 1920, shortly after the end of hostilities, a young German bandleader from Dortmund was hired to play dance music in a Swiss luxury hotel. The first-person account of his difficulties, published in 1926, confirms many of the points made above regarding the early reception of jazz:[37]

Even at the beginning of 1920, at a time still within recent memory, there was scarcely a single musician in the whole of Germany who knew what a jazz band or a shimmy actually is. For those who doubt this claim I can offer my own experiences as proof. Let me begin, however, by stressing that the German musician should not be reproached for his ignorance. The main reason for it lay in the sad fact that at that time Germany was still sealed off from its "enemies abroad," even though that gigantic mental fermata, also known as the World War, was well and truly over. Our opinion of the nature and properties of the jazz band was therefore based on very vague and obscure rumours.

Germany's isolation, we shall see, was not only political but cultural and economic. Having received his contract, our musician hired his sidemen, packed his library, and moved to St Moritz, where he proceeded to play antiquated German foxtrots

(*Fuchstänze*) to fashionable audiences from England and France. He soon discovered that he would have to modernize his repertoire:

We were regaled with whisky sodas for our serenades and Ave Marias, but our *Fuchstänze* were only greeted with puzzled expressions. One evening after we had primarily obliged our audiences with *Fuchstänze*, an Englishman approached the bandstand and courteously asked for a foxtrot. Astonished, I asked him with equal courtesy whether he hadn't noticed that we had been playing nothing but foxtrots for the last hour. He replied, with an embarrassed smile, that he had followed our playing with utmost attention: just what we had played he couldn't very well say, but he could say with certainty that there wasn't a foxtrot amongst it. . . . Only too soon was I to discover that the Englishman was right, and that our German foxtrots of the time turned out on closer inspection to be nothing more than somewhat exotically syncopated *Rheinländers* and *Rixdorfers* in disguise.

Our musician, then, lacked an up-to-date repertoire. The way he went about acquiring it is revealing of the double dependence of German dance musicians on Anglo-American publishers and on the printed page:

Before the war broke out I had possessed, for many years running, a standing order with the London publishers Francis & Day, who sent me new Anglo-American titles *en masse* for a fixed annual sum. My attempts to renew this subscription after the war, from Dortmund, failed miserably: my letters brought no answers at all since at that time any Englishman considered it beneath his dignity to enter into business relations with a German. . . . From St Moritz, however, the standing order went off without a hitch, and in a matter of days I received a pile of the latest English and American foxtrots, a pile so large that I had to add a zwieback crate to my navy locker.

In short, our Dortmund musician obtained his repertoire, not by consulting recorded examples or listening to other musicians, but by turning to foreign music publishers. At this point, still in the year 1920, he confronted the word "jazz" for the first time:

Hardly had we rounded the foxtrot cliffs when a new danger reared its head. One day the hotelier let drop that he intended to re-engage us for the coming winter season and that the contract was ready to be signed. Then he added a condition: I would have to play "jazzband" (he actually said *Tschetzpend*). I heard this exotic word for the first time in my life, and I hadn't the foggiest notion what it meant. Since, however, my principle is the Horatian maxim *nil admirari* (never be fazed) I replied with the iron mien of an Assyrian charioteer: "But of course, Herr Direktor, we'll play *Tschetzpend*!". . . Done! We both signed the contract which stipulated, in black and white, that I was to play *Tschetzpend*. . . . My hunt for the *Tschetzpend* began.

His first instinct was to search for new publications of dance music. Writing to the musicians' union in Berlin, he was informed that jazz was a new dance style accompanied by the latest German foxtrots, played at a racing tempo. Once again, his international audience in Switzerland told him otherwise:

We rushed at Derby Gallop tempo so that the dust never settled on the dance floor. The audience looked quizzical. Aha, I thought, the jazz is working its magic. But when several people asked me what I was playing and I proudly replied that we'd just played jazz, I began to see that all-too-familiar embarrassed smile once again. And when a nervous guest, full of *vino* and *veritas*, retorted that what we had played was nonsense but not jazz, my daemon whispered into my ear: the man's right, our Berlin jazz isn't up to snuff. My embarrassment reached a climax when a little Parisienne asked us to play a shimmy. She had just come from Paris, she added, where shimmy and jazz band were all the rage. . . . I expressed my regret with a shrug of the shoulders, and the little Parisienne pursed her brightly painted lips in disdain.

Jazz, as our musician could not have guessed, was not so much a repertoire of printed dance numbers, still less a form of social dancing, but rather a new rhythmic basis, instrumental timbre, and performance style. Enlightenment finally came from an unusual and, for our purposes, revealing quarter:

I had just bought my customary morning newspaper in a [St Moritz] bookshop when I noticed a pile of sheet music on the next table: French and English dance music for piano, with droll, colorful pictures on the title pages. I leafed through it without a thought in my head. Suddenly I stumbled on a foxtrot with the photograph of an orchestra on its title page and the explanatory caption that this was the celebrated London jazz band N.N., whose repertoire includes the above-mentioned foxtrot. No Egyptologist could have taken his papyrus more lovingly in hand or scrutinized it more closely than I did this jazz-band photograph. . . . At long last I saw what a jazz band is. Seven blokes in sport dress: piano, violin, two banjos, saxophone, trombone, and percussion. I entered into a dialogue, diplomatically conducted on my part, with the bookdealer, who proved to be an enthusiastic devotee of the new music, and learnt all I needed to know about a jazz band down to the last detail. I was saved! Everything relating to jazz that has since become obvious to any musician but was still vague and enigmatic at the time was revealed at a stroke.

This amusing report confirms a number of points regarding the early reception of jazz in Germany. Note, for instance, the importance of France and England as arbiters of German taste: they were to remain so for the rest of the decade, far more so than America. Note also that our musician at no point turned to recordings or to authoritative foreign musicians for his knowledge of jazz: there were none in Germany at that time to consult. Finally, note his dependence on printed piano music, the primary medium for the dissemination of early jazz in Germany. Ultimately, our early German jazz authority created his own style of German jazz on the basis of printed pop songs, visual evidence, and lore.

It was under these circumstances, then, that German commercial musicians created the music that fed the jazz craze of the early 1920s. And it was under the same circumstances that Hindemith, Krenek, and Weill, as well as the second rank of Wilhelm Grosz, Erwin Schulhoff, Karol Rathaus, Max Brand, and their younger contemporaries Paul Dessau, Boris Blacher, Karl Amadeus Hartmann, and Rudolf Wagner-Régeny, all formed the image of jazz that they incorporated in their *Kunstjazz*.[38] On the one hand there were the so-called *Radaukapellen* or semi-professional "racket bands" (the term, antedating World War I, is George Grosz's)[39] who created jazz by disfiguring Wilhelmine march and salon numbers and peppering them with unmotivated explosions or sound effects from the drummer, from police sirens to pistol shots (one of which found its way into the opening of Weill's *Mahagonny Songspiel*). On the other hand there was printed dance music from abroad, not to mention an active indigenous publishing industry that soon turned out American hits and German imitations at a phenomenal rate to satisfy Weimar Germany's demand for jazz. Just as Stravinsky, surrounded by rags and cakewalks in Paris, had to wait for a printed stimulus to take up ragtime during his Swiss exile in 1917,[40] so young German composers of the Jazz Age took their stimulus from the printed page. There is nothing in Krenek's early foxtrot from Op. 13a, nor in Weill's unpublished, and perhaps unperformed, early essays in popular dance styles, to suggest the influence of a live performance or gramophone recording, but much − the accuracy of the part-writing, the conservative handling of harmony, the choice of instrumentation and timbre − to indicate the influence of printed dance music. This influence will be examined more closely below. First, however, it is essential to discuss the least well-known of Weimar's musical mass media, the music publishing industry.

V

What sort of music did the German sheet-music industry turn out for Weimar Germany's jazz consumption? Of the thousands upon thousands of titles issued during the decade, only a tiny fraction has been examined, and to date no attempt has been made to codify, quantify, or evaluate this vast and seemingly monotonous repertoire. However, a few words can be ventured as to the impact of American popular music on the German scene and how German commercial musicians responded to it. At first, German dance-band leaders generally bought piano editions, or lead sheets, which they then arranged for the use of their own ensembles. Later, especially from the mid-1920s, printed arrangements, some of them by well-known American or British arrangers, were available in large numbers from English and German publishers. A German bandleader, depending on his standards and ambitions, had the option of playing these arrangements as written, or altering them to meet the special needs and abilities of his own musicians. Indeed, the pages of *Der Artist* as well as much of Paul Bernhard's book-length study *Jazz: eine musikalische Zeitfrage*, mentioned earlier, are full of practical tips to bandleaders for recasting printed arrangements for their ensembles. Usually these arrangements contained written out "improvisations" known as *Jazzstimmen*, which were then handed to the jazz specialists in the band. Example 7.10 conveys a good impression of what these jazz parts looked like at the end of the decade: a mechanical application of syncopation to a given melody, a catchy instrumentation (in this case a clarinet trio, reminiscent not so much of Ellington's *The Mooche* but rather of countless Ferde Grofé arrangements for Paul Whiteman), and an absence of free melodic invention. The melody being improvised upon is Kurt Weill's well-known "Alabama Song" from *Mahagonny*.[41]

Example 7.10 Kurt Weill: "*Alabama Song*" *aus Aufsteig und Fall der Stadt Mahagonny (*special arrangement by R. Etlinger)

More often than not, however, the dance-band musician worked from sheet music for piano, which had the advantage that it could easily be shipped from abroad and carried about on tour. In 1923–24, for example, during and just after the hyperinflation, Weimar pop culture was seized by a hit tune called "Vater liebt Muttern, Mutter liebt Vatern," a quaint title that plays on a pun on *Muttern*, the obsolete accusative declension of "mother" and the German word for "bolts". Incorporated in a revue called *An Alle* and anthologized in a widely circulated annual collection of dance numbers, *Zum 5 Uhr Tee*, it began as in Example 7.11, with an ear-catching emphasis on the blues seventh.[42]

Example 7.11 "Vater liebt Muttern, Mutter liebt Vatern" (*Zum 5 Uhr Tee,* No. 14)

Those familiar with America popular music of the 1920s will have no difficulty recognizing the 1923 hit tune (and subsequent dixieland standard) "Papa Loves Mama, Mama loves Papa" by Cliff Friend and Abel Baer. Within a year of its appearance in America, then, this Tin Pan Alley tune had been "Germanized" and transformed into a popular song at the peak of Weimar Germany's shimmy craze. In that same year it was recorded by, among others, the then leading German jazz musician Eric Borchard[43] and the first American bandleader known to have toured Germany (at the belated date of 1924), Alex Hyde.[44] But it is not simply the song's level of popularity that is relevant to this study. The above quoted introduction merely repeats an immediately recognizable rhythmic figure that dominates the entire refrain: the Jonny figure.

Krenek's unassuming woodblock figure, then, had firm roots in German popular music. It was also associated, temporally at least, with the shimmy. And it could even lay claim at one remove to an American pedigree. As might be expected, "Vater liebt Muttern" immediately found home-grown German imitators and was replicated throughout the dance music of these years, which also witnessed the genesis of Krenek's *Sprung über den Schatten* and *Jonny spielt auf*. The same volume of *Zum 5 Uhr Tee* included a newly written German popular song, "Jede Gnädige, jede ledige trägt den Bubikopf" (Every single girl wants to wear a page boy), celebrating the flapper's page-boy hairstyle (another American import and expression of the Jazz Age). Its opening bars, likewise extracted from the refrain (see Example 7.12), are obviously intended to capitalize on the familiarity of the "Mama loves Papa" rhythm.[45]

Example 7.12 "Jede Gnädige, jede ledige trägt den Bubikopf" (*Zum 5 Uhr Tee,* No. 11)

In the world of German commercial music in 1923–24, years that saw the rise of the jazz opera, the Jonny figure, though unnamed and not associated with any particular dance form, was thus virtually ubiquitous. Krenek simply quoted a rhythm so familiar, and so closely associated with jazz, as to obviate special comment.

But Germany's printing industry aided the burgeoning jazz culture in another way as well. By the mid-1920s there had already begun to appear a number of jazz primers to help Germany's commercial musicians master the mysteries of improvisation and syncopated rhythms. It is these to which we shall now turn in our exploration of the Jonny figure.

VI

One of the most striking features of the new music from America, at least from the vantage point of Weimar Germany, was that it was improvised. This fact alone set it apart from the music then in use, whether on the concert stage or in the dance hall, and led to much editorializing about the "democraticization" of music. Jazz, after all, did not require a conductor. The musicians were not beholden to the printed page but could express themselves freely – it was thought – without regard for the rules of harmony, counterpoint, or ensemble sonority. There were no accompanying musicians, only soloists. Even the weak beats of the bar had been liberated in the march to four-beat jazz. Jazz was as remote from the music of the Wilhelmine period as was universal suffrage from the rule of the Iron Chancellor.

Yet these journalistic effusions overlooked one important point: German commercial musicians generally did not improvise. Apart from those schooled in the gypsy traditions of Austro-Hungarian cafés, German musicians – even the jazz specialists, as we have seen – dutifully played what was written on the page and expected to continue doing so. A number of German jazz recordings from the early 1920s reveal that such "improvised" solos as did exist were learnt by rote and played like small concert études, especially if they involved difficult new techniques such as growl and plunger-mute effects.[46] Clearly, if German jazz was to live up to its democratic image a tradition of improvisation would somehow have to be inculcated.

Part of this task fell to the jazz primers that began to appear from late 1925, at a time, we should recall, when the first American jazz musicians traveled to Germany and the matrix-exchange program was beginning to make the American item more familiar to a larger public. Three names stand out in particular: Mátyás Seiber, Alfred Baresel, and Arthur Lange.

Mátyás Seiber (1905–60), by far the most familiar of these three musicians today, was suddenly thrust into the political limelight when he took over a newly-established jazz course at the Hoch Conservatory in Frankfurt and found his name heatedly discussed in the German Reichstag.[47] Though he claimed to have learnt jazz on a transatlantic steamer he was in fact a thoroughly trained conservatory composer who later had a respectable career in exile in England. His pedagogical instincts are reflected in a number of piano études prefaced by "knocking exercises" (*Klopfübungen*), which are interesting today in that they neatly summarize the rhythmic clichés of Weimar social-dance forms.[48] More importantly, he also wrote a purportedly definitive textbook on jazz percussion which, being largely an introduction to musical notation and musicianship, was clearly meant to lend a pedigree to his jazz seminar in Frankfurt.[49] Yet apart from an injunction to play "very accurately," Seiber shows no understanding of real jazz drumming at a time when Baby Dodds and Zutty Singleton were exploring new possibilities of swing. This is, however, not to underestimate his importance: Seiber was the first jazz instructor at an officially recognized musical institution; he legitimized jazz for a number of Weimar musicians who felt uneasy with the music's lowborn beginnings and apparent lack of a theoretical basis; and he served as jazz adviser to Theodor Adorno, who was likewise based in Frankfurt and whose misunderstanding of *Scheintaktigkeit* (secondary rag) can be directly traced to Seiber's teachings, as can his bizarre claim that the rhythmic achievements of jazz are present in Brahms.[50]

Far more important, though less well-known than Seiber, was Alfred Baresel (1893–1984), a conservatory professor and freelance music journalist who heroically took on a one-man campaign to liberate jazz from what he called the "sins of its youth" and to champion the cause of *Kunstjazz*. Baresel's influence on commercial musicians, and even conservatory-trained composers, was as remarkable at the time as it is forgotten today. His voluminous writings in the 1920s for scholarly journals, trade rags, and the popular press reveal an energetic and enquiring mind with a firm understanding of jazz's improvisational basis and a belief in its ability to rejuvenate both art music and commercial music – if properly cultivated. This latter proviso led him to assume an advisory position at the Leipzig publishing house of Zimmermann, from which he issued a flood of teaching publications that all bear reading today: textbooks on jazz percussion, collections of pseudo-improvised instrumental breaks, piano études in various dance styles, exemplary small-band arrangements, even primers for jazz accordion, all of them in inexpensive editions to be bought and read in large quantities.[51] But the most important of these works from our present perspective is his *Jazz-Buch* of 1925, the first comprehensive textbook on jazz in any language.[52]

The *Jazz-Buch* was phenomenally successful. First issued in December 1925, it had already entered a revised fourth edition before a year had passed, and four more editions were to follow over the next two years. Baresel kept his book abreast of new developments, especially with regard to the "arranger's jazz" that began to take hold in the latter part of the decade with the increased influence of Whiteman and Red Nichols. By 1929 the *Jazz-Buch* had been so often altered and extended that Baresel wrote an entirely new book which resembles its predecessor only in its title: *Das neue Jazz-Buch*.[53] This book still stands as a compendium of Weimar jazz as understood by one of its most intelligent and committed observers. Of the many insights it offers the present-day reader, two stand out in particular as they affect our assessment of Weimar's *Kunstjazz* as a whole. The first is that there is no difference in principle between the rhythms of the dance forms variously known as shimmy, foxtrot, black bottom, ragtime, and so forth. All make use of the same repertoire of snappy rhythmic figures that had entered German commercial music under the banner of ragtime and jazz. What did distinguish these dance forms however – and this is the second point – was their tempos, which Baresel proceeds to list for the convenience of his readers, most of whom were dance-band musicians who needed to know this information for eminently practical reasons.[54] We tend to forget that the various genres of jazz – foxtrot, shimmy, and so forth – were social dances first and musical forms second, and that the music supplied for them had to be played at tempos that would accommodate the steps of the dancers. An equally revealing list of tempos comes, in fact, from the German Society of Dance Instructors (Allgemeiner Deutscher Tanzlehrer-Verband), which could be expected to know about such things as it codified the steps officially used in Germany's dance schools and competitions.[55] If we want to know why Kurt Weill called Mackie Messer's "Moritat" a blues it helps to bear in mind that the blues, to a musician of Weimar Germany, was not a twelve-bar form with call-and-response patterns and a fixed sequence of harmonies, but a tempo mark of roughly 33 bars per minute.[56]

To introduce his readers to the essence of jazz, Baresel systematically led them from the straight pulse of march music to the first inklings of jazz syncopation, gradually increasing the difficulties until the music becomes quite heavily syncopated. The initial step away from march music deserves our closer attention. Example 7.13 shows Baresel's first "Variant of the Basic Rhythm", given to piano and banjo.[57]

Example 7.13 Alfred Baresel: *Das neue Jazz-Buch*, p. 74

It is, of course, the rhythm of Jonny's shimmy. For the German commercial musician, then, the Jonny rhythm was anything but unfamiliar. On the contrary, it represented the first step away from his Wilhelmine background into the new uncharted territory of jazz.

The third leading authority of Weimar's jazz culture was not a German at all but an American: Arthur Lange (1889–1956). This popular dance-band arranger became famous from mid-decade for his printed small-ensemble arrangements, which could be purchased from England.[58] Lange's small-group arrangements were considered models of their kind, and far more practical than the more pompous and ornate, if more famous, arrangements by Ferde Grofé for Whiteman. His greatest fame, however, came from a definitive study of dance-band arranging which he published privately in April 1926 in a limited edition of 500 signed copies: *Arranging for the Modern Dance Orchestra*. (One year later the book was taken into the catalogue of the mass publisher Robbins in New York.) Though difficult to obtain and very expensive, this book soon acquired a definitive reputation among insiders in Germany's musical life, both high-brow and low-brow.

Lange's manual is rooted in the tradition of symphonic jazz practiced by Paul Whiteman and his staff arrangers. But it is just as revealing of contemporary practice as Baresel's *Jazz-Buch* and strikes the present-day reader as remarkably modern. Lange, for example, divides the dance orchestra into three parts: rhythmic unit, saxophone unit, and brass unit. Readers familiar with 1920s jazz will have no difficulty recognizing the basic distinction between reed, brass, and rhythm sections said to have been achieved by the black-American bandleaders Fletcher Henderson and Don Redman half a decade later. If only to show the influence of white dance-band music on the genesis of black orchestral jazz – an influence sensed by several jazz historians but never pursued in depth[59] – Lange's book repays careful study. Although rhythmic practices are beyond its topic, a book with hundreds of music examples in score cannot fail but shed light on dance-band rhythms as well. And here we discover the following example of what Lange calls "concerted rhythm," meaning a basic rhythm played simultaneously by the entire rhythm section (see Example 7.14).[60]

Example 7.14 Arthur Lange: *Arranging for the Modern Dance Orchestra*, p. 91

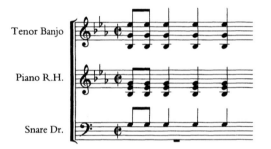

Once again, we note that the Jonny figure, to retain the name we gave it at the beginning of this paper, appears as one of the basic and most elementary forms of jazz rhythm. Krenek's Jonny and Weill's Jimmy, it would seem, presented themselves to Weimar Germany's audiences with a rhythmic formula that underlay the very essence of jazz.

VII

How widely distributed were these jazz manuals, not only among practicing commercial musicians but also among the composers of Weimar's *Kunstjazz*? As so often with questions of reception history, we are forced to rely on indirect evidence. The many editions of Baresel's *Jazz-Buch* suggest that its press runs were soon exhausted. That the book gave Baresel almost celebrity status among commercial musicians is attested by his regular appearances in the pages of *Der Artist*. Baresel, for the world of German dance music, was the recognized authority on jazz technique, improvisation, and the historical and aesthetic significance of the new music.

The same applied to Lange in the related realm of dance-band arrangement. Even the rare private first edition of his book was announced in *Der Artist* in words of highest praise immediately upon publication,[61] a clear indication of Lange's popularity among professional insiders. The book was available on special request from a jazz specialty shop in the Berlin district of Charlottenburg, though admittedly the price – 25 Reichmarks – put it beyond the reach of all but the most successful dance-band leaders.[62] This was, however, a period in which band-leaders even in Germany were expected to produce distinctive and immediately identifiable sounds by writing their own arrangements or, as was more often the case, by adapting published arrangements to the needs and tastes of their ensembles. For these bandleaders, Lange's book acquired the status of *vademecum* to the most arcane secrets of the arranger's art, from a recognized authority in the field. Baresel lists the original private edition in the bibliography of his *Neues Jazz-Buch* of 1929, and around the same time a long synopsis, in German, was serialized in the pages of *Der Artist* by a musicologist and conductor Eugen Rosenkaimer (the author of a dissertation on Scheibe's *Critischer Musicus*), who also promised a German translation of the entire book.[63] In the end, Rosenkaimer's translation never materialized, doubtless because of the change of taste in commercial music that left jazz, like other forms of Americana after the Wall Street Crash, out of favor by 1930.[64] Eventually the ascent of National Socialism put an end to any demand for such a translation. Today, as one indication of the book's rarity during the 1920s and of the predations of the 1930s, there is not a single copy extant in German libraries.

Lange's book, however, was also familiar to conservatory-trained composers. An orchestration manual written in 1928 by the young Egon Wellesz simply defers to Lange in all questions related to jazz-band writing:[65]

Finally we should mention the jazz orchestra, as used by Wilhelm Grosz in *Baby in der Bar*, Kurt Weill in *Die Dreigroschenoper*, and Max Brand in *Maschinist Hopkins*. These adaptations require a knowledge of the nature of jazz ensembles and their methods of playing, which, as intimated above, are dealt with most thoroughly in Arthur Lange's study *Arranging for the* [modern] *dance orchestra* (New York, 1926).

For the new genre of *Kunstjazz*, represented in Wellesz's book by examples, in score, from *Jonny spielt auf* and *Der Zar lässt sich photographieren*,[66] Lange was thus the recognized master of instrumentation. Moreover, like Baresel, Wellesz's bibliography cites the 1926 private edition of the work, indicating that at least one of the 500 signed copies found its way into Viennese *avant-garde* circles. Lange, then, was clearly a crossover figure with authority in both commercial and art music.

Except in one prominent instance to be discussed in due course, it is unclear to what extent art musicians drew directly on these jazz manuals or other commercial publications for their knowledge of the new music. Krenek, as we have seen, distanced himself in later life from his jazz creations, claiming that, at the time, jazz music was "anything that came out of America."[67] Though undoubtedly correct from the standpoint of reception history, this remark offers little insight into the sources of his knowledge of jazz texture and techniques. Susan C. Cook, among others, has drawn attention to Krenek's familiarity with printed American popular songs supplied to him by Arthur Schnabel, who collected them on his American tours of 1921 and 1922–23.[68] This is consistent with the piano writing in his "Foxtrott" from Op.13a and the revue number in *Sprung über den Schatten*, both of which date from this period and rely on pianistic "stride" bass patterns. As with Krenek's involvement in the performance edition of Mahler's Tenth, however, the world of scholarship will have to wait until his autobiography – now on deposit in the Library of Congress – and his estate become open to the public before the means by which he assimilated American popular music can be properly surveyed.

In the case of Kurt Weill we must lament the irreparable loss of his European library. It would doubtless have contained many of the same kinds of items with which this supremely gifted assimilator mastered the style of American popular song. His American library, now in the Beinecke Rare Book Room at Yale University, included harmony manuals, books on boogie-woogie piano style, and even notebooks with exercises in the distinctive harmonic idiom of America's popular song industry.[69] It is hard to imagine that his European library did not include at least Baresel's manual, which had been favorably mentioned in *Die Musik* and *Melos*, and in the pages of *Anbruch*, the house organ of Weill's own publisher, Universal.[70] Examples 7.15 and 7.16 reveal a close similarity between Weill's jazz-piano writing and a break prescribed in a contemporary manual once located in the personal library of a Berlin commercial musician.[71]

Example 7.15 Kurt Weill: "Ballade vom angenehmen Leben"

Example 7.16 Art Shefte: *Up-to-the-Minute Jazz Breaks*, p. 18

Fortunately, in the case of one leading composer we are not forced to resort to this sort of guesswork. Shortly after Alban Berg had begun work on his opera *Lulu* he wrote, as a sort of study for the Wardrobe Scene, the concert aria *Der Wein* (May–July 1929). Here he tried his hand at assimilating certain jazz instruments (alto saxophone, novelty piano, drum set) as well as some syncopated rhythmic practices of current dance music. To acquaint himself with this new idiom of a younger generation he consulted a jazz textbook, reading it from cover to cover and annotating it throughout, even correcting a few misprints. His annotated copy of the book is now preserved in the Austrian National Library; it was, as might be expected, Baresel's *Jazz-Buch*.[72] Berg, a composer personally acquainted with Gershwin, interested in the music of Kurt Weill from a very early date,[73] and, unlike his teacher Schoenberg, keenly aware of developments in light music, proceeded to master jazz by systematically studying, not recordings or live performances, but Alfred Baresel's jazz primer.

VIII

Berg's annotations fall into four categories: tempo, rhythm, piano texture, and instrumentation. Without attempting to be exhaustive, a few of them may be illustrated for the purposes of this essay, pending a longer study to be undertaken elsewhere.

Baresel, as mentioned above, laid down tempos for the more popular social dance forms of his day. One of these Berg took quite seriously: the tango, said by Baresel to be played at quarter note = 46.[74] Berg underscored this figure, entered it elsewhere in the booklet as a reminder, and on one occasion doubled it to 92. Doubtless he was especially struck by the fact that Baresel's metronome mark is a multiple of that fateful number 23 that pervades so much of his late music.[75] This same tempo, slightly modified to quarter note = 46–52, is prescribed in the "Tempo di Tango" sections of *Der Wein* and forms the work's *Hauptzeitmaß* or "principal tempo."[76]

Berg was also fascinated by Baresel's discussion of syncopation and secondary rag, a "clever type of syncopation" that Baresel traced back to the ambiguity of

3/2 and 6/4 in the courantes of Bach's French and English Suites.[77] Doubly underscoring Baresel's simple example, Berg later elaborated it into a complex rhythmic étude spread over two staves.[78] An excerpt of this étude is given in Example 7.18, alongside Baresel's original example as marked by Berg (Example 7.17).

Example 7.17 Alfred Baresel: *Das Jazz-Buch*, 4th edn, p. 24 (with Berg's annotations, indicated by dotted lines)

Example 7.18 Alban Berg: Rhythmic study (Ms Alban-Berg Fond., Box 21 Berg 80/IV, fol. 40)

etc.

Berg's exercise, intended to show the distribution of secondary-rag groupings in an ensemble, also found application in the scores of *Der Wein* (e.g. bars 43ff.) and, later, *Lulu* (bars 1005ff.). It is interesting to note that, as in Kurt Weill's writing for voice, none of these rhythmic devices was applied to the vocal part. There were, as it turns out, good stylistic reasons for this. As Baresel remarks, and as Berg underscored: "When a vocal part is present, syncopation and embellishment are restricted to the accompanying middle parts."[79] This strange injunction, which negates the rhythmic achievements of early jazz and blues singers, is fully in keeping with the popular 1920s singing style known as crooning, and was adhered to by composers of popular songs and *Kunstjazz* alike.[80]

Berg also followed many of Baresel's suggestions regarding jazz-piano texture. The parallel fourths so favored by ragtime and novelty pianists of the time captured his attention, as did the "crushed" appoggiaturas and the general doubling of the melody line in octaves. These features, too, found their way into the piano writing of *Lulu* and *Der Wein*. The fourths in the passage from *Lulu* shown in Example 7.19 (bar 1046) are typical of the sort of piano figuration that Berg circled in Baresel's examples (see Example 7.20).[81]

Example 7.19 Alban Berg: *Lulu*, full score, ed. H. Apostel, Act I, m. 1046

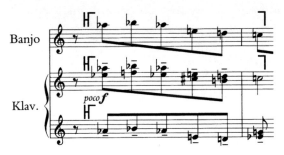

Example 7.20 Alfred Baresel: *Das Jazz-Buch*, 4th edn, p. 19 (with Berg's annotation, indicated by dotted line)

Even certain obscure features of Berg's piano texture can be traced to Baresel's manual. The quote in Example 7.21, from bar 60 of *Der Wein*, inverts a piano figure from the *Jazz-Buch*, which Berg underscored and to which he added, as if to remind himself, the term "Klavier" (see Example 7.22).[82]

Example 7.21 Alban Berg: *Der Wein*, full score, m. 60

Example 7.22 Alfred Baresel: *Das Jazz-Buch*, 4th edn, p. 14 (with Berg's annotations, indicated by dotted lines)

Kennzeichnung der Originalmelodie.

And the remarkable piano passage from bar 50 of *Der Wein*, marked *brillant*, is obviously a dodecaphonic elaboration of the virtuoso breaks for which Baresel, with his *Jazz-Buch* and 77 *Klavier-Breaks*, had become the acknowledged German expert. The same applies to the "introductory break" leading into the tango section of *Der Wein* (bar 38, see Example 7.23),

Example 7.23 Alban Berg: *Der Wein*, full score, 37–8

which might have been adapted from Example 23 of Baresel's break method (Example 7.24):[83]

Example 7.24 Alfred Baresel: 77 *Klavier-Breaks*, p. 10

Indeed, the similarities between Berg's jazz-piano writing in *Der Wein* and *Lulu* as a whole and Baresel's manuals are too obvious to be entirely coincidental.

Finally, the question of instrumentation seems to have caused Berg no end of trouble and second thoughts. In the event, after much experimentation, he assembled his own combination of instruments from Baresel's suggestions, adding only the vibraphone, which was too new to be mentioned in the 1926 edition of the *Jazz-Buch*.[84] After some vacillation he settled on Baresel's fifth variant for an eleven-to-twelve-piece jazz orchestra: piano, percussion, two–to-three saxophones, violin, two trumpets, trombone, banjo, sousaphone, and double bass.[85] A comparison with the offstage jazz band in *Lulu* reveals that Berg adopted this same scoring, not excluding parts for banjo and sousaphone, merely adding another reed instrument (clarinet) and two extra violins to amplify the violin part.[86] The percussion section is likewise adopted from Baresel, who, in a passage underscored twice by Berg, specifies a "kombiniertes Jazz-Schlagzeug" consisting of bass and side drums, woodblock, tom-tom, and cymbal, with optional *Stahlbesen* (wire brushes) as a noise effect.[87] Berg's offstage jazz band for *Lulu* adopts almost the identical wording for the instrumentation of his "Jazz-Schlagwerk": bass and side drums, two temple blocks (low- and high-pitch), and wire brushes.[88] Baresel's contrast of idiophone and membranophone (woodblock and tom-tom) has merely given way to two idiophones of contrasting pitch level.[89]

Berg, in sum, learnt his jazz from Baresel. And the influence is not merely limited to compositional devices. In an interesting polemical afterword, heavily underscored by Berg, Baresel argues on behalf of the tango as a modern-day erotic equivalent of the eighteenth-century minuet. Berg, intent on creating a female counterpart to *Don Giovanni*, must have been struck by the parallels with his own projected work. Both operas use dance bands extracted from the main orchestra in scenes that demonstrate the destructive erotic powers of their title characters, and both do so with the current dance forms of their day.[90] If *Lulu*, as Hans Ferdinand Redlich has suggested, was conceived in the Wardrobe Scene,[91] it may well be said that one of its midwives was Alfred Baresel.

IX

Berg's jazz studies were not limited to the *Jazz-Buch*. To deepen his knowledge of jazz he turned to another body of material recommended by Baresel and easy enough to obtain: the instrumental *Kunstjazz* published by his younger colleagues at Universal. As surprising as it may seem, Weimar Germany's art composers were far more readily inclined to consult each other's works, and the works of their French colleagues, as jazz sources than to turn to the live performances or studio recordings of dance-band musicians. Just as Baresel could include a passage from Ravel's *L'enfant et les sortilèges* among his jazz breaks,[92] German composers were constantly enjoined to study the growing body of recognized *Kunstjazz* for hints and inspiration. We have already mentioned the classical status attained by Kurt Weill's carefully crafted scores as examples of jazz instrumentation.[93] Similar classical authority attached to Zez Confrey's well-known novelty piano piece of 1921, *Kitten on the Keys* (regarded by Adorno as one of the two lasting musical achievements of the Jazz Age[94]), and to a small corpus of pieces drawn without exception from the Universal catalogue: Milhaud's *Trois Rag-Caprices* for piano (1922), Wilhelm Grosz's *Jazzband* for violin and piano (1924), Erwin Schulhoff's piano cycles *Cinq études de jazz* (1927) and *Six esquisses de jazz* (1928), and *The Daniel Jazz* (1924), a solo cantata by the Russo-American composer Louis Gruenberg, whose American background and German training established him briefly among Viennese intellectuals as a jazz expert.[95] To German art composers this body of study materials held out several advantages: the authors had unimpeachable musical pedigrees; the pieces were easily obtainable in music shops; and, most importantly, the works were codified in writing, and hence could be examined and analyzed by composers who were equally accustomed to think of music not as a performer's art but primarily as a musical text in staff notation.

Berg was fully aware of these exemplary works of *Kunstjazz*. At the same time that he studied Baresel's jazz manual he also wrote out a number of excerpts from works by Schulhoff (the aforementioned *Etudes* and *Esquisses*) and Wilhelm Grosz (*Baby in der Bar*), conscientiously noting the various dance types involved: shimmy, blues, tango, rag, and Charleston. These excerpts, written in a clear hand for his own future reference, occupy no fewer than four sides of manuscript paper in the Berg estate.[96] They supply convincing evidence that one of the principal sources for the assimilation of jazz among German art composers was, paradoxically, the work of other art composers. One of Berg's chosen examples immediately catches our attention. Painstakingly written out under the heading "shimmy" is the same passage from Grosz's *Baby in der Bar* that we quoted above as a further instance of the Jonny figure (see Example 7.4). For Berg, as for Krenek, Rathaus, Grosz, Weill, and many other composers of Weimar Germany's *Kunstjazz*, the Jonny figure, so remote from the legitimate American jazz of the time, was evidently as integral and unquestioned a part of the language of jazz as were the saxophones and blue sevenths he underscored in Baresel's primer.

With this final occurrence of Jonny's shimmy figure the essay comes to a close. We have traced this seemingly insignificant rhythm from the opera stage to the popular song and recording industries, from these industries to the jazz primers and textbooks, and from these textbooks to instrumental *Kunstjazz* and back to the opera stage. All of these levels of Weimar Germany's musical culture worked in interaction to create the music that undergird the German Jazz Age and the works of art that arose from it. Our view of the history of jazz in Weimar Germany has shifted from conventional sources of jazz reception to others that have received less notice: from legitimate jazz to commercial dance music, from American popular music to German surrogates, from live or recorded performances to printed sources, and finally to Weimar Germany's jazz textbooks and performance aids, a primary source for its commercial music and art music alike. Jazz in Weimar Germany, then, grew in parallel with, but quite separately from, the music of America's Jazz Age. From untutored beginnings in the post-war *Stehgeiger* and "racket bands", drawing on distant American sources filtered through the recording and sheet-music industries, always beholden to opinion in London and Paris, German jazz of the Twenties developed a distinctive arsenal of conventions and techniques capable of being codified in textbooks, assimilated by the lowly dance-band musician no less than the composer of genius, and transmuted into supreme works of art as far-ranging as *Lulu* and *Mahagonny*.

8

THE IDEA OF *BEWEGUNG* IN THE GERMAN ORGAN REFORM MOVEMENT OF THE 1920S

PETER WILLIAMS

In 1928 Günther Ramin, organist of St Thomas, Leipzig, and thus someone with great influence in the lively and energetic spheres of church music, organ-playing, and conservatory education, published one of the many essays inspired by the decade's newer attitudes to organs and organ repertory. His pamphlet includes the following remarks:[1]

Our period is moving rapidly in regard to evaluation and reassessment of artistic complexes, and one is almost taken aback at how big and far-reaching the Organ Renewal Movement has become in the space of six years. May this [haste] not be a sign that this renaissance has come about as one of the many spiritual currents of fashion in the post-war era, rather may the true kernel and genuine enthusiasm of this process of change be preserved!

Many themes can be discerned in these remarks, representing certain views commonly held at the time. These views were that there was a discrete *Orgelbewegung*, one that was only six or so years old at that point; that despite (probably) being a "fashion" it had a "kernel of truth" and the character of a "renaissance"; that it related specifically to the postwar period, a period of general reevaluation in Germany; and of course that it was a subject on which the organist of the Bach church could usefully offer thoughts to the musical community. Each of these themes is a subject for contemplation today, not least insofar as they still exist in the minds of musicians who seem barely aware of the broader musical interests that were being developed in other countries at that time. The *Orgelbewegung* was and is a national movement that often exposes the limitations of cultural centrism at the very moment it is being original and "enlightened". As such it is something of a case-study for the assumptions that underlie an important, well-populated sphere of practical music-making in the 1920s, and indeed underlie a good deal of performance inside and outside Germany over the rest of the twentieth century.

A DISCRETE *BEWEGUNG*?

That Ramin's booklet, despite the apposite nature of its contents, has been almost entirely absent from recent literature concerning the *Orgelbewegung* is itself a sign of one of the *Bewegung*'s most powerful traits: just as it promoted certain attitudes about organs and organ music presented as the canonic or official view, so it created a narrow canon of literature on the subject, in particular the writings of Albert Schweitzer, Wilibald Gurlitt and Christhard Mahrenholz.[2]

Gurlitt's and Mahrenholz's analysis of the change in tastes in which they saw themselves as taking a leading role became, and has continued to be, a German orthodoxy for understanding a decade of monumental musical developments in which organs and church music assumed, frankly, only a marginal part. More recent German writing has modified this position only in certain details: an author might now point out that Schweitzer's credit ought to be shared by another Alsatian reformer, Emile Rupp, or that in any case Schweitzer's position has been misunderstood and that he had little sympathy with back-to-the-past interests.[3] In general there still appears to be little awareness of the broader background, those events preceding the German *Orgelbewegung* which were described by L. F. Tagliavini already nearly thirty years ago now.[4] Particularly dominated by this canon and following entirely in its footsteps have been writers in those countries traditionally dependent on established German norms, including Denmark, Holland, and (during the years of partition) East Germany. This is the more surprising because Denmark in particular was producing "historically aware" organs here and there already in the 1920s,[5] so that for many years, as far as new organs were concerned, one could more nearly approach the spirit of Buxtehude in Denmark than in Germany. That in effect Schweitzer and Rupp themselves challenged German orthodoxy by claiming Widor as the greatest organ-composer after Bach[6] – and therefore implied that his organist-type was of paramount importance to modern builders – did nothing much to convince leaders of the movement to broaden their ideas, one imagines. To them, it was such a claim as this that must have seemed provincial.

Questions about the received view of the German Organ Reform Movement can be raised under various heads. These include its attitudes towards historical performance, towards *Urtext* editions of music, and towards the work of writers elsewhere and to what extent it sympathized with extant old instruments that were too small or too quaint for the music of Bach.

On the attitude to *historical performance*: to a large extent this depends on the other attitudes (to *Urtext* editions, old instruments, etc.) and it seldom if ever appears as a topic beyond the details of organ registration. For the organist the question of timbres (stop registrations) does no doubt loom large, but it is striking what a minor part was played in earlier phases of the reform by the questions that occupy so many pages in today's publications, such as mechanism or temperament or articulation.

On *editions of music*: it is strange that in referring to Karl Straube's collection *Alte Meister des Orgelspiels* (1904)[7] Gurlitt should imply approval for its editorial techniques, for if one bears in mind the standards already established by the Guilmant-Pirro series *Archives des Maîtres de l'Orgue* (1901–), Straube's editing amounted to little more than making updated arrangements. Perhaps it was politeness or partiality (Gurlitt had been a Straube pupil), but just as likely is that old French music was still regarded as too frivolous for Gurlitt to find Guilmant's work important. Nor was it only the *Archives des Maîtres* that were (as far as I know) nowhere acknowledged by the canonic *Orgelbewegung* writers, for the better German scholarly editions do not seem to enter much into their deliberations either, except as sources for popular editions. It is otherwise difficult to see why in his Pachelbel edition of 1928 Karl Matthaei should treat Seiffert's impeccable DTB volumes of 1901 and 1903 in this way. According to Matthaei, in this edition "all signs, phrasing, registration, tempo markings and so on are the result of careful study on the Praetorius organ" – Gurlitt's 1921 organ at Freiburg, stoplist in Appendix 1 – and registrations have been added such as were "partly outlined" by Straube in his recitals on that organ (Bärenreiter Edition 238, preface). This sounds as if Matthaei-Gurlitt-Straube were setting out to create a received view of Pachelbel. If so, it was one that would put back the idea of performances faithful to Pachelbel, since neither the Freiburg Praetorius organ nor the old instruments known to Straube would go very far in illuminating what Pachelbel had taken for granted in Erfurt and Nürnberg.

On the *work of writers elsewhere*: important though the achievements of major new German organ monographs were in the 1920s,[8] they were not alone. Equally concerned with great instruments of the past, with the mature repertories of music composed for them and, by implication, with a renewed sense of the lessons they could teach modern builders, was the work of individual writers such as Félix Raugel in France.[9] Various French studies of old organ cases, though perhaps superficial musicologically, also evince a respect for such lessons, as does the first great study of the organ as art-object, Arthur Hill's *The Organ-Cases and Organs of the Middle Ages and Renaissance*, 2 vols (London, 1883, 1891).[10] From time to time in such books, explicit criticisms are made of the then contemporary standards of design and workmanship, and derogatory comparison is made between them and the work of the past. Such criticism is an *eminence grise* behind much of the performance practice interests of the time and became a prime mover of *Orgelbewegung* philosophy: but it certainly did not originate there, nor is it acknowledged by its writers.

On *old organs of little use to Bach*: the *Orgelbewegung*'s interest in or awareness of the historic position of extant old instruments in general – other than those fit for major works of Buxtehude and Bach – should by no means be taken for granted. The smaller old organs of East Friesland raise questions about the Movement's principles, for while the attention paid them in the 1920s by certain *Orgelbewegung* leaders was useful, nevertheless many of the fine instruments since restored there were declared by those leaders at that time to be irreparable and hopelessly antiquated.[11] It should be clear from the instruments particularly associated with *Orgelbewegung* philosophies – the Freiburg "Praetorius organ" and the Marienkirche, Göttingen (see Appendix 2) – that despite the claims made by its spokesmen, the Movement's organological understanding was not at all fully alerted to earlier periods. Only the stoplist of these organs and the new timbres created by the old-style stops suggest anything historical: the mechanism and other structural details betray no awareness that the organ as we know it is a historical phenomenon to modify too many parameters of which is to change it beyond the definition of "organ". (Only in the last thirty years, and only by certain craftsmen, has something of this sort been recognized for harpsichord and other keyboard instruments.) Without an understanding of the historical periods of the organ it is difficult to imagine an understanding of historical performance or those elements in it that follow as a matter of course from particular types of instrument.

"FASHION" VERSUS "KERNEL OF TRUTH"

That for some time the Schweitzer-Gurlitt-Mahrenholz sequence dominated the thinking of certain historians is clear from the writings of Gurlitt's successor in Freiburg, when in 1967 the university hosted another organ conference. Showing the *Orgelbewegung* to be no mere movement for a return-to-the-distant-past, H. H. Eggebrecht isolated three elements in the broad concept of such a "movement" in the 1920s: *protest* against certain developments in the recent past, *affirmation of values* chiefly on behalf of earlier music against the "collapse" of music during the postwar years, and *the fixing of norms* in order to establish "canonic" views as to what was correct or not.[12] By extracting such elements in the thinking of the period, Eggebrecht is able to quote aptly from a writer of 1933:

[In this sense would] the German Music Movement come fully into its own only through the push forward of National Socialism[13]

Not surprisingly, Eggebrecht also found that Adorno claimed a *Gemeinschaft* or "common purpose" between at least one musical movement (the *Singbewegung*) and fascism. But conceivably in Italy, too, the totalitarianism of that period could have provided a "climate" for a certain degree of "norm-fixing,"[14] and yet no new explicit organ movement emerged there. It seems that neither is conformity itself a sign of incipient Nazism nor did the *Orgelbewegung*, however much it coerced organists into conforming with what certain musicologists told them, lead to uniformity. It took another war to reduce German organ builders to a repetitious and dismal utility in their instruments, reflecting both the impasse that German organ music had reached and the fact that for so long afterwards the enterprising builders of the West were cut off from the old masterpieces of Saxony.

The "kernel of truth" behind the "fashion" for rethinking the organ, as it showed itself in central Germany in the 1920s, was both international and by no means new. There had been signs pointing in this direction for some time. Shortly after 1900 Italian journals were carrying appreciations of the old Italian organ (particularly its *ripieno* and mechanical action),[15] and it would be difficult to find a more suitable summary of ideas in the Germany of the 1920s than those published in an English book of 1915:[16]

The [old] church organs . . . had that power based on sweetness which constitutes majesty. The change came on, and for the sake of louder tone, pressure of wind was doubled and trebled. The same pressure acting on the valves which let the wind into the pipes made them too heavy for the fingers to move through the keys. A machine was then invented which did the work at second hand . . . Personal touch, which did so much for phrasing and expression, was destroyed.

Then fashion decreed that the organ should be an imitation of the orchestra . . . but without the life that players instil into their instruments . . . Modern compositions are intended for this machine, and all is well with them; but it is a revelation to hear Handel's or Bach's music on a well-preserved old organ.

An important element in Arnold Dolmetsch's pathbreaking book is that his remarks on the organ come third in his overall survey of "the musical instruments of the period." He was enabled by experience and skill to view the organ in a context of other instruments, but this ability was virtually unknown to the *Orgelbewegung* and is still by no means common in German thinking. Nevertheless, Dolmetsch already identifies two of the themes that were characteristic of the *Orgelbewegung*: the dislike of higher (i.e., unnatural) wind pressure[17] and the complaint that organs imitated orchestras – which, as Mahrenholz later pointed out, was nothing new for organs.[18] Dolmetsch's remarks were also aimed at performance itself, but what he said concerning sensitive action, like Raugel's emphasis on the quality of workmanship in old French organs, took many years before finding echoes in Germany.[19] Earlier still, Schweitzer was speaking of the contrapuntal clarity given by older styles of organ voicing (see below, concerning the Kronenburg organ of 1908), but it took a Dolmetsch to see the picture in the round.

The tentative moves towards historical performance practice in the Germany of the 1920s rarely if ever became as focussed as they were for Dolmetsch. Such a focus must have sprung from Dolmetsch's practical experiences as both a maker and player, a combination not often found. On the contrary, in Germany in the

1920s the humanist academic-musicological training for men of influence was not practical in the same way and would tend instead to encourage broad philosophical overviews that can appear vaguer the more they are contemplated. Arnold Schering ("today's most prominent representative of German musicology," according to Gurlitt in 1929[20]) was not alone in saying such things as:

As the music of our period approaches in many details the principal feature of baroque music . . . the old organ becomes the symbol of a musical conception whose consequence lies in the future.

Schering's "music of our period" must be far removed from most of the repertories discussed elsewhere in the present volume and gives the impression that his readers knew nothing of the advanced music of the 1920s.[21] Was he thinking of the dead-end contrapuntalism of a Hindemith, as during the interwar years were so many of the advanced organists and church-composers, such as Hugo Distler in Lübeck?

Quite what a German musicologist of the 1920s such as Schering would call a "principal feature" of "baroque music" other than a certain kind of counterpoint and a certain regular phraseology characteristic chiefly of German music, is not always clear. But Schering certainly thought of the organ chiefly in connection with protestant church practice, as is clear from another remark he made at that period:[22]

For if we compare the near-to-earth sound of a baroque organ with the far-from-earth of a romantic, then it has to be inevitably accepted that the protestantism of the romantic period was to just the same degree as far from that of the baroque in decisive points of the religious experience as the one sound-ideal was from the other.

Such an attractively broad view belongs to the same national flair for the wide *aperçu* that would soon produce an Adorno – indeed, it is a view that helps to illustrate the culture that could produce the phenomenon Adorno. But in their lack of specificity – in their leaving the mere practical details to the artisan (*Bauer, Restaurator)* – such remarks give little guidance. Those craftsmen are left to their own devices, while academics are encouraged to survey grandly landscapes they themselves have never mapped on the ground. By no means has this situation much changed in the last seventy years, and insofar as a few recent organ builders have set standards for the restoration and understanding of old instruments (such as Jürgen Ahrend in East Friesland), little credit can go to any *Bewegung* theorists of the 1920s except as they eventually provided something for later, better educated builders to react against.

Meanwhile, however, it was not least in their language that the *Orgelbewegung*'s writers effectively influenced the future in a subtle way, in particular with the term "baroque organ". It was and is a phrase that would otherwise have been barely conceivable – except in some art-historical or metaphorical sense – to native English, French and Italian users. The *Orgelbewegung's* terms "baroque organ" and "romantic organ" are good examples for any theory one might have that period labels have been invented to help with two of the music historian's great problems: to develop a good grass-roots knowledge (actually getting to know the label-defying range of instruments and music of the seventeenth and eighteenth centuries) and to have to deal with vastly diverse amounts of music (a need to marshall under a *label* what it is one does know). Dolmetsch did not call and would never have called his book *The Interpretation of Baroque Music.*[23]

Even if a "kernel of truth" in the *Orgelbewegung* is that it helped alert musicians of one particular profession and one particular country to issues arising in the new historicism, it could be that its writers (Gurlitt, Mahrenholz) and players (Straube, Ramin), plus the new performance-practice scholars (Schering, Haas), did in effect promote a received canon of acceptable attitudes. And these attitudes would not only hold back development but would contribute to that division of labor characteristic of much German music-study. Now one could claim that division of labor – keeping to one's specialism – leads to the fullest development in the long run. Early specialized experimental work in England on the history of pitch[24] has turned out to contribute directly or indirectly to the best of today's understanding of crucial aspects of instrument history.[25] Or the specialized positivistic coverage of details in Curt Sachs's handbook on instruments,[26] written and revised exactly over the period of the *Orgelbewegung*, forms a firm basis for today's detailed monographs written by professional organologists.[27] Or any professional, technical study open to subsequent detailed revision can at least lead directly to later interpretation and "truer" understanding.[28] But in the broad field of performance-practice studies, division of labor could lead to too small a base from which to draw useful conclusions: neither a performer nor a scholar *simpliciter* would have enough experience for authoritative interpretation.

A good example of this can be found in certain coverage of figured-bass playing. The treatment of figured bass in Dolmetsch may appear to be less thorough than the comparable treatment in Schering,[29] where the *musicologist* has carefully selected amongst German repertories and theorists to give the reader some historical coordinates. But Dolmetsch's coverage bespeaks the more experienced musician. In drawing briefly but tellingly upon a finely selected group of imaginative and practical authors – Praetorius, Mace, d'Anglebert, Forqueray, Geminiani (apropos Handel), and Bach (? BWV 203) – Dolmetsch gives a far livelier and inspiring view of the arts and styles involved in the art of playing figured bass. It is true, as Schering says, that no thorough coverage of the subject *auf historischer Grundlage* had so far appeared, but even when something of the kind did appear (also in 1931, but not in Germany and presumably not known at the time to Schering),[30] it could not improve on Dolmetsch as far as the responsive player was concerned, and it must have lain unused on the library shelves of English conservatories.

A useful comparison of these three *continuo* writers – Dolmetsch, Schering, and Arnold – can be made in the way they handled Praetorius's realization of the bass in the second section of his motet "Wir glauben's" (not so identified by Schering). For Schering (p. 149), it seems to be simply a four-part realization of a full-choral movement, for which he cross refers to a further theorist (Bianciardi). For Arnold, who alone quotes and translates the whole passage (vol. I, pp. 47–48, eagerly identifying parallels in the harmony!), the reference is much fuller though not as full as he intended, because he could not find (as he laudably wished to) a full set of Praetorius's vocal parts with which to check and compare it. But for the pioneering Dolmetsch (pp. 342–44), Praetorius's realization is more useful for the musical performer himself. It "gives a noble example [and] the working out is free . . . just right for effect;" furthermore, it remains an important source because most books of the period "hardly say anything about the practical and artistic sides of the question," which are what Dolmetsch was interested in and wished to write about.

It may be unrealistic, however, to suppose the *Orgelbewegung* to have led organists to feel involved or knowledgeable in such issues as stylistic figured-bass playing. Whether Günther Ramin or Karl Straube studied the work of Max Schneider on Bach's figured bass, I do not know.[31] To that period, too, belonged D. F. Tovey's piano realizations of Bach continuo (so admired by Arnold – see his preface to vol. I, p. xiii), and it is very unlikely that he followed the manner described by early eighteenth-century writers. These big musicians of *ca*1930 would pay no attention to a Heinichen or Mattheson. Nor do organists appear to have seen that new attempts to understand aspects of *Aufführungspraxis* meant a crucial part for old organs in the picture as a whole. Non-organists certainly did not see it, for although one might now assume *Die Orgelbewegung* and *Aufführungspraxis* to be related, neither Schering nor Haas had much to say on organs, particularly as a token for any back-to-the-past movement there might have been. Their references, generalized and not very expert, are to its participation in early repertories. Once past the period of Abt Vogler,[32] Haas does not refer to organ at all, and his remarks on *neuromantische* music concern only the orchestra.

"IN THE SPACE OF SIX YEARS"

What Haas called *neuromantisch*, Schweitzer's erstwhile colleague and later critic Rupp called *neudeutsch*: such was the music of the *Fortschrittspartei* of Liszt and Wagner (1859), as distinct from the late classics up to and including Brahms.[33] It can only have been by some kind of fancied analogy that Rupp could coin the phrase *die elsässisch-neudeutsche Orgelreform*, since most of the New German composers themselves had only the most tenuous connection with the organ. Yet insofar as Rupp thought it wrong to want to return to the "Bach-Silbermann" organ or the French (baroque?) church organ, desiring instead a complex of several organ types for "us New German builders and players,"[34] he may have been less than correct himself, for Liszt's own organ interests centered on late-classical instruments much less technologically developed than those admired by Rupp. Ramin's phrase "space of six years" suggests that he was thinking not of Rupp nor of Schweitzer but of the 1921 "Praetorius organ" in Freiburg, an instrument offering little to *neudeutsche* interests. On the contrary, it was neo-baroque in the very respect that can have been only marginal to the modern composers but fascinating to the *Orgelbewegung* organists: its timbres and the taste for "old sounds" it encouraged.[35]

Although J. S. Bach was the spoken and unspoken household god being appeased by the true believers' sacrifice of high-pressure orchestral organs, a longer musical lineage was most often invoked by the writers, that of Scheidt-Buxtehude-Bach-Reger. (This lineage is still fundamental to church musicians.) These four were not evaluated equally, of course, and the sequence sustained the idea of Bach as "the culmination of an era." In Ramin's words:[36]

If one observes the history of the development of church music it becomes clear that the great appearance of J. S. Bach signifies a goal, a fulfillment, and that the essential steps of development are to be sought *before* him.

Such belief led Schweitzer and Gurlitt to very different recommendations for organs, and yet both could claim to be justified by what they understood to be "the Bach organ." Schweitzer knew the Silbermann connection to be important, but reasoned that the best of recent French-Alsatian organ building was more appropriate. If for him Bach was "a mystic, a model, and an educator for mankind," then what was wanted was a "true" or "artistic" organ, something perhaps corresponding to the masterpieces of the 1850–1880 period (with a swell manual and good action), not some historicist reconstruction. If there was a particular historical figure for the French Alsatians to emulate, it was Andreas Silbermann, an imitation of whose pipe-voicing Schweitzer was pleased to announce already in the Strasbourg-Kronenburg organ of 1908, on which instrument fugal inner parts were "remarkably clear."[37] In all such discussions, there must have been elements of geographical rivalry – Rhineland *versus* Prussia, Alsace *versus* Thuringia – and it is not difficult to suspect this rivalry to be lurking behind many apparently pure musical preferences. Thus Gurlitt, a Freiburger surely not ignorant of Alsatian organ tone, focussed more on the old pure German organs of Thuringia and

Lower Saxony and found in Praetorius an appropriate starting point for an understanding of the Scheidt-Bach sequence, i.e., the more purely German pedigree removed from Alsace. Because of such "geographical rivalry," Bach devotion could lead devotees in several directions.

But there is an enormous difficulty encountered when the music of Bach is the reference point for organ builders, advisers, and players: no one knows what any of the organs he played regularly were like. A second difficulty is that virtually everything about them – size, timbre, pitch, tuning, compass, touch, playing dimensions, accessories, acoustic, the general and the specific sound – varied in the course of the half century during which Bach can be assumed to have been composing organ music. Rarely do any of the 1920s writers on organs, organ-music, or performance practice ever betray an awareness that, for example, the Passacaglia and the E-flat Prelude and Fugue were composed with very different organs in mind, or that very different organs were associated with the composer over the decades in which he produced such music. This is an approach that has still not been very thoroughly worked out, even today. Ernst Flade, author of one of the more valuable monographs of the period,[38] came near to it when he remarked at the Freiburg Conference of 1926 that indeed various organ types were appropriate for the various periods within the Bach œuvre, but he compromised by claiming that the early works "could be played" on the next-generation instruments of Gottfried Silbermann. Wilhelm Fischer also explored the idea a little but necessarily suffered from the day's understanding of the Bach chronology.[39] Insofar as the 1920s were aware of the chronological factor, organists seem to have recognized it only in terms of tonal character – what different stops or manuals could be found on organs respectively of the 1690s and 1740s – and not with respect to other details of performance, such as whether keyboards and therefore articulation changed in the course of Bach's life.

In *Orgelbewegung* theory, Gurlitt's Praetorius organ of 1921 took the player as far as the early works of Bach, while Mahrenholz's Göttingen organ of 1926 gave one the total sequence of Scheidt-to-Reger (see Appendix 2).[40] Straube, perhaps bearing in mind Flade's praise of Gottfried Silbermann and criticism of that "inborn German tendency for the speculative" which could lead to a "shoving aside of the tested-and-true of old,"[41] evidently became enthusiastic for Gottfried Silbermann, and re-registered his collection of old organ music according to the Silbermann organ(s) in Rötha (1718), a village only a short drive from Leipzig. (One wonders what attention Straube had paid these nearby organs before they became acceptable to the *Orgelbewegung*. His registration for the "Eight Little Preludes and Fugues" of Bach[42] shows no knowledge of Silbermann's own recommendations.) Silbermann organs in Dresden, Großhartmannsdorf, Helbigsdorf, and Freiberg were visited by members of the 1927 Conference, and meanwhile a masterpiece of the northern master Arp Schnitger was also being invoked: the Jakobikirche, Hamburg (1693). This was an organ celebrated ever since it had been completed, associated with one of Bach's job applications, admired by local experts such as Hans Henny Jahnn but now thrust into the *Orgelbewegung* limelight by Günther Ramin and Karl Straube (1923–24).[43]

To some extent one can see the support for Praetorius, G. Silbermann, and Schnitger as a response to the Schweitzer-Rupp emphasis on Andreas Silbermann, in particular the organ in Ebersmünster (Alsace). That there were nationalistic elements at play for at least some of the antagonists seems clear from Rupp's preface, which is free of German references of any kind.[44] And for other critics, the Freiburg *Orgelbewegung* was too one-sided, even provincial.[45] Of course, old organs had been continuously played, and Ramin cannot have been the only musician to ask how it came about that suddenly everyone admired them (see p. 34, n1). The answer was: because an agenda was being created around them, publicized by conferences and those that dominated them.

Ramin's "space of six years," then, coincides with the opening of the Praetorius organ in the University of Freiburg and follows the interpretation of events as developed by the conferences and confirmed – a suitably canonic term – by both the cantor and the organist of St Thomas, Leipzig. At that point, musicology and organology had not yet come together to give guidance on, for example, questions of dual pitch, transposition, and temperament such as were relevant to the organ's part in Bach cantatas,[46] but the general move away from the "factory organ"[47] would naturally lead to a refinement of understanding on many such fronts. The first of the spate of books on old organs in the German regions (Burgemeister on Silesia, Haacke on Mecklenburg[48]) relate or refer to another and more openly antiquarian conference, the *19. Tage für Denkmalpflege und Heimatschütz* held at Breslau in 1925, in which Gurlitt and Burgemeister participated and which typified the renewed interest in the older crafts generally and the museum priorities they would lead to. Without doubt, such interests were still those of a small minority, and in those same months most organists would have seen the new giant organ of Passau Cathedral (the "largest church organ in the world") as far more indicative of progress and of that technical know-how for which German organ builders had long been widely admired.[49] The biggest organ in the world before World War I, the Breslau Jahrhunderthalle, had required special electrical engineering,[50] and it cannot have been easy in the 1920s to deliberately shun such well-established and proud technologies.

But a *geistige Bewegung*, as at the time Jacques Handschin claimed the *Orgelbewegung* to be,[51] could consciously turn away from material excess, especially if it were the excess of southern Roman catholicism (Passau Cathedral) or of industrial-municipal pride (Breslau Jahrhunderthalle), and towards the technical craft elements or superfine workmanship of old protestant instruments (G. Silbermann). Thus, at the Freiburg Conference, Paul Rubardt (later director of the ex-Heyer Collection of Historical Instruments, Leipzig) called for a fundamental technical study of all the extant Schnitger work, especially its scaling.[52] Pipe-scale in particular interested the earliest *Orgelbewegung* writers, being a technical question they could get their teeth into. An irony of Mahrenholz's booklet on the Göttingen organ (see Appendix 2) is that there are several pages in it devoted to scaling theory while the organ itself was an unrefined compromise: electric console, Victorian gothic *Hauptwerk* and a new *Rückpositiv* very coarsely designed (after the Hamburg Jacobiorgel?). Perhaps scaling interested the *Orgelbewegung* writers for the same reason it had the Benedictine theorists of the tenth century: pipe-scale gives a scientific *locus* for the attention of humanistically trained and literate authors, while out there in the workshops the actual organ makers find and have always found so many other technical and technological details quite as pressing, if not more so.

It is tempting to think that another development of the period also helped focus attention on the specifics of organology and performance practice: the summary-like but newly comprehensive descriptions of certain musical repertories, as represented by Karl Fellerer's two volumes on organ-music.[53] Nothing in other countries compared with this wide-ranging coverage of music, and in one particular respect it surpasses most *Orgelbewegung* writings: unlike them it does not merely nod towards other, non-German repertories,[54] merely in order to regard Bach as the consummation devoutly to be wished. However, whether Fellerer's discussion of other repertories did directly influence developments is doubtful, if only because even today the fullest understanding of e.g. French elements in the organ music of J. S. Bach is unlikely to be found in any part of Germany.

The nationalism that was inherent in the Bach devotion of the 1920s and 30s had the effect of bequeathing a narrowness of outlook towards the beloved composer, since it demoted the non-German elements in his music and led musicians to think that they could quickly summarize them. What was written about the neo-baroque organ of Bremen Cathedral in 1939 (that it was the significance of Bach that had led to the lively re-awakening of German baroque music and its organ-ideal, hence to a renaissance of old German organ music) could still be found in a comparable pamphlet today.[55] Another idea still valid in German historiography is Ramin's "space of six years": 1921 and the Freiburg Praetorius organ are still regarded today as the starting points for well-researched studies of organ music,[56] as if a *Movement* can be so exactly dated.

REEVALUATION IN THE INTERWAR YEARS

Long after the events of 1933, the step between "nationally-aware" and "nationalistic" can appear very small. Is it only the associations of the Third Reich's gothic book-type in 1935[57] that make such phrases as *das ganze Reich* (when speaking of organ regions) or *im klassischen Lande der Orgelkomposition, des Orgelspiels und der Orgelbaukunst* seem to have taken that small step? Is it only the associations of autumn 1939 that suggest Müller-Blattau's reference at that period to Strasbourg and the Rhineland as *eine rechte deutsche Orgellandschaft*[58] to be bolstering certain political agendas? That it is easy to draw hasty conclusions about what is politically significant is clear from the 1927 Freiberg Conference's talk of *das deutsche Volk* and of the education *des Volkes* (Freiberg conference papers, pp. 87–88, 91 [see n.2]): as it happens, these were not new political slogans at all but quotations from Schoenberg's *Richtlinien für ein Kunstamt* (Vienna, 1919), and they bore no obvious relation to the National Socialists' peculiar adoption of these words.[59]

But the "reevaluation" characteristic of the *Orgelbewegung* for Ramin was moral-political when it meant that its "historical strengths" (*geschichtliche Kräfte*) were there to expose the "historically alien and fickle revolutionizing and americanizing of the organ" (*geschichtsfremden und geschichtsflüchtigen Orgelrevolutionierung und -americanisierung*) and thus to make it possible for "the German organ and its music [to become] again a genuine, leading force in European musical life" (*die deutsche Orgel und Orgelmusik wieder zu einer wahrhaft führenden Macht im europäischen . . . Musikleben*).[60] In this way, Schweitzer's dislike of high wind pressures and electric actions would now have a spiritual dimension, since these modern devices make it impossible for an organist to "speak the impulses of the soul."[61] Cultures that produced the *americanized* (cinema) organ would be anathema, and it is difficult to believe that such views were free of political or even military overtones. In 1933, when addressing a leader of the party-friendly "Confessional Reform Movement" or *Glaubensbewegung* (the so-called *Deutsche Christen),* Hans Henny Jahnn – poet, playright, philosopher, visionary, organ builder, and occasional anti-Semite – not only took up the theme of a Germany deploringly gripped by *Amerikanismus* but also unwittingly revealed the kind of historiography (abetted by short-cut simplifications such as period labels) that must surely have encouraged political thuggery. Any visionary who spoke in favor of a "German rebellion against Christian confinement" as it had once been personified by Charlemagne (whom he called "Emperor Charles the Saxon-killer") and who rejoiced in a future rebellion that would originate in Baltic lands where the "Hanseatic spirit met northerly power-streams," was playing with fire, even if on this occasion he was only giving his views on organ-building.[62]

That Jahnn himself was discredited by the Nazis[63] does not lessen the danger of such historiography, for any sense of indisputable national right conveyed by such theorists or practitioners will not remain confined to arcane arguments about mechanical organ action. Jahnn's personal visions – particularly of the life-pervading validity of Pythagorean proportion, or of that "cosmic transmission" that was last represented by J. S. Bach, etc. – may have seemed a manifestation of cultural bolshevism to some,[64] but those to whom it did were the kind of people who also had their own ethereal *visions*, though of a deadlier kind. It was not necessarily a big step from describing the moral character of German music to hinting at – even encouraging – contemporary political developments. When Schütz's music was seen as something that had signalled "the beginning of capitalist enterprise" in an Erzgebirge whose "bourgeois and courtly music-making" was developing with the "new High German language" after the original "German colonialization" of Thuringia-Saxony,[65] was it so big a step to go on to support a more active form of *Ostpolitik* in that period (1935)? With the benefit of hindsight, it does not appear to have been so. While the Buxtehude Complete Edition founded in 1925 may not have been planned because this "unprecedently healthy music" was thought at the time to contrast with the modern *Nervenmusik,* it was only a decade or so later that it was said to be doing precisely this.[66] An organist would play such healthy music in as healthy a manner as he could by means of a mechanical organ action – which would more easily convey its "northerly power-streams." And the "clean lines" of an *Orgelbewegung* organ as designed and built in the 1930s would sustain the "cleanliness" metaphors. In the circumstances one is bound to wonder how far removed from this was the desire to *clean out* the synagogues.[67]

Whatever its connection to later political developments, the idea of "re-evaluation" in the 1920s takes various forms in *Orgelbewegung* literature, and presumably the organ playing that went with it. Gurlitt himself speaks of the situation "for the youth returning from the war" and of the musical effects of the *Jugendbewegung.* Surely not alone at the time, he also makes the point that the losers in World War I were not the "Powers of Central Europe" but the whole of Europe.[68] All this would not seem to have much to do with organs were it not that the writers themselves made certain connections. Thus the Göttingen Marienorgel was important to *die ganze Jugendmusikbewegung* since it offered an amalgam of German achievements in the present and the past and was thus a kind of model.[69] Perhaps there may not appear now a very clear relationship between organ stops and the *Wille . . . in der kirchenmusikalischen Erneuerungsbewegung,*[70] but by 1938 the relationship was there for Mahrenholz:[71]

In its origins, the Organ Movement is naturally a child of its time, the time after the Great World War and the collapse of our people. . . . Much of that which the civilized world before 1918 had possessed with pride, appeared vain . . .

One *reaction to the collapse* meant a *return to natural things* and away from the articifial. For some, this meant a turn against machine-like instruments with their high wind pressures and organ consoles that looked like the control panel of a railway marshalling yard. For others, it somehow meant on the contrary an admiration for the large organ as purveyor of some *Gesamtmusikreich,* as J. Müller-Blattau put it at the second Freiburg Conference, now in 1938:[72]

As the most comprehensive instrument of our musical culture, the big organ draws in to the great halls of our political festivals and ceremonies . . . [It is] a total music empire . . . the symbolic instrument of the community. It is a "political" instrument in the highest sense.

Alas for Müller-Blattau, this was less likely to be alluding to the early Christian Fathers' idea of the organ as an allegory for "the community of souls"[73] than to Günther Ramin playing the 220-stop Walcker organ in Nürnberg Luitpoldhalle (1936) to Hitler and his admiring crowds.

   It is hardly feasible to guess how far such sentiments of 1938 were an inevitable result of a *Bewegung*'s "reevaluation" in the 1920s, but what one can say is that over this period there is no sudden change of direction, no obvious moral jolt from positive to negative nationalism. In the 1920s young musicology was taking another look at history, particularly that German protestant music history which naturally gravitated around cantors and their worlds. This did not have to lead either to an empty historicism[74] or to fascism, but in helping to reestablish the organist and the organ as musical-cultural forces, it did mean resisting the "American" cinema-organ,[75] which in turn led to moral scorn for the popular (often black) musical idioms that went with it. Similarly, the apparently harmless call for *Hausmusik* in the 1920s became one more element in the politically correct family ideology developed after 1933,[76] and, unbelievable though it may now seem, playing Telemann's recorder sonatas came to have a hidden political agenda. After all, if by 1938 the most influential musicians such as Müller-Blattau of Freiburg found themselves playing a part in reconciling music and its philosophy to the mentality of Bavarian beerhall putschists, they had the model of the Freiburg *Rektor* Heidegger before them.

   In such presentations, there is only indirect reference to the *Aufführungspraxis* concerns of the period, to the fact that the *Jugendbewegung* was actually prewar in origin, and to the earlier moves towards historical awareness in musical matters that one could have found in other countries. The more the *Jugendmusikbewegung* merged into the *Hitlerjugend-Musikpflege* the less likely it was to develop any understanding of historical idioms and purely musical matters arising from trying to play them. Perhaps for many Germans the work of Dolmetsch in London or Erard in Paris had been an empty historicism, without any of the moral force of a *Bewegung*? The word *Bewegung* had long had the aura of didactic or moral improvement about it, chiefly – as far as the world of learning and teaching was concerned – through the *pädagogische Bewegung in Deutschland* of the second half of the nineteenth century. It continued to have this aura throughout the Nazi period, not least with the journal *Die Bewegung: Zentralorgan des NSD-Studentenbundes* (1933–1945).

RAMIN AS ORGANIST OF ST THOMAS, LEIPZIG

It is possible that no one in the Upper Rhineland in the 1920s knew of the work of Dolmetsch or Erard in various fields of early music activity, including making harpsichords and giving historically conceived concerts. In fact, a curious element in the whole story of the *Orgelbewegung* is its apparent indifference to (ignorance of) harpsichords and the questions being asked by musicians and craftsmen working with other keyboard instruments and their equally monumental repertories.

Several reasons for this are possible. Firstly, few old German harpsichords survived or aroused wide interest outside museums, although the Heyer Collection was presented to the University of Leipzig in 1927, the very period under consideration. Secondly, the organ world was self-contained and its *Bewegung* was inspired by professional or liturgical concerns, not therefore as part of a broader interest in historical conditions of performance as such. Thirdly, Bach's harpsichord music had become so firmly entrenched in the nation's piano repertory (the Old Testament to Beethoven's New) that organists would no more turn to the harpsichord for it than Italian organists would reject the piano for Scarlatti. And fourthly, the German organ up to World War I had become so excessive and dreary that it required more urgent attention than the organs of any other country did. This last is not expressed quite so bluntly at the time, although writers less personally committed then or now to the *Orgelbewegung*'s claims for authority have not hesitated to say something of the sort.[77] They could show how much more necessary it was to insist on traditional sliderchests in Germany than in England or Italy because in those countries the more recent factory-made organ chests had never become so popular.

When, therefore, Ramin writes as the current organist of the Bach church, he is giving the whole question a certain cathedral authority and stamping it as a church concern, one for which Bach is the touchstone. At the Freiberg Conference (conference papers, p. 113 [see n.2]), Gurlitt made a classic summing up of the kind that sees J. S. Bach as the "culmination of an era"[78] and reinforces the protestant nature of the *Orgelbewegung*. After complaining that Sweelinck (teacher of Scheidt and thus the *deutscher Organistenmacher*) was too little valued, he points out that a study of Sweelinck supplies "a fundamental connoisseurship" (*eine gründliche Kennerschaft*) of the Netherlandish-Venetian *a cappella* style as it was "originally coined by Josquin" (*ursprünglich Josquinscher Prägung*) and as it then formed the basis of European organ art up to the late chorales of Bach. Not irrelevant to Gurlitt in this breathtaking historical sweep was the English virginal music, for with its new kind of instrumental technique it had become and "remains exemplary" *(vorbildlich bleibt)* for protestant organ music. This kind of interpretation of history – which would surely have surprised Byrd, Bull, and Phillips – aims to show that various national schools can be briefy summed up before the real point is reached, which is: that they all contribute to a fuller understanding of J. S. Bach.

So canonic a view did this become that all too often to this day it affects how other keyboard repertories are approached in so many German and therefore not a few American *Musikhochschulen.* Furthermore, it has also had the effect of delaying the appreciation of French elements in Bach for those readers who rely on German studies,[79] especially as the French *manière* is so much more a practical matter for the performer than for the scholar or theorist. Although by the time of the second edition of Hans Klotz's organ history (1975)[80] writing on the Bach oeuvre has become much broader and more circumspect, the old canonicism still means that the final section of the book is devoted to *Die Orgelkunst Johann Sebastian Bachs,* as if it were for this that the reader had been waiting throughout the various gothic, renaissance, and baroque periods. The phrase "culmination of an era" is not used by Klotz, but it seems that an awareness of Bach's cosmopolitanism – he rises *aus der mitteldeutschen Tradition . . . der norddeutschen, der italienischen und der französischen Musik* (p. 375) – only confirms the same underlying idea. In the Nazi period, such interpretations must have slipped effortlessly into being politically correct: Rücker's book of 1940 on the organs of the Upper Rhineland (see n.58) goes through the motions of referring to other cultures (pp. 6, 8) but is at pains to confirm the *innerdeutsch* influences – as distinct from Dutch – on the organs of North Germany (pp. 93–94). This is poor history in two respects. It is superficial from the point of view of performance practice, since a major theme to explore is precisely the cross-border similarity in musical habits *ca*1500, in particular the nature of public concerts (organ recitals) at the time and the instruments used in them. And it is anachronistic in supposing that in *ca*1500 one could speak of a single "Germany" and that organs of other countries, like other elements in their culture, were marginal or could be easily dealt with.

POSTSCRIPT

Try as one might to see the *Orgelbewegung* in the broader musical context of the 1920s inside and outside Germany – particularly its focus on performance-practice issues – today's move by certain German scholars born after World War II to find Nazi skeletons in revered musicians' closets[81] is sure to make their motives appear other than purely musical. Of course, a posthumous witch-hunt might be unpleasant, but equally, any positivist or uncritical account of the *Orgelbewegung*'s aims[82] does seem inadequate, missing its political character and failing to illustrate the nature of the nationalistic *Moment* of the time. Musicians themselves were often quite willing to mix music and party politics.[83] It seems to be only now in the new anti-Nazi literature that certain basics become clear, such as that the Movement was only ever associated with certain people, of whom the unreliable H. H. Jahnn was one; there was strong resistance in Berlin already by 1928.[84] In turn, this suggests that the broad basis claimed for the *Orgelbewegung* by West German writers immediately after the twelve years of what is now called The Aberration (1933–45) was no more than a chimera, political wishful thinking, some kind of point-scoring.

APPENDIX 1

Organ in the Institute of Musicology, University of Freiburg.

Planned by W. Gurlitt, drawing on M. Praetorius's second volume (*De Organographia*, Wolfenbüttel 1619, pp. 191–92), built by Oskar Walcker, dedicated by Karl Straube, 4 December 1921, destroyed 27 November 1944.

Oberwerk (II)		*Rückpositiv (I)*		*Brust*	
Principal	8	Quintadeena	8	Klein lieblich	
Octava	4	Blockflöit	4	Gedacktflöit/	
Mixtur	IV	Gemshörnlein	2	Rohrflöit	2
including Octav	2	Zimbel doppelt	II	Baerpfeiff	8
and Quint	1⅓	very small & sharp		Geigend Regal	4
Grob Gedackt/		Spitzflöit or			
Rohrflöit	8	Spillflöit	4		
Nachthorn	4	Krumbhorn	8	*Pedal*	
Schwiegelpfeiff	1			Untersatz, strong	16
Rancket, or quiet				Posaunenbaß	16
Posaun	16			Cornett	2
Gemshorn★	4			Dolzianbaß★	8

Couplers: I/II, P/I, ★P/II
★ stops not in Praetorius
Electric-pneumatic action; cone-chests; utility casework
Details taken from Praetorius include pipe measurements, materials, construction, sound and wind pressure.

Ref: A. Riethmüller, "Die Praetorius-Orgel der Universität Freiburg i. Br.', in ed. H. H. Eggebrecht, *Orgelwissenschaft und Orgelpraxis: Festschrift zum zweihundert-jährigen Bestehen des Hauses Walcker* = Veröffentlichung der Walcker-Stiftung 8 (Murrhardt: Musikwissenschaftl. Verlags-Gesellschaft, 1980), pp. 27–59.

APPENDIX 2

Organ in the Marienkirche, Göttingen

Planned by Christhard Mahrenholz, built by Furtwängler & Hammer 1925 (enlarged in 1928)

Hauptwerk		*Rückpositiv*		*Oberwerk*	
Grossgedackt	16	Bordun	8	Geigend Prinzipal	8
Prinzipal	8	Quintade	8	Lieblich Gedackt	8
Viola da gamba	8	Salizional	8	Fernflöte	8
Holzflöte	8	Prinzipal	4	Prinzipal	4
Oktave	4	Gedacktflöte	4	Rohrflöte	4
Gemshorn	4	Schweizerflöte	4	Nasat	2⅔
Oktave	2	Rohrflöte	2	Waldflöte	2
Mixtur	V	Scharf	III	Nachthorn	2
Kornett	V	Sesquialtera	II	Zimbel	II
Trompete	8	Rankett	16	Dulzian	16
		Krummhorn	8	Oboe	8
		Tremulant		Regal	8
				Tremulant	

Pedal					
Prinzipal	16	Cello	8	Posaune	16
Subbass	16	Oktave	4	Schalmei	2
Quinte	10⅔	Sifflöte	2	Dulzian	16
Oktave	8	Rauschpfeife	IV	Oboe	8
Gedackt	8	Bärpfeife	32	Regal	4

Seven couplers, Zimbelstern
Hw: originally with nineteenth-century case. *Rp*: new.

Ref: Christhard Mahrenholz, *Die neue Orgel in der St. Marienkirche zu Göttingen* (Göttingen/Augsburg, 1926: Bärenreiter; Kassel, 2/1931): 1926 edn, especially pp. 9 (stoplist), 17 (case), 30ff (scalings), and 63 (electric console).

NOTES

ABBREVIATIONS

The following abbreviations are used in the notes.

AM   *Allgemeine Musikzeitung*
DJD   *Die deutsche Jugendmusikbewegung in Dokumenten ihrer Zeit von den Anfängen bis 1933* (Wolfenbüttel: Möseler, 1980)
MGG   *Die Musik in Geschichte und Gegenwart*, ed. F. Blume (Kassel and Basel: Bärenreiter, 1949–68; suppl. 1973–79)
NG   *The New Grove Dictionary of Music and Musicians*, ed. Stanley Sadid (London: Macmillan, 1980), 20 vols.
ZfM   *Zeitschrift für Musikwissenschaft*

PREFACE

1 A. J. Rydeer, *Twentieth-Century Germany: from Bismark to Brandt* (New York: Columbia University Press, 1973), p. 231. Ryder hastens to add that, later on, a form of government censorship was reinstated.

1 STAGE AND SCREEN: KURT WEILL AND OPERATIC REFORM IN THE 1920S

1 H. H. Wollenberg, *Fifty Years of German Film* (London: Falcon Press, 1948; repr. New York: Arno Press, 1972), p. 16. In 1927 the United States produced 743 feature films, Japan 407, and Russia 141. In Europe the top five producers were Germany (241), France (74), Great Britain (44), Poland (17), and Austria (15). That year also began a period of decline for the German film industry. UFA (*Universum Film AG*), a large umbrella organization for numerous smaller film companies, was on the brink of financial ruin, and it was bought out by Alfred Hugenberg, the right-wing chairman of Krupp. His ideological stamp on UFA became increasingly strong. 1927, moreover, marked the birth of the first full-length talking picture (*The Jazz Singer*), and, few realized it at the time, the silent-film era would soon come to a close.

2 Hans Gutman, "Young Germany," *Modern Music* 7 (1930), p. 7. According to Gutman, the November Revolution had ushered in a new audience. Traditional concert life – with its emphasis on nineteenth-century music – had passed into the class of luxuries

154

"reserved for the entertainment of the upper classes and [had] ceased to be an integral part in the life of the people."

3 Arnold Schoenberg, "Gibt es eine Krise der Oper?," *Musikblätter des Anbruch* 8 (1926), p. 209. "Die Krise des Theaters ist zum Teil bewirkt durch den Film: und durch ihn befindet sich auch die Oper in dieser Lage: die Konkurrenz mit dem dort gebotenen Realismus nicht mehr aufnehmen zu können. Der Film hat das Auge des Zuschauers verwöhnt: man sieht nicht nur Wahrheit und Wirklichkeit, sondern auch jener Schein, der sonst der Bühne vorbehalten blieb und der nur Schein sein wollte, stellt sich in phantastischer Weise als Wirklichkeit vor."

4 Letter to Hugo von Hofmannsthal (16 August 1916) in *Richard Strauss-Hugo von Hofmannsthal: Briefwechsel*, ed. Willi Schuh, (5th edn Zurich: Atlantis, 1978), p. 359. By summer 1916 Strauss, who was sketching the last act of *Die Frau ohne Schatten*, had grown weary of its intricate symbolism and mythology. As early as 28 July he declared: "Let us resolve that *Die Frau ohne Schatten* will be the last Romantic opera." See *Briefwechsel*, p. 354.

5 See Strauss's preface to *Intermezzo* in *Betrachtungen und Erinnerungen*, ed. Willi Schuh (Zurich: Atlantis, 1981), p. 149.

6 Strauss originally worked on the libretto with Hermann Bahr, but ended up writing the text himself. At one point during their collaboration the composer sent Bahr some sketched out scenes, which Strauss suggested were "fast nur Kinobilder." See letter of 1 January 1917 in *Meister und Meisterbriefe um Hermann Bahr*, ed. Joseph Gregor (Vienna: H. Bauer, 1947), pp. 99–100.

7 "Das Theater unserer Zeit [1927]," in *Erwin Piscator: Aufsätze, Reden, Gespräche*, Erwin Piscator Schriften 2, ed. Ludwig Hofmann (Berlin: Henschelverlag, 1968), pp. 23–24: "Wenn die Besucher unseres Theaters das Haus betreten, so soll die Welt nicht hinter ihnen versinken, sondern sich auftun. . . . Die *Verbindung zwischen Film und Bühne* geschieht nicht aus Sensationslust oder Effekthascherei, sondern mit der Absicht, die Totalität eines politischen Weltbilds anschaulich zu machen."

8 "Bühne der Gegenwart und Zukunft [1928]," in *Aufsätze, Reden, Gespräche*, p. 36: "Gerade die Verbindung von Bühne und Film, von epischer Schwarzweißkunst und der Dramatik des gesprochenen Wortes und des dreidimensionalen Menschen, scheint mir das wesentlichste Mittel zur Erreichung dieses Zieles." Piscator no doubt savored the dialectical flavor of the term "Schwarzweißkunst."

9 C. D. Innes, *Erwin Piscator's Political Theater* (Cambridge: Cambridge University Press, 1972), p. 108.

10 Ernst Krenek, "Opera between the wars," *Modern Music* 20 (1943), p. 104. Krenek was not the only German-speaking composer to laud the innovations of *L'Histoire*. In *Die neue Oper* (1926), Kurt Weill looked to Stravinsky's stage piece as possibly an important, concrete step in the direction toward a new opera, a work that "stands on the boundary between play, pantomime, and opera." See *Kurt Weill: Musik und Theater. Gesammelte Schriften*, ed. Stephen Hinton and Jürgen Schebera (Berlin: Henschelverlag, 1990), pp. 29–30. Theater critic Alfred Jhering found a connection between *L'Histoire* and not only film but (foreshadowing Krenek's remarks) epic musical theater: "A line leads from film to Stravinsky's outstanding *L'Histoire du Soldat*, from *L'Histoire du Soldat* to the lively, contemporary, crucial *Dreigroschenoper*." (Vom Film führt eine Linie zu Strawinskys herrlicher "Geschichte vom Soldaten", von der "Geschichte vom

Soldaten" zu der heiteren, gegenwärtigen, springenden "Dreigroschenoper".) See "Zeittheater [1929]", *Der Kampf ums Theater* (Berlin, 1974), pp. 301–02.

11 Eileen Bowser, *The Transformation of Cinema, 1907–1915* (New York: Scribner's, 1990), p. 19.

12 See *Weill Gesammelte Schriften*, pp. 28–32.

13 Stephen Hinton suggests how Weill's interest in operatic reform, which rejected Wagner as a point of departure, was "aided and abetted by Busoni." See "The concept of epic opera: theoretical anomalies in the Brecht-Weill partnership," in *Das musikalische Kunstwerk: Geschichte, Ästhetik, Theorie (Festschrift Carl Dahlhaus)*, ed. Hermann Danuser et al. (Laaber: Laaber-Verlag, 1988), p. 291.

14 Beyond the general concept of a non-illustrative, autonomous music, Weill's use of the term "konzertante Musik" remains unclear. Busoni's *Entwurf einer neuen Ästhetik der Tonkunst*, Weill's likely source, offers an important context. In the essay Busoni criticizes the present-day post-Wagnerian opera orchestra for its superficial illustration, for "seeking to repeat the scenes passing on the stage, instead of fulfilling its own proper mission of interpreting the soul-states of the persons represented. When the scene presents the illusion of a thunderstorm, this is exhaustively apprehended by the eye. Nevertheless, nearly all composers strive to depict the storm in tones – which is not only a needless and feebler repetition, but likewise a failure to perform their true function. . . . The storm is visible and audible without aid from music; it is the invisible and inaudible, the spiritual processes of the personages portrayed, which music should render intelligible." See *Sketch of a New Esthetic of Music* [1911], transl. Theodore Baker, in *Three Classics in the Aesthetic of Music* (New York: Dover, [1962]), p. 83. (Der größte Teil neuerer Theatermusik leidet an dem Fehler, daß sie die Vorgänge, die sich auf der Bühne abspielen, wiederholen will, anstatt ihrer eigentlichen Aufgabe nachzugehen, den Seelenzustand der handelnden Personen während jener Vorgänge zu tragen. Wenn die Bühne die Illusion eines Gewitters vortäuscht, so ist dieses Ereignis durch das Auge erschöpfend wahrgenommen. Fast alle Komponisten bemühen sich jedoch, das Gewitter in Tönen zu beschreiben, welches nicht nur eine unnötige und schwächere Wiederholung, sondern zugleich eine Versäumnis ihrer Aufgabe ist. . . . Das Gewitter ist sichtbar und hörbar ohne Hilfe der Musik; was aber in der Seele des Menschen während dessen vorgeht, das Unsichtbare und Unhörbare, das soll die Musik verständlich machen.") *Entwurf einer neuen Ästhetik der Tonkunst*, ed. Wolfgang Dömling (Hamburg: Karl Dieter Wagner, 1973), p. 19.

15 Kim Kowalke, *Kurt Weill in Europe* (Ann Arbor: UMI Press, 1979), p. 101.

16 "Musikalische Illustration oder Film Musik?," an interview with Lotte H. Eisner (1927) in *Weill Gesammelte Schriften*, pp. 297–99.

17 Two years after *Sumurûn* Hofmannsthal devised an opera libretto with direct regard for Reinhardt (*Ariadne auf Naxos*) that focusses, in part, on the pantomimic world of *commedia dell'arte*. Strauss and Hofmannsthal revised the work in 1916, just a year before Busoni's two *commedia dell'arte* operas *Arlecchino* and *Turandot*. Increased interest in the relationship between pantomime and opera is suggested by Busoni's addendum of 1922 to his *Entwurf*. To the discussion of opera he adds that "it ought to be possible to consider the form of a scenario accompanied by music and illustrated by song, without words, producing a kind of 'sung pantomime.'" It is important to view Weill's *Der Protagonist* (1925) from this perspective. See Hinton, "The concept of epic opera," p. 291.

18 Paul Bekker, "Der Film," in *Klang und Eros* (Stuttgart and Berlin: Deutsche Verlags-Anstalt, 1922).

19 A scene from this production is reproduced in Walter Panofsky, *Protest in der Oper* (Munich: Im Laokoon, 1966), p. 151. The intertitle reads: "Miß Lucia erwartet Edgardo zu einem geheimen Stelldichein" (Miss Lucia awaits Edgardo for a secret rendevous).

20 Kowalke, *Kurt Weill in Europe*, p. 41.

21 Parallels between *Der Protagonist* and *Ariadne* are illuminating. Both libretti involve two plays (one comic, the other tragic) within a play as well as the realm of *commedia dell'arte*. See note 17.

22 "Sie ist ganz tänzerisch, unrealistisch, mit übertriebenen Gesten darzustellen, im Gegensatz zu der späteren, zweiten Pantomime, welche durchaus dramatisch, mit lebendigem Ausdruck und leidenschaftlicher Bewegung gespielt werden soll."

23 Hanns-Werner Heister, "Der Protagonist – Ein Akt Oper von Georg Kaiser, Musik von Kurt Weill," in *Höhepunkte der Dresdner Operngeschichte* (Dresden: Hochschule für Musik Dresden, 1989), p. 986.

24 "*Der Protagonist*: Kurt Weill in der Dresdner Staatsoper," *Berliner Zeitung am Mittag* (20 March 1926).

25 This reference to the silent-film piano player is foreshadowed in Weill's 1925 cantata, *Der neue Orpheus* (which premiered with *Royal Palace*). In the last of seven variations mid-way through the piece there is a textual reference to Orpheus "In suburban movie houses on the / 'Torture-piano' / He has the Pilgims' Chorus lament / The death of the virgin." See Kowalke, *Kurt Weill in Europe*, p. 283. The surrealistic poem was by Iwan Goll, who had written another poem (Goll called it "Eine Filmdichtung") entitled *Die Chaplinade* (1920). In this equally surrealistic work a likeness of Charlie Chaplin comes to life, literally stepping out of a movie poster.

26 Paul Stefan, "Weill: Royal Palace," *Musikblätter des Anbruch* 9/3 (1927), pp. 133–34: "Krenek bietet den Zauber rasch wechselnder Schauplätze, nähert sich also dem Film, Weill führt diesen geradezu ein: Royal Palace ist in diesem Sinn wohl die erste Film-Oper."

27 Siegfried Günther, "Gegenwartsoper: Zur Lage des heutigen Opernschaffens," *Die Musik* 20/10 (1928), p. 725: "Überall bemerken wir das Zielen in eine Reihe geschlossener Bilder, die optische Rundung haben und also Folge filmischen Gesetzen unterstehen."

28 Hinton cogently argues that in dealing with the concept of epic theater one must make a distinction between ends and means. The end result of the *Royal Palace* film scene may not be epic in the Piscatorian or Brechtian sense, but the technique – with its interruption of dramatic continuity – certainly is. Hinton explores this distinction at length in "The concept of epic opera," pp. 285–94. Weill, like his teacher Busoni and unlike Brecht, saw the eighteenth-century number opera (with its emphasis on segmentation) as proto-epic in its technique. Thus pantomime as well as film episode may be considered as epic devices even if the end result was not intended to be epic theater.

29 Brecht's fascination with gangster films continued beyond the twenties. Hanns Eisler noted that in 1935, when he and Brecht were in New York, "we drove off to 42nd Street and had a look at the gangster films featuring James Cagney, *Public Enemy Number One* and so on." See John Willett, *Brecht in Context: Comparative Approaches* (London and New York: Methuen, 1984), p. 108.

30 According to Willett, these unrealized film treatments (from 1921) were *The Mystery of the Jamaican Bar*, *The Diamond Eater*, and *Three in a Tower*. See *Brecht in Context*, p. 109–10. In 1922 Brecht collaborated with the comedian Karl Valentin on a short-subject film entitled *Mysteries of a Barbershop*; it has been preserved. See *Brecht in Context*, p. 110, and John Fuegi, *Bertolt Brecht: Chaos according to Plan* (Cambridge: Cambridge University Press, 1987), p. 45. Fuegi suggests a love-hate relationship between Brecht and film. On the one hand the genre fascinated him, but on the other most of his assays in the medium were primarily for financial gain "in much the way he went into writing advertisements in the same period."

31 In "The concept of epic opera" (p. 290) Hinton suggests parenthetically that "given the extent of Chaplin's influence on Brecht, the latter's written titles may well have been inspired by silent films, irrespective of the fact that here, as for Weill, their use was largely a matter of expediency."

32 The *Mahagonny Songspiel* was part of an evening of various chamber operas: Hindemith's *Hin und Zurück*, Ernst Toch's *Die Prinzessin auf der Erbse* and Darius Milhaud's *L'Enlèvement d'Europe*. Hindemith's *Hin und Zurück* (There and back) represented a clever spoof on contemporary film. Midway through this "Sketch mit Musik" the action goes "backward," as if a projectionist decided to reverse the film. Susan Cook rightly suggests that this little quasi-cinematic satire barely suggests Hindemith's profound interest in film and film scoring. During the late twenties in Berlin he taught a course on film music techniques. See Cook, *Opera for a New Republic: The Zeitopern of Krenek, Weill, and Hindemith* (Ann Arbor: UMI Press, 1988), p. 154.

33 David Drew's preface to the Universal Edition of the *Songspiel* and his subsequent remarks about it in *Kurt Weill: A Handbook* (Berkeley and Los Angeles: University of California Press, 1987) indicate the difficulty in attributing the production notes (in a copied piano-vocal score at the Weill/Lenya Archive at Yale University), which Drew first assumed were for the original Baden-Baden production.

34 "The *Regie* by the author was a brilliant achievement . . . " (Hermann Ensslin, "Deutsche Kammermusik Baden-Baden 1927: 15.–17. Juli," *Neue Musik-Zeitung* 48/22 [1927], p. 493.) "The production under Brecht's Regie was extraordinary." (K. L., "Ausklang in Baden-Baden. Musikalische Bühnenwerke," *Neue Badische Landeszeitung*, 19 July 1927).

35 Kristine Stiles has pointed out that the term "action" would be used in a different context (during the 1960s and '70s) by German visual artists who pioneered what later became defined generically as "performance art." The production concept for the *Mahagonny-Songspiel* (i.e., actions, projections, titles) might be seen as an important antecedent for these later German artists' work, which focussed on the problems of action as body, title as language, and projection as image – the three unified elements of performance art.

36 It should be added that the later, full-length *Aufstieg und Fall der Stadt Mahagonny* (1930) expands some of the cinematic techniques foreshadowed in the *Songspiel*. There are, indeed, projected titles between all scenes of the opera. Moreover, the filmic aspects of *Aufstieg und Fall* were not lost on Jonathan Miller, whose 1989 production of the opera (Los Angeles Music Center Opera) placed it not in its original Florida Gold Coast setting but rather in a Hollywood studio of the silent-film era. According to Miller: "I was thinking about how [Weill] and Brecht and others saw America. Obviously, they got their ideas from the movies, the Keystone Cops, Chaplin. You

think of these guys sitting in poky little movie houses in Central Europe in the 1920s watching these flickering images." Otto Friedrich, "Ferocious parable: a Weill opera goes Hollywood," *Time* (25 September 1989), p. 76.

37 "Verschiebungen in der musikalischen Produktion [1927]," in *Weill Gesammelte Schriften*, p. 47. Kowalke translates this essay in *Kurt Weill in Europe*, pp. 478–81: "Ich bin auch überzeugt, daß auf Grund der neu erlangten inneren und äusseren Unkompliziertheit im Stoff und in den Ausdrucksmitteln ein Zweig der Oper sich zu einer neuen epischen Form entwickelt, wie ich sie gemeinsam mit Brecht in dem Songspiel *Mahagonny* anwende. Diese Form des musikalischen Bühnenwerkes setzt zwar eine von Hause aus theatralische Musik voraus, sie ermöglicht es aber vollends, der Oper eine absolut musikalische, sogar konzertante Gestaltung zu geben. Auf diesen und auf anderen Gebieten der neuen Oper zeigt sich deutlich, daß die musikalische Entwicklung vom Theaterfilm eine neue Befruchtung erlangt."

38 Roland Barthes, "Diderot, Brecht, and Eisenstein [1974]," in *The Responsibility of Forms* (Berkeley: University of California Press, 1991), p. 92.

39 Ibid, p. 93.

40 V[sevolod] I. Pudovkin, *Film Technique* [1928], trans. Ivor Montagu (London: George Newnes, 1935), p. xiv.

41 In a recent study of Brecht's work with the sound film *Kuhle Wampe* (1932), Roswitha Mueller finds a compelling similarity between Brecht's theatrical techniques and Eisenstein's theory of montage. Eisenstein's fundamental source is Marx's definition of investigation: "True investigation is unfolded truth, the disjuncted members of which unite in the result." Thus, Eisenstein recognizes an organic relationship between the shot and the larger political truth being told in the film. For Brecht the organic relationship is between the *Gestus* and the "total event of the play," or the fable. See Mueller's "Montage in Brecht," *Theatre Journal* 39 (1987), p. 474.

2 RETHINKING SOUND: MUSIC AND RADIO IN WEIMAR GERMANY

1 "Antwort auf eine Rundfrage," translated as "The radio: reply to a questionnaire," (1930) in *Style and Idea*, ed. Leonard Stein (Berkeley and Los Angeles: University of California Press, 1972), pp. 147–48.

2 The contemporary literature on music and the radio mainly deals with three areas of interest: technical developments of the medium, aesthetic correlates for performance and composition, and sociological implications for programming and the audience. The principal focus of this essay is upon the first two areas, though an attempt has been made to indicate the scope and importance of the third.

3 The link between German radio and the state was firmly established during the last two years of the First World War, when Germans had made military use of radio technology on the Western front. After the war the radio evolved into a state-run enterprise under the pioneering direction of Hans Bredow (1879–1959), "father of the German radio," whose writings on the medium, including his autobiographical book *Aus meinem Archiv* (Heidelberg: Vowinkel, 1950) are important sources for radio history in Germany. The following discussion also draws upon Kurt von Boeckmann, "Organisation des deutschen Rundfunks," in *Kunst und Technik*, ed. Leo Kestenberg (Berlin: Volksverband der Bücherfreunde Wegweiser-Verlag, 1930), pp. 219–42.

4 Germany's nine stations administered among them twenty-one regional transmitters, each with its own capacity for producing programs locally.

5 It should be noted that the Bayerischer Rundfunk in Munich enjoyed a greater degree of autonomy in questions of administration, since it was not a stock company but a private limited liability company directly answerable not to the Reichs-Rundfunk-Gesellschaft but to the Bavarian postal ministry. Dealings between the Reichs-Rundfunk-Gesellschaft and radio stations abroad were coordinated through the Union Internationale de Radiophonie (Weltrundfunkverein), founded in April 1925 in Geneva to regulate the allotment of frequencies, as well as a range of legal, artistic, and technical matters.

6 By 1932 Berlin alone had eight weekly private radio journals: the *Arbeiterfunk, Arbeiter-Sender, Der deutsche Rundfunk* (for which Kurt Weill wrote essays and broadcast reviews), *Der deutsche Sender, Europa-Stunde, Funkwoche, Die Sendung,* and *Sieben Tage*; a ninth Berlin journal, *Rufer und Hörer,* appeared monthly.

7 The radio guides of the German stations were *Bayerische Radiozeitung und Bayernfunk* (Munich), *Deutsche Welle* and *Funk-Stunde* (Berlin), *Königsberger Rundfunk und Ostdeutsche Illustrierte* (Königsberg), *Die Mirag* (Leipzig), *Die Norag* (Hamburg), *Schlesische Funkstunde* (Breslau), *Südwestdeutsche Rundfunkzeitung* (Frankfurt), *Südfunk* (Stuttgart), and *Werag* (Cologne).

8 *Dokumente zur Geschichte des deutschen Rundfunks und Fernsehens,* ed. E. Kurt Fischer (Göttingen: Musterschmidt, 1957), pp. 201–02; translated in Wolf von Eckardt and Sander L. Gilman, *Bertolt Brecht's Berlin* (Garden City, New York: Anchor Press/ Doubleday, 1975), p. 57.

9 Ibid.

10 "The radio: reply to a questionnaire," p. 147.

11 Adolf Weissmann, *Die Entgötterung der Musik* (Stuttgart, Berlin, and Leipzig: Deutsche Verlags-Anstalt, 1928), pp. 16ff.

12 It is revealing that after a tour of the Ruhrgebiet in 1921 Franz Schreker entertained the plan to write an opera on the subject of modern technology.

13 See in particular Bekker's "Musikalische Neuzeit," first published in the *Frankfurter Zeitung* on 29 July 1917 and reprinted in Bekker's essay collection *Kritische Zeitbilder* (Berlin: Schuster & Loeffler, 1921), pp. 292–99. The following remarks summarize some of the conclusions of the author's "Musical Expressionism: the search for autonomy," a paper delivered at the Manchester International Festival of Expressionism in March 1992.

14 Jost Hermand, citing in particular the writings of the composer Heinz Tiessen (1887–1971), arrives at a similar conclusion in his article "Musikalischer Expressionismus," in *Beredte Töne* (Frankfurt am Main: Verlag Peter Land, 1991), pp. 97–117.

15 "Form ist Gestaltwerden der Materie gemäß den ihr selbsteigenen Gesetzen und zu keinem anderen Zweck, als zur Darstellung eben dieser Materie." See "Was ist 'neue' Musik," in *Organische und Mechanische Musik* (Stuttgart, Berlin, and Leipzig: Deutsche Verlags-Anstalt, 1927), p. 12.

16 In this regard Weill's theories on the gestic qualities of rhythm, Toch's work with mechanical instruments, and Hindemith's evolving ideas about "music for use" were all inspired not by music's emotional or psychological characteristics but by its physical properties and their application as cognitive affect, structural articulation, and social function.

17 In his article "Musik im Rundfunk," *Anbruch* (Sonderheft *Musik und Maschine*) (October–November, 1926), pp. 374–79, esp. 378, Frank Warschauer pointed out that the microphone had had the effect of thrusting the music of the past and the present onto the same plane.

18 These contributions included constructing the first electromagnetic telegraph in 1831, the first telephone in 1860, the first gramophone in 1887, the first cathode tubes in 1906, attempting the first telegraphic transmission of pictures in 1907, undertaking the first experiments with wireless telephones in 1906, constructing the first transmitter tube in 1914, engaging in early experiments in broadcasting music and language in 1919, being among the first to develop electrical recording, and creating the first sound film in 1922. Even television was already a practical reality in Germany by 1923.

19 Walter Benjamin, whose influential article "The work of art in the age of mechanical reproduction" first appeared in 1936 (in *Zeitschrift für Sozialforschung* 5/1, pp. 40–46), was but one of many philosophers and aestheticians, including Eberhard Zschimmer, Max Eyth, and Ernst Cassirer, who devoted their attentions to the implications of technology. For an enlightening review of Theodor W. Adorno's reception of recording technology in the twenties and thirties see Thomas Y. Levin, "For the record: Adorno on music in the age of its technological reproducibility," *October* 55 (Winter 1990), pp. 23–47; in the same issue of *October* Levin translates three Adorno articles, "The curves of the needle" (1928), "The form of the phonograph record" (1934), and "Opera and the long-playing record" (1969), pp. 49–66. Of general interest for the effect of recording and radio technology upon the perception and manipulation of sound is the stimulating collection of essays and documents in *Wireless Imagination; Sound, Radio, and the Avant-garde*, ed. Douglas Kahn and Gregory Whitehead (Cambridge, Mass.: The MIT Press, 1992).

20 This is, of course, essentially the technology of the telephone, whose signals are sent by wire. Through the twenties, however, the telephone laid only modest claims to sonic fidelity; its poor transmission of upper partials, so important for consonants like "s" and "f", made even speech intelligibility at times problematic.

21 "Ich muss Dir gleich schreiben, wie begeistert ich von der Oper bin. Leider waren wir beim Einstellen etwas nervös und haben vieles schlecht gehört. Aber was wir gehört haben war herrlich! . . . Trotz der schlechten Übertragung hatte man den Eindruck einer wundervollen Aufführung, besonders gegen Schluß. Das Duett war leider fast unhörbar, es scheint wegen der andern deutschen Stationen auf einer andren Welle gestellt worden zu sein, und obwohl wir den ganzen Nachmittag aus lauter Angst, es könnte im letzten Moment nicht gehn, bei dröhnenden Männerchören und Blas-orchestern, Wacht am Rhein, etc. verbracht haben, wars vom Augenblick an, wo die Oper war, leise und fortwährend wechselnd. . . . Wir haben den ganzen Tag, wie schon lange nicht, an Dich gedacht: jetzt zieht er sich an, jetzt freut er sich, dass er keinen Frack braucht, oder soll er nicht doch einen Frack anziehen? und haben gezittert, als ob es nebenan wäre. Das macht das Radio, das ist für mich ein grosser Zauberkasten." Letter of 28 February 1930, Library of Congress; translated by the author.

22 Letter of 1 March 1930; translated in *The Berg-Schoenberg Correspondence*, ed. Juliane Brand, Christopher Hailey and Donald Harris (New York: Norton, 1987), pp. 394–95.

23 The headset continued to offer the best reception, since most of the distortion in reception came from the speaker amplification of the radio receiver.

24 "Meine Erfahrungen vor Trichter und Mikrophon," *Ton- und Schallplatter-Magazin*, (May 1931), pp. 11–14. It was in fact during the 1920s that the flute began to assume the prominent position it has since occupied in the literature of twentieth-century music.

25 "Prüfen wir nun daraufhin die fast beispiellos schnelle Verbreitung des Saxophons, das jahrzehntelang unbeachtet blieb und nun plötzlich als 'Mann seiner Zeit', dank einer undefinierbaren, aber dennoch zweifellosen Klangfarbenaktualität zum volkstümlichsten Blasinstrument unserer Tage geworden ist . . ." See "Antiphonie," *Anbruch* (Sonderheft *Musik und Maschine*) (October–November, 1926), pp. 350–53, esp. 352.

26 Karl Gerstberger, in his article "Technik und Recht im Bereiche der Musik," *Kunst und Technik*, pp. 157–74, went so far as to claim (p. 167) that the radio so distorted music that no broadcast of any works by a living composer should take place without explicit permission. Others such as Max Butting argued that repertory less suited to the radio should not be performed without substantial rearrangement to permit its musical content to emerge with clarity.

27 In his article "Moderne Musik im Rundfunk" (1933), translated as "Modern music on the radio," in *Style and Idea*, pp. 151–52, Schoenberg pointed out that radio was also better able to accommodate performances of single, shorter works.

28 "Manche Partitur unserer jüngeren Autoren sieht aus, als ob sie eigens für den Rundfunk geschrieben wäre." See "Das Verhältnis des schaffenden Musikers zum Rundfunk," *Kunst und Technik*, pp. 279–98, esp. 291.

29 See also Hermann W. von Waltershausen, "Allgemeine musikalische Probleme des Rundfunks," in *Kunst und Technik*, pp. 299–322, esp. 309.

30 "Modern music on the radio," p. 152.

31 During his tenure as General Music Director in Königsberg (1928–31) Hermann Scherchen was particularly active in cultivating new music in that city, and in Frankfurt and Berlin Hans Flesch, intendant first of the Südwestfunk and then of the Funk-Stunde, was an avid proponent of new music.

32 A second version of the work for which Weill recomposed the sections set by Hindemith was given a Berlin concert premiere in November 1929 by Karl Rankl.

33 ". . . ein Grad der Exaktheit, der durch menschliches Spiel niemals erreicht werden kann; die vollkommene Versachlichung, die vollkommene Entpersönlichung des Spieles. Nichts unterläuft, was nicht durch Tonhöhe, Metrum, Rhythmus, Tempo, Dynamik in den *Noten* fixiert ist: jede Spur einer Spontaneität, eines Sentiments, eines Impulses ist hinausgedrängt." See "Musik für mechanische Instrumente," *Anbruch* (Sonderheft *Musik und Maschine*) (October–November 1926), pp. 346–49, esp. 348.

34 Published in *Anbruch* (January 1929), pp. 36f.

35 "Franz Schreker und Professor Gatz," *Der deutsche Rundfunk* (13 March 1927), reprinted in *Kurt Weill: Ausgewählte Schriften*, ed. David Drew (Frankfurt am Main: Suhrkamp, 1975), p. 117.

36 "Damit ist ein neues Material konstituiert, das bestimmte Eigentümlichkeiten aufweist, die bei keinem andern zu finden sind." See "Der schaffende Musiker und die Technik der Gegenwart," *Kunst und Technik*, pp. 141–55, esp. 144. However, regarding "funk-gerechte Musik," Krenek states later in the article (p. 146) that "here, too, the stimulation is actually more negative in that the microphone, like all musical machines, has the tendency to neutralize timbre and transform it into that characteristically muffled, somewhat nasal, monotone, and muddled sound characteristic of all these

contrivances. To write something specifically for this paltry sound spectrum will probably not offer even an occasional incentive to creation." (Aber auch hier sind die Reize eigentlich mehr negativ, indem das Mikrophon, wie alle Musikapparate, die Eigenschaft hat, Klangfarben zu neutralisieren und in jenen charakteristischen gedämpften, etwas nasalen, monotonen und wirren Tonfall zu verwandeln, den all diese Vorrichtungen an sich haben. Für diese dürftige Klangskala eigens etwas zu schreiben, wird wohl nicht einmal gelegentlich einen Anreiz zum Schaffen ausüben.)

37 ". . . und wenn es nur soweit wäre, als die Ablehnung oder Aufnahme gewisser Einzelheiten . . ." See "Das Verhältnis des schaffenden Musikers zum Rundfunk," p. 291.

38 Ibid, p. 281.

39 Ibid, p. 290.

40 "Allgemeine musikalische Probleme des Rundfunks," p. 318.

41 "Jede Kunst hat gewissermaßen ihr Schwarzweiß; dies ist immer Herbheit, Ehrlichkeit, Geradheit, Sachlichkeit im guten und wahren Sinn, das heißt Sachlichkeit dem stilistischen Problem gegenüber. . . . Die Besinnung auf das musikalische Schwarzweiß wird als reinigendes Bad wirken." See "Das Verhältnis des schaffenden Musikers zum Rundfunk," p. 319.

42 "Das Verhältnis des schaffenden Musikers zum Rundfunk," p. 289. Naturally there were discussions about the feasibility of opera on the radio. In his article "Musik im Rundfunk," Frank Warschauer predicted (p. 378) that radio might influence opera in the direction of oratorio. In this sense both the epic theater of Brecht and his musical collaborators and aspects of works such as Schoenberg's *Moses und Aron* may reflect an increased focus upon purely aural, narrative effects.

43 Ibid, p. 208.

44 *Buildings for Music. The Architect, the Musician, and the Listener from the Seventeenth Century to the Present Day* (Cambridge, Mass.: The MIT Press, 1985), p. 271.

45 "Das Ich und das All stehen sich unvermittelt gegenüber. Es läßt sich nicht leugnen, daß darin eine neue Erhabenheit ruht. Eine Erhabenheit, die vollkommen jener Erhabenheit entspricht, die sich auch in den Werken der Technik überall findet: im Luftschiff, im Riesendampfer, im Wolkenkratzer, kurz überall. Es ist die Erhabenheit der exakten Präzision." See "Radio und Musik," in *Deutsche Musikpflege*, ed. Josef Ludwig Fischer (Frankfurt: Verlag des Bühnenvolksbundes, 1925), pp. 95–97, esp. 97.

46 "[. . .] die nicht aus dem Material 'Sprache' herausarbeiten, wie Bildhauer aus dem Stein, sondern ihre Wirkungen aus andern Bezirken holen." See "Sprache und Technik," in *Kunst und Technik*, pp. 183–96, esp. 190f.

47 "Musikpädagogik im Rundfunk," in *Kunst und Technik*, pp. 243–78, esp. 248.

48 See Waltershausen, "Allgemeine musikalische Probleme des Rundfunks," p. 308. Waltershausen goes on to add that "proper singing depends on producing the purest tone with the least ambient noise." (Richtiges Singen beruht eben auf der Produktion möglichst reiner und von Nebengeräuschen freier Töne.)

49 "Die Substanz jeder musikalischen Leistung ist allein dasjenige, was sich im reinen Klanglichen objektiviert." See "Musik im Rundfunk," pp. 377f.

50 "Meine Erfahrungen vor Trichter und Mikrophon," p. 14.

51 "Radio und Musik," p. 96.

52 One might argue that structural hearing is a function of this experience, just as dramatic improvements in sound fidelity helped inspire the current preoccupation

with authentic performance practice with its heightened sensitivity to the quality of timbre as an integral part of compositional conception.

53 "Die erste Stufe dieses Prozesses der Einbeziehung der Kunst ist durch die naive ästhetische Freude an der Maschine, an sich bewegenden Material gekennzeichnet. Die höchste Stufe ist erreicht, wenn die technischen Mittel in der künstlerischen Form aufgehen, in ihr geradezu verschwinden." See "Vorwort," in *Kunst und Technik*, pp. 5–12, esp. 7.

3 "OVERCOMING ROMANTICISM": ON THE MODERNIZATION OF TWENTIETH-CENTURY PERFORMANCE PRACTICE

1 Artur Schnabel, *My Life and Music* (New York: Dover, 1988), p. 157.

2 Jacques Handschin, "Die alte Musik als Gegenwartsproblem" (1927), in *Gedenkschrift Jacques Handschin: Aufsätze und Bibliographie*, ed. Hans Oesch (Bern: Haupt, 1957), pp. 338–341: "Drei Strömungen sind es, die unser Musikleben beherrschen . . . der klassisch-romantischen . . . der radikal-modernen und der retrospektiv-historischen . . . wie die radikal-moderne Strömung, so will auch die retrospektiv-historische in ihrer Art aus dem Gewohnten hinaus in neue Welten führen. . . . Es scheint jedenfalls, daß wir nunmehr den Höhepunkt der mit der Romantik eingeleiteten Doppelbewegung erreichen. Nicht umsonst klingt uns das Wort von der 'Überwindung der Romantik' in den Ohren; anderseits wird es nicht bloßer Zufall sein, daß gerade der mittelalterlichen Musik 'Sachlichkeit' im höchsten Maße eigen ist. Gewiß liegt in diesen Schlagworten unserer Zeit ein Teil Übertreibung, aber sie spiegeln doch reale Entwicklungstendenzen wider."

3 See Richard Taruskin, "On letting the music speak for itself: some reflections on musicology and performance", *Journal of Musicology* 1 (1982), pp. 338–49, and "The pastness of the present and the presence of the past", in *Authenticity and Early Music: A Symposium*, ed. Nicholas Kenyon (Oxford: Oxford University Press, 1988), pp. 137–210; and Rose Rosengard Subotnik, *Developing Variations: Style and Ideology in Western Music* (Minneapolis: University of Minnesota Press, 1991), especially the first and fifth essays.

4 Cf. Susan McClary, "The blasphemy of talking politics during Bach Year," in *Music and Culture*, ed. Susan McClary and Richard Leppert (Cambridge: Cambridge University Press, 1987), pp. 13–62, esp. 18.: "We find ourselves today embedded in a society that is very anxious to secure for itself order in the face of potential or actual violence, in the face of pluralistic claims of the right to cultural production. Our theories of music (the means by which institutions train musicians) try to account for all events in a piece of music as manifestations of self-contained order, rather than as a more complex dialectical relationship between conventional norms and codes on the one hand and significant particularities and strategies on the other. And, consciously or not, our performance practices for the most part are designed to produce literal, note-perfect, reassuring but inert renditions of virtually all musics, whether originally affirmative or oppositional." Compare with Donald Francis Tovey, *A Musician Talks: 1. The Integrity of Music* (London: Oxford University Press, 1941), pp. 132–33: "Mozart is now in fashion, largely because romanticism is out of fashion. Romanticism is out of fashion because at present we are tired of the unexpected and the catastrophic, and we delight in things that are punctual, predestined, and exact."

5 The piano pedagogue J. Alfred Johnstone (*Essentials in Piano-Playing and Other Musical Studies* [London: W. Reeves, n.d.], pp. 51–53), gives us a view of the effect of "tasteless" playing on a contemporary witness, one with an essentially late-romantic outlook: "There is one special feature of modern piano-playing which illustrates strikingly this obtuseness of sensibility for mood and style in music. It is a feature particularly pronounced in the attempts to render the romantic music of such a composer as Chopin. *Tempo rubato*, instead of being the spontaneously recognised, the instinctively felt, delicate variations arising naturally from the changing moods of the music, is made an altogether stiff, arbitrary and palpably artificial interference with the time of the composition at certain selected parts of its progress. It is a stereotyped process which the observant hearer soon learns to predict with accuracy; it comes, as it were, with the automatic regularity of work done by machinery. This curiously artificial device may be described thus: the first few notes of the passage selected for the operation are taken slowly, and then, during the remainder of the passage, the pace is gradually increased until the regulation speed is attained. In this account there is, unhappily, no exaggeration. . . . This senseless and artificial device, for all the world reminds me of the regularly donned artificial accommodation of the facial features adopted for the purposes of conventional social amenities by many hollow-hearted people, to represent what, with sincere people, is a pleasant smile. No artifice or conceit which is adopted to simulate reality can be of any value in expressing the sincere and strong emotions of our great-hearted composers." Johnstone is criticizing here a deficiency similar to that known in rhetoric as "isotony": the too-regular rising and falling of the tone of voice. See Nikolaus Schleiniger, *Grundzüge der Beredsamkeit*, 5th edn (Freiburg: Herder, 1896), p. 266.

6 Alessandro Moreschi (1858–1922), Bach-Gounod "Ave Maria", recorded in Rome, April 1904, reissued in *A Record of Singers*, Part 1, Record 1, Side 1, Band 1 (EMI RLS 7705, published 1982), and in the Opal CD 9823, *Moreschi: The Last Castrato*.

7 See for example Artur Rubinstein's recording (1930) of Mozart's A Major Piano Concerto KV 488 with the London Symphony Orchestra under John Barbirolli, reviewed in *Music and Letters* 13 (1932), p. 115, by Scott Goddard, a reviewer often critical of interpretive liberties: "A sensitive solo performance and an alert, discreet accompaniment make this a conspicuously good record, worth using carefully." In the first movement, extreme tempo changes contribute to a sense of dialogue between soloist and orchestra, but they are unsettling to modern listeners. Rubinstein's pre-World War II playing is controversial today. Though widely regarded as immature, his playing during this period is held by some to be his best. For an anthology of Rubinstein's solo playing from the late 1920s and early 1930s, see the Pearl CD 9464, published by Pavilion Records. The Rubinstein/Barbirolli performance of KV 488 was released as an LP by EMI Italiana (1986) as no. 5 of a series entitled "Mozart & Mozart," contrasting this performance with one by Arturo Benedetti-Michelangeli.

8 My personal working definition goes further, calling "early" any repertoire in which a cleft can be sensed between the performance values operative at the time of its inception and those of the present; this window of actuality for a repertory and its performance practice seems to be a span of about thirty years. In the 1990s, the compositions and performance practice of the 1960s are gradually coming to be seen as "historical", thus entering the category of "Early Music".

9 Hans Haaß, "Über das Wesen mechanischer Klaviermusik," *Musikblätter der Anbruch* 9 (1927), vol. 8/9, p. 351: "Man ist vielfach der Meinung, daß mechanische Musik in engste Verbindung mit den Begriffen Objektivität und Sachlichkeit zu bringen sei. Ich möchte hier noch einmal kurz die Frage aufwerfen: Was ist objektive Musik? Jedenfalls ist das Hauptmerkmal dieser Musik die vollständige Befreiung von jeder Individualität, d.h. die Ausschaltung willkürlicher und unwillkürlicher Auffassung sowohl des Interpreten, als auch . . . des Komponisten selbst. Demnach wäre das Problem der rein sachlichen Musik gelöst, wenn uns Kompositionen zur Verfügung ständen, bei denen man von Anfang bis zu Ende auf jede schattierende Dynamik und jeden Tempowechsel innerhalb des Stückes und der einzelnen Phrasen verzichten könnte."

10 Herbert Lichtenthal, "Musical Interpretation," *Music Review* 4 (1943), pp. 163–170, esp. 170.

11 Marcel Dupré, *Philosophie de la Musique* (Tournai, Belgium: Collegium Musieum, n.d. p. 43: "L'interprète ne doit jamais laisser paraître sa propre personalité. Aussitôt qu'elle transperce, l'œuvre est trahie. En s'effaçant sincèrement devant la caractère de l'œuvre à mettre en lumière, plus encore que devant la personalité de l'auteur, il sert ce dernier et impose l'œuvre. Il est tenu: 1) à la fidélité du texte; 2) au respect des nuances demandées par l'auteur; 3) à une parfaite clarité, jamais sacrificiée par la rapidité du mouvement." Dupré's organ-roll performances from 1922/1923 for the Welte-Philharmonie organ of works by J. S. Bach (Intercord CD 860.858) are stylistically modernist, scarcely distinguishable, but for the instrument used, from legato-school organ performances common since the Second World War.

12 Virgil Thomson, *A Virgil Thomson Reader* (Boston: Houghton Mifflin, 1981), p. 197. For performances by Lhévinne on the Ampico B reproducing piano system, see the Newport Classics CD NC 60020 *The Performing Piano* (1986). Lhévinne's playing on acoustic records can be heard on the Novello Records CD NVLCD 902 *Josef Lhévinne: The Complete Recordings*. The liner notes by Cyril Ehrlich intone a veritable list of both anti-romantic and modernist clichés: "There is none of the excessive rubato, sentimentality, empty rhetoric, and self-indulgent posturing which are often associated with late romantic pianists. Instead there is discipline, line and texture. It is modern, indeed timeless art. . . ."

13 "Sentimentality in the performance of absolute music: Pablo Casals's performance of the Saraband from Johann Sebastian Bach's Suite No. 2 in D Minor for unaccompanied cello, S. 1008," *The Musical Quarterly* 73 (1989), pp. 212–48.

14 Karl Leimer, *Modernes Klavierspiel nach Leimer-Gieseking* (Mainz: Schott, 1931), author's preface to 3rd edn, p. 9: "die Natürlichkeit des Vortrags . . . ist es, die das Spiel Giesekings besonders kennzeichnet. . . . Mittlerweile hat sein Spiel Schule gemacht, der manierierte, überromantische Vortrag ist immer mehr in Mißkredit geraten und eine wohltuende Rückkehr zur Natürlichkeit des Musizierens scheint sich anzubahnen. . . . Ich hoffe, daß meine Aufzeichnungen auch mithelfen werden, den manierierten Vortrag zu bekämpfen und für sinn- und notengetreues einfach schönes Spiel zu werben."

15 Eric Blom, *A Musical Postbag* (London: G. M. Dent, 1941), p. 239.

16 While a clear case can be made for degeneration of taste in other respects, musical and otherwise, in the course of the nineteenth century, the issue here is whether we are free to apply this notion of degeneration to performance practice, given that we have

no recordings from before about 1890 by which we might judge for ourselves. It is common for witnesses in one era to reject the performance practice of the preceding one as "tasteless". We do not identify with the sentiments behind such epithets as they were voiced, for example, by nineteenth-century writers with respect to the playing style of Mozart, or by early eighteenth-century writers to the playing style of the seventeenth century, yet we allow ourselves to remain influenced by the attitude of early twentieth-century modernists towards standards of taste in nineteenth-century playing. That we are in a position to have an opinion ourselves about late-romantic performance practice at all is only possible because recording technology happened to be introduced as romantic practices were dying out. Contemporary advocates of the late-romantic ethic understood degeneration of taste in performance practice in connection with the advancement of academicism as an aesthetic virtue. This process has been completed in our century, as academically correct musicianship has become the dominant paradigm in the form of historicist performance practice. See the remarks by Paul Bekker in the appendix to this chapter.

17 Hans Sittner, *Österreichische Musikzeitschrift* 20 (1965), vol. 4, p. 189: "Der neue Name schien uns . . . weniger autoritär und doktrinär zu sein und mehr das gemeinsame Erarbeiten von Interpretationsrichtlinien zu betonen, zu denen wir uns nicht 'auf Anordnung', sondern aus wissenschaftlich fundierter Ueberzeugung bekennen. . . . Die virtuose Paraphrase und agogische Freiheit der Lisztschule sind dem Original und der metrischen Strenge gewichen, die Busoni-Artikulation bei Bach, die sich verheerend auf die einst von keinem Geringeren als Beethoven in Wien vorgeführte Legato-Kultur ausgewirkt hat, ist wieder in die ihr zukommenden Grenzen verwiesen; Chopin, der von hemmungslosen 'Ausdrucksmusikern' bis hart an die Salonmusik herunterinterpretiert wurde, konnte als ein an Mozart orientierter Musiker klassischen Formats erkannt werden."

18 Eugen Schmitz, *Musikästhetik* (Leipzig: Breitkopf & Härtel, 1915), chapter 10: ("Stilcharakter und Vortrag", pp. 206–10), 207: "Der Vortrag erstreckt sich besonders auf die Wahl des Tempos und seiner Modifikationen, auf die Dynamik, auf die Phrasierung, auf die klangliche Schattierung . . ., sodann aber überhaupt auf alle Seiten äußeren wie inneren Ausdrucks. Seine Richtungslinien aber gewinnt dieser Vortrag aus dem Stilcharakter des Kunstwerkes. . . . mit der Erfüllung des Technischen [ist] erst die primitive Grundlage der tieferen geistigen Auffassung des Kunstwerkes seitens des Vortragenden erfüllt. Auch hierfür sind zunächst die historischen Gesichtspunkte maßgebend: das Kunstwerk muß im 'Geiste seiner Zeit' verlebendigt werden. . . . Aber auch die Individualität des Schöpfers, soweit sie sich im Stilcharakter ausprägt, muß im Vortrag zur Geltung kommen. Je subjektivistischer beispielsweise die Komposition ist, desto mehr soll der Vortrag einer freien Improvisation ähneln . . . [p. 210:] sind somit die objektiven Voraussetzungen stilgemäßen Vortrages durch den Stilcharakter des Kunstwerkes teils direkt, teils indirekt gegeben, so kann bei ihrer tatsächlichen Verwirklichung doch auch die Phantasie des ausübenden Künstlers noch in weitgehendem Maße sich frei betätigen. 'In Bezug auf Auffassung,' sagt X. Scharwenka mit Recht, 'ist die Musik die toleranteste von allen Künsten, und wenn auch gewisse Grenzen gezogen werden müssen, so bleibt doch ein ganz gewaltiger Spielraum für die verschiedensten Individualitäten übrig. Daher kommt es, daß das Publikum im Konzertsaal nicht müde wird, dieselben Kompositionen immer wieder von anderen Virtuosen

zu hören, denn alle diese verschiedenen Auffassungen sind gewissermaßen so viele verschiedene Spiegel, die das Phantasiegebilde des Komponisten zurückwerfen und immer
wieder neu erscheinen lassen.' In der Tat läßt z.B. schon die Phrasierung manchmal
die Wahl zwischen mehreren gleichberechtigten Lesarten offen; desgleichen sind in der
Dynamik auch bei unverrückbar festgelegten Grundlinien unendlich viele feine und
feinste Abstufungen möglich, ebenso wie das Tempo, ohne seinen Grundcharakter zu
verlieren, Verschärfungen nach Seite des Langsamen und Schnellen zuläßt, ganz
ungerechnet der zahllosen Möglichkeiten agogischer Schattierung. Auf solche Weise
kann also wirklich ein und dasselbe Tonstück unter der Hand verschiedener Interpreten
ein verschiedenes Gesicht gewinnen. Wo hierbei die Grenze der Willkür ist, läßt sich
nur von Fall zu Fall entscheiden; im allgemeinen ist lediglich negativ zu sagen, daß der
Stilcharakter in keinem Falle verwischt werden darf. An seiner richtunggebenden
Bedeutung ändern also auch die subjektiven Möglichkeiten des Vortrags nichts."

19 Ignace Paderewski, "Rhythm is life," in *They Talk about Music*, ed. Robert Cumming,
(Rockville, New York: Bellville/Mills, 1971), vol. 1, pp. 107–12, esp. 110f. Paderewski's
views about the "loss" of time in tempo rubato are shared by many of his contemporaries, who legitimized their use of tempo rubato by citing its use in the eighteenth
century, yet at the same time questioned the feasibility of a rubato practice where "the
left hand keeps strict time and the right hand plays freely." Mathis Lussy's "excellent
book on musical expression" is the *Traité de l'expression musicale* (Paris: Heugel, 1874).

20 Adrian C. Boult, obituary for Arthur Nikisch in *Music and Letters* 3 (1922), pp. 117–21.
Wilhelm Furtwängler, in (*Vermächtnis: Nachgelassene Schriften* (Wiesbaden: F. A. Brockhaus,
1956, p. 106), cites the opinion of Richard Strauss on Nikisch's musical art: "Nikisch
has the ability to draw a sound out of the orchestra that the rest of us do not have. I
don't know how he does it, but it is an undeniable fact." ("Nikisch hat die Fähigkeit,
aus dem Orchester einen Klang herauszuholen, die wir andren nicht besitzen. Ich
weiß nicht, worauf es beruht, aber es ist unbezweifelbar Tatsache.") Furtwängler
elsewhere (p. 104) defended Nikisch: "It used to be said that a conductor like Arthur
Nikisch was putting on airs. Now, I can testify out of my personal acquaintance with
this conductor – and it was a very close acquaintance – that for Nikisch, striking an
attitude was foreign to his character, whereas other conductors, who unlike Nikisch
conducted in a pedantic manner, were not free from posing, since they, with their
relatively primitive technical orientation, had time to think about the public,
something that a conductor like Nikisch could never have in mind. Finally, he was
attending to the sound as such, to the creation and formation of the sound."

(Man hat früher immer behauptet, ein Dirigent wie Arthur Nikisch wäre posiert.
Nun, ich kann aus persönlicher Kenntnis dieses Dirigenten – und diese meine Kenntnis
ist sehr genau – bezeugen, daß Nikisch jede Art von Pose fremd war, wogegen andere
Dirigenten, die im Gegensatz zu Nikisch schulmäßig dirigierten, nicht frei von Pose
waren, denn sie hatten bei relativ primitiven technischen Einstellungen Zeit dazu,
nebenbei an das Publikum zu denken, etwas, was einem Dirigenten, wie Nikisch es
war, nie in den Sinn kommen mochte. Er hatte schließlich mit dem Klang als solchem,
der Bildung und Gestaltwerdung dieses Klanges zu tun.) For a recording by Nikisch as
conductor, see his performance of Beethoven's Fifth Symphony with the Berlin
Philharmonic Orchestra (1913), reissued on *Berliner Philharmonisches Orchester: 100
Jahre Jubileum* (Deutsche Grammophon, out of print).

21 Richard Aldrich, *The New York Times*, 6 November 1908: "A large audience, enthusiastic and appreciative, listened to him in Carnegie Hall. . . . He still commands all his old marvel of 'touch', his old magic of delicate, filmy iridescent tone, of sighing pianissimo, of purling, rippling passages, of clear articulation, to transform the piano into a celestial instrument. It is pretty, wonderfully pretty, ravishingly pretty, and it beguiles the senses of the listener in a way that hardly any other piano playing can do. . . . Mr. de Pachmann chose . . . music that submits graciously to his conceptions and methods; but [in] . . . Mendelssohn's *Rondo capriccioso* in E . . . he put a certain sticky *tempo rubato* that was probably far from Mendelssohn's idea of the rhythm and flow of his absolutely symmetrical measures, designed for absolutely symmetrical playing, although the transparent delicacy and fleetness of the music under Mr. de Pachmann's fingers were delightful. . . . His Chopin group . . . need raise no doubts or the feeling of a loss of emotional power in his interpretation. Probably nobody plays Chopin's music more nearly as Chopin himself played it, in scale of conception and quality and subtlety of tone." Richard Aldrich, *Concert Life in New York* (New York: G. P. Putman, 1941), pp. 332–34. An impression of Pachmann's pianism may be gained from the CD *Vladimir de Pachmann* Opal 9840, published by Pavilion Records. For a reissue of Mendelssohn recordings by Pachmann originally made between 1909 and 1912, including a 1909 recording of the *Rondo Capriccioso* in E Major, Opus 14, see the Pearl LP *Great Virtuosi of the Golden Age: Vladimir de Pachmann*, GEM 103.

22 Richard Aldrich, *Concert Life in New York*, p. 229–30: "Mr. Lhévinne's playing . . . is marked by a remarkably sure and accurate technique, a complete grasp of . . . technical problems . . ., and an equally remarkable command of the peculiar resources of the tone of the modern pianoforte. . . . He is a conscientious and unpretending artist; he is absolutely absorbed in the music he is playing, and there is no suggestion in his performance of personal display, of any appeal to the wonder of the unthinking. He is now, as he has been in the previous seasons he has played here, deficient in imagination, in poetical feeling. His readings give every evidence of being carefully thought out and very little of being inspired by any flight of imagination or fired by enthusiasm. They are all cautious, all most commendably planned, all well laid out in detail, but they present little that kindles the ardor of the listener. Herein was found the limitation that beset all the more important performances he gave. . . . When the matter in hand demanded little exposition of emotional content, as in the three arrangements of pieces by seventeenth and eighteenth-century composers, the well-ordered clarity of his playing gave more satisfaction."

23 For Albert Schweitzer's interesting view of the use by "academicists" of J. S. Bach's music as a Wagnerian antipode (including Schweitzer's views on the outlook of Philipp Spitta in this regard), and the consequences for the general perception of Bach's music and performance practice, see his *Aufsätze zur Musik*, ed. Stefan Hanheide (Kassel: Bärenreiter, 1988), especially pp. 123–24.

24 Hermann Kretzschmar, "Einige Bemerkungen über den Vortrag alter Musik," in *Gesammelte Aufsätze aus den Jahrbüchern der Musikbibliothek Peters* (Leipzig: Peters, 1911; repr. 1973), pp. 100–19, esp. 103: "Die Schwierigkeiten, die die alte Musik dem modernen Musiker bietet, gehen sämtlich auf den Fundamentalunterschied zurück, der zwischen der künstlerischen Stellung des heutigen und des früheren Virtuosen besteht. Heute sind Sänger, Spieler und Dirigenten in der Entfaltung ihrer Begabung

an enge Grenzen gebunden. Sie dürfen alle den vorgelegten Noten nichts zusetzen, nichts davon weglassen, nur die Behandlung der Akzente und Stärkegrade gestattet dem Temperament und der Intelligenz einen kleinen Spielraum, erlaubt, daß sich das höhere Talent vor dem geringeren auszeichne. Schon einer freieren, selbstständigeren Behandlung des Tempos werden die Schreckensworte vom 'objektiven' und 'subjektiven' Vortrag zugedonnert."

25 The problem of how a musician's playing changes as he or she ages is complex. Making music involves physical habit, suggesting that it becomes less likely that one would change these habits as one ages, unless one were to subscribe to a new outlook. None of the musicians mentioned immediately above is known for having undergone such a change of outlook in later years. I myself heard in 1991 a harpsichordist in her late seventies, educated in Geneva in the 1930s, who has lived in comparative isolation on the Lago Maggiore since the early 1950s. She played for me on the Pleyel harpsichord she purchased after World War II, in a vivid, intact "authentic" harpsichord style of the 1930s, uninfluenced by subsequent developments in thinking about harpsichord playing and interpretation, but persuasive and enjoyable on its own terms.

26 Eugen d'Albert "Klavier und Pianistentum", *Musikblätter der Anbruch* 9 (1927), vol. 8/9, pp. 371–72: "Früher legte man den größten Wert auf die Individualität und auf die seelische Vertiefung beim Spiel, heute kümmert man sich immer weniger darum. Man legt den Hauptwert auf ein fehlerloses, perlendes Spiel und auf eine saubere, glatte Technik. Man ist dem Pianolavortrag immer näher gekommen, und in dem Maße, wie alles Mechanische weiter Fortschritte macht, werden wir wohl bald nur Pianola-Konzerte haben, deren es in England und Amerika heute schon viele gibt. Man wird davon abkommen, von einem schwitzenden Kunstarbeiter sich seelisch erregen zu lassen und wird vorziehen, in ungetrübter Seelenruhe eine nichtssagende, aber tadellose Maschine anzuhören, welche einen vorübergehenden, faden Genuß erzeugt, ohne jede Aufregung. Die Zukunft wird uns gewiß überraschende Erzeugnisse auf diesem Gebiete bringen. Wir werden uns dann immer mehr von der Gehirn- und Seelenarbeit entfernen, welche bekanntlich nicht mechanisch wiederzugeben ist." From our vantage point, we could say that d'Albert's vision of the machine replacing the artist has been fulfilled by an epigonal culture of musicians who have become difficult to distinguish one from another, and who excel at reproducing in live performance the brilliant and impeccable but sterile effect of studio recordings.

27 Hans Pfitzner, *Werk und Wiedergabe*, Gesammelte Schriften, Band 3 (Augsburg: Benno Filser, 1929), pp. 225–26: "Dieses unmerkliche Auf-und-ab, diese Elastizität des Ab-und-zugebenkönnens bildet die Freiheit, die in der Musik jeder Wiedergebende haben muß, der nicht ganz darauf verzichten will, etwas von Geist und Seele, von Geschmack und Gefühl in seinen Vortrag einfließen zu lassen. Je mehr diese Möglichkeit, die wie gesagt, eine Hauptvoraussetzung eines jeden wirklichen Vortrages ist, abgeschnürt wird durch die agogische Notierungsbeschaffenheit der Komposition, die den Ausübenden zwingt zu nur technischen Leistungen, zu Eiertänzen auf unmöglichen Taktarten, – desto mehr muß das ganze Gebiet der musikalischen Wiedergabe einer bloßen Sportsleistung verfallen, einer Richtung, die unsere Zeit schon längst deutlich einschlägt, und deren erste Anfänge in dem Stil der Salome- und Elektramusik zu finden sind. Eine Musik, die solche kalte Sportlichkeit, aber auch anderweitige Seelenlosigkeit nicht verträgt, erfordert also gebieterisch diese Modifikationen, die

weiter nichts sind, als Artikulationen der musikalischen Rede, Schmeidigungen der musikalischen Linie, die einerseits zu fein, andererseits zu selbstverständlich sind, als daß man sie durch Angaben vorschreiben könnte oder durch Notierung festlegen, also etwa durch 'rit.' 'accelerando', durch eingeschobene 1/8 Takte und dergleichen. Es ist die Kunst des Vortrages – das Gebiet des ausübenden Künstlers. So gut, wie es zu Bachs Zeiten und früher überhaupt keine Vorschrift des Zeitmaßes gab, weil das Finden des richtigen dem Musiker und Musikfreund von damals aus dem Notenbild allein zugetraut wurde, so gut gab es später, giebt bis auf unsere Zeit, gewisse Vortragsselbstverständlichkeiten, wie etwa die Verlangsamung der Schlußkadenz, Vorbereitung eines neuen Themas, gewisse Halte, Rücksicht auf Wort und Gesang und unzählige mehr. All das sind wir eben dran zu verlieren."

28 Heinrich Boell, "Die Bach-Interpretation im Wandel der Anschauungen," in *Von deutscher Tonkunst: Festschrift zu Peter Raabes 70. Geburtstag*, ed. Alfred Morgenroth (Leipzig: Peters, 1942), pp. 164–70, esp. 169: "Keinesfalls aber dürfen die wieder-gewonnenen beglückenden Erkenntnisse einer dem originalen Bachschen Klang entsprechenden Wiedergabe ... dazu führen, daß dabei die Forderung nach innerlich lebendiger Interpretation vernachlässigt und durch die Forderung nach 'unromantischer' Objektivität ersetzt wird. Begründet wird diese letzte Forderung mit dem Hinweis auf die erhabene Objektivität des Bachschen Geistes, die wie überhaupt die Musik des Barock strengste Sachlichkeit verlange. Daß dies völlig abwegig ist, lehrt schon die flüchtigste historische Betrachtung. Schon Heinrich Schütz verlangt nicht Sachlichkeit, sondern stets und immer den denkbar stärksten Effekt; und die offizielle Ästhetik der Bach-Zeit verlangt von jeder Musik zunächst, daß sie rührend und 'ausdrückend' sei (ausdrucksvoll würden wir heute sagen). .." [With respect to the expressive intensity of the cantata "Herr, wie Du willst": Boell goes on "der größte Sachlichkeitsfanatiker [müßte] verstehen, was es mit der sogenannten Bachschen Objektivität auf sich hat. ... Neigung zu innerlich unbewegter, abgeklärter Sachlichkeit war sicherlich das letzte, was die Leipziger ihrem temperamentvollen, von seiner Behörde amtlich als 'inkorrigibel' bezeichneten Kantor nachsagten."

29 Paul Bekker, *Klang und Eros* (Stuttgart, 1922), essay "Improvisation und Reproduktion", pp. 291–307. P. 297f. ". . . die Gegenwart beschäftigt sich noch auf intensivste Art mit Beethoven, und doch vermissen wir an ihr . . . gleichviel ob es sich um orchestrale, kammer-musikalische oder pianistische Leistungen handelt, jene souveräne Produktivität der Wiedergabe, wie sie dem Dirigenten und Pianisten Bülow, dem Geiger und Quartettführer Joachim eigen war. . . . Wenn also ein Rückgang als allgemeine, talentmässige Verarmung nicht zugegeben werden soll, andererseits die künstlerischen Aufgaben eine äußerliche Wertverminderung nicht erfahren, die Leistungen der ausübenden musikalischen Kunst aber zweifellos nachgelassen haben, so bleibt nur eine Erklärung: daß nämlich die Art, wie die Gegenwart sich den gegebenen Kunstwerken gegen-überstellt, den ausübenden Künstler zur Betonung seiner materiell talentmäßigen Gaben auf Kosten seines Menschentumes drängt. Wir haben augenscheinlich die Fähigkeit produktiven Schauens und Erfassens eingebüßt, und der Ausübende entbehrt dadurch der auftreibenden Kraft, die seine Nachahmungsfertigkeit zur Persönlichkeits-kundgebung steigert.

Die Ursachen solcher Abstopfung befruchtender menschlicher Steigerungskräfte sind mannigfacher Art. . . . Die geschäftliche Organisierung des Musikbetriebes . . .

das Überhandnehmen mißverstandener sozialer, gewerkschaftlicher Bestrebungen . . .
Die ausübende musikalische Kunst ist ihrem Ursprung und Wesen nach eine Kunst
der Improvisation. Sie schafft aus der Eingebung des Augenblickes, mehr noch, sie ist
überhaupt unmittelbare Erfassung eines zu intensivsten Lebensgefühl gesteigerten
Augenblickes. Musik ist eigentlich nicht anders als im Augenblick des Erklingens erst
entstehend zu denken. . . . [With reference to interpretive attitudes of Baroque
musicians, p. 301:] Es ist selbstverständlich, daß für solche Auffassung der ausübenden
Kunst, bei der das Schwergewicht in der augenblicklichen Phantasietätigkeit des
Vortragenden lag, keine strengen Anforderungen bezüglich der Korrektheit der
Vorlage galten. Sie war Untergrund einer Transkription, deren Gestaltung freies
Recht des Spielers blieb. . . . Der letzte Improvisator großen Stiles . . . war Liszt, aber
auch bei späteren außergewöhnlichen Künstlern finden wir das Prinzip der freien
persönlichen Vortragsgestaltung wieder. Mahlers Instrumentationsänderungen namentlich
bei Beethoven, die nur dem Augenblick hingegebene impulsive Stabführung von
Richard Strauß, die koloristisch üppige, aus stark sinnlichem Klanggefühl sich
erregende und sättigende Interpretationsart eines Nikisch gehen immer wieder auf das
Improvisationsrecht des ausübenden Künstlers zurück. . . . Dieses Improvisationsideal
geht dem Sinn nach darauf aus, das Musikstück durch innige, schöpferische Ver-
schmelzung von Komponist und Darsteller als im Augenblick des Erklingens entstehend
erscheinen zu lassen und dadurch mit dem ursprünglichen Schaffenswillen in Einklang
zu bringen. Ihm ist in der zweiten Hälfte, eigentlich erst im letzten Drittel des 19.
Jahrhunderts ein neues Ideal entgegengestellt worden: die Reproduktion . . . die
Möglichkeit einer Reproduktion in der bildenden Kunst [ist] wenigstens denkbar. In
der Musik ist sie auch das nicht. . . . wer sich an das Klavier setzt, um ein vom
Komponisten bis auf die minutiöseste Einzelheit bezeichnetes Werk in aufmerksamster
Treue, unter strengster Enthaltung von jeglicher eigener Regung auszuführen – er wird
unweigerlich seine Individualität der des Komponisten nicht nur beimischen, er wird
sie ihr überordnen. Was er reproduziert, sind nur Noten und Zeichen, der lebendige
Odem kommt aus ihm selbst. . . . [p. 303:] Der Improvisator fordere für sich das
Recht der Willkür und Eigenmächtigkeit gegenüber dem Texte, während das Streben
des heutigen Reproduzieren dahin ziele, sich völlig in den Dienst des Schaffenden zu
stellen, nur dessen Weisungen zu folgen und so ein getreues Abbild, eben die
Reproduktion des schöpferischen Willens zu bieten. Das klingt sehr bestechend und
tugendhaft, ist aber in Wirklichkeit unerfüllbar . . . mehr als ein Fingerzeig, als eine
Andeutung, als ein ungefährer Hinweis kann auch das subtilste Vortragszeichen
niemals sein. . . . Wenn aber schon diese primitiven Elementarbezeichnungen
unzuverlässig sind, was soll man dann gegenüber solchen Angaben sagen, die bereits in
sich selbst den Begriff des Schwankenden, Unbestimmten tragen, etwa Ritardando,
Accelerando, gegenüber einer Fermate? Man muß sich die Relativität dieser, überhaupt
aller Vortragsangaben, ihre rein subjektivistische Deutbarkeit klarmachen. Dann zeigt
sich, daß zwischen der scheinbar peinlichst genauen Bezeichnung Beethovens und dem
Mangel fast aller Vortragshinweise bei Bach im Grunde genommen kein Unterschied
ist, daß der Ausübende hier wie dort lediglich sich selbst überlassen bleibt. Es zeigt sich
weiter, welch ungeheuerliche Anmaßlichkeit in dem Begriff der sachlich korrekten,
notengetreuen Reproduktion liegt. Anmaßlichkeit und – Talentlosigkeit, diese im
Sinne fehlender Persönlichkeitskraft. Tatsächlich entstammt der Begriff der sachgetreuen

'Reproduktion' einer der schlechtesten Geschmacksperioden, der Zeit, da man an den amtlichen Pflegestätten der musikalischen Kunstbildung, den Hochschulen und Akademien, in Opposition trat zu dem 'freien' Vortragstil Wagners, Liszts, Bülows, Rubinsteins, da man die eigene Nüchternheit und Phantasiearmut zur Tugend erhob und das trockene Notenbild heilig sprach, weil man sich außerstande fühlte, es innerlich zu beleben, es aus dem Rausch der Improvisation neu zu gebären. Dazu kam als Unterstützung eine zu falschen Folgerungen ausgesponnene Wissenschaftlichkeit der Kunstbetrachtung, gipfelnd in der Lehre von der unabänderlichen Stetigkeit historischer Stilgesetze, nach denen das Ideal der 'Reproduktion' schließlich zur mechanischen Kopie einstiger Ausführungsgepflogenheiten, zum Museumsobjekt wurde.

Nun soll keineswegs geleugnet werden, daß in der bewußten Betonung der Achtung vor der Originalfassung angesichts der Gefahr einer Überwucherung durch Bearbeitungen ein positiver Wert lag, namentlich im Hinblick auf die erzieherische Wirkung. Die Einschränkung subjektiver Willkür, die Unterbindung launenhafter, die Vorlage zum nebensächlichen Objekt persönlicher Eitelkeit herabwürdigender Spielereien, der Zwang zur Unterordnung unter gegebene unverrückbare Anweisungen war zunächst ein achtenswertes Moment der Besinnlichkeit, des Respekts gegenüber der Meisterforderung. Bedenklich aber wurde sie, als sie die Bedeutung ausschließlicher kanonischer Geltung beanspruchte, als sie zum höchsten Gesetz für die ausübende Kunst erhoben wurde. Diese Sachlichkeit des Scheines bedeutete in Wahrheit Nivellierung der entscheidenden Persönlichkeitswerte zugunsten eines imaginären Objektivitätsbegriffes, Mechanisierung der Methode und der Ziele ausübender Kunst, Umstürzung der Qualitätsbegriffe, Förderung der Mittelmäßigkeit, kunstmoralische Verdächtigung und Beargwohnung des Außergewöhnlichen. Der üppig wuchernde Konservatoriumsbetrieb mit seinem Ziel der Massenproduktion von Durchschnittstalenten entsprach dieser Entwicklungsrichtung, und die äußeren Umstände wirtschaftlicher und sozialer Art gaben ihr die erforderliche reale Festigung. So wirkten alle gegebenen Faktoren gegenüber der ausübenden Kunst als Hemmungen der selbstständigen Persönlichkeit. Der Künstler, durch die Art seiner Veranlagung in natürlichem Abhängigkeitsverhältnis zur Außenwelt stehend, empfing von ihr keinen Antrieb zur menschlich individuellen Entfaltung seines Talentes, sondern sah sich immer mehr zum mechanischen Funktionär herabgedrückt. Viele unserer besten Talente mit schönen Anlagen zu echter, großliniger Virtuosität sind auf diese Weise zu dem fatalen Typ des sogenannten 'guten Musikers' zurückgeschraubt worden, die schöpferische Phantasie ist unter Vormundschaft der sachlichen Wissenschaftlichkeit geraten und die keusche Langeweile wurde zur obersten Tugend ernannt. [p. 306: All that can be done against this] . . . ist die Verhütung der Irreleitung eines auf Abhängigkeit angewiesenen Naturtriebes durch falsche Kunstideologie. Solche aber liegt in dem heute geltenden Begriff der sachlichen Reproduktion. Sie ist eine philiströse Selbsttäuschung und in der Musik etwas Unmögliches. Wir können freilich nicht zurückkehren zur freien Improvisation der klassischen und früh-romantischen Zeit. . . . Das Problem der ausübenden Kunst unserer Tage liegt darin, vom pädagogischen Schulbegriff der Reproduktion aus zu einer neuen, sachlich gefestigten und doch persönlich ungebundenen Improvisation zu gelangen. Das mag theoretisch formelhaft klingen, und doch ist schon außerordentlich viel gewonnen, wenn wir es nur wagen, den Begriff der Improvisation als der eigentlich höchsten und einzig wahrhaften Art der Kunstübung anzusprechen und festzustellen. Der Weg dazu wird um so leichter zu finden sein, je intensiver die ausübenden Künstler sich mit der schaffenden Kunst der eigenen Zeit beschäftigen. Aus ihr, nicht aus der historischen Wissenschaft fließen für uns die Gesetzte des Vortragsstiles auch der älteren Kunst. Aus ihr ist der Stil der heutigen Improvisation zu finden, und nur an dem Mut, sich ihr zuzuwenden, kann auch die Kraft der Persönlichkeit wieder erstärken."

30 The identification of performer with the creative moment of the composition is regularly identified as a value in the eighteenth and nineteenth centuries. Heinrich Christoph Koch's definition of the term "Begeisterung" or "inspiration" comes close to describing the state we must recreate in "improvisatory" interpretation: "When the powers of the spirit, called genius, become so animated through the imagination of a particular object that they bring forth a whole with extreme ease and without awareness of intent or of rules, such that the whole is pleasing in form and awakens interest, then one says that the artist is in a state of inspiration." (Wenn die Kräfte des Geistes, die man Genie nennt, durch die Vorstellung eines bestimmten Gegenstandes in eine solche lebhafte Bewegung gesetzt werden, in welcher sie mit außerordentlicher Leichtigkeit, und ohne Bewußtseyn von Absicht und Regeln, ein Ganzes hervorbringen, welches durch seine Form gefällt und Interesse erregt, so sagt man, der Künstler sey in dem Zustande der Begeisterung.) *Kurzgefaßtes Handwörterbuch der Musik für praktische Tonkünstler und für Dilettanten* (Leipzig: J. F. Hartknoch, 1807, facs. repr. Hildesheim: Olms, 1981), p. 53.

31 This is not to say that certain performance styles of the past did not operate under highly regulative codes – e.g. the French Baroque – but rather it is to say that we cannot assume that the music-making of the past was governed by assumptions essentially like ours, thus yielding results essentially like ours. In my view, the difference lies in the emphasis in the past on the effect, or *Wirkung*, of the music on the listener, an aspect which today receives scant attention from classical musicians concerned with producing "absolute music". One point of reference is H. C. Koch's definition of the term "Rührend" (*Kurzgefaßtes Handwörterbuch*, p. 302). Koch cites Schnell, who cites Eberhard: "The first character trait of something stirring or moving is that when it has this effect, we are more aware of the effect of being stirred or moved than we are of the object or thing that is the cause of the effect." (Der erste Zug in dem Charakter des Rührenden . . . ist, daß wir uns, wenn es auf uns wirkt, mehr dieser Wirkung, womit es uns affiziert, als des Gegenstandes, der auf uns wirkt, bewußt sind.) This definition is one very useful index for gauging the artistic success of musical performance.

32 The practical and theoretical foundation of hierarchic metric accentuation constitutes a strong inner connection uniting the performance practice for the entire period in which tonality and affective expression defined the countenance of music. Modern-day performance practice – whether classical-romantic, radical-modernist, unfortunately even most retrospective-historicist – has become anti-hierarchical in its treatment of accent. We pay lip service to the idea that strong and weak inflection of the beat naturally alternate, but its practical expression is no longer second nature. The assumption of highly differentiated hierarchical relationships between stronger and weaker beats is the foundation of an intelligent Baroque performance practice. How the hierarchic relationships are expressed, whether through stress accent, duration of

the note on an accented beat, or more extreme forms of beat and tempo modification, is for the artist to decide; the cliché of the pure stress accent realization of the hierarchy is outdated. Walther Dürr and Walter Gerstenberg's assertion (see the article "Rhythm" in *MGG*, reprinted in *NG*, vol. 15, p. 818) that "the displacement of a single rhythmic series . . . which is characteristic of Baroque polyphony, establishes a pulse in which all the beats are equally heavy, except those on which a new harmony falls. Bach's music lacks differentiated nuances of emphasis; its rhythm moves evenly, 'objectively', without personal additive – in short, like a heartbeat. The performer allows it to express itself and take effect without actually obstructing it; he does not rebel against its authority by placing an accent contrary to it" certainly describes how Bach and Baroque music generally was played in the mid-twentieth century when the statement was written. Historically speaking, however, while this outlook as applied to music before the twentieth century is a fiction, it has regrettably become aesthetic fact in our time, and no longer just for Baroque music.

A still-living tradition of metric-hierarchic observance in late-romantic performance practice is witnessed by treatises of the time (for example Adolph Christiani, *The Principles of Expression in Pianoforte Playing* [Philadelphia: Theodor Presser, 1895]), but more importantly is found documented in expressive reproducing-piano rolls, first brought to a high technological level by the Welte firm in Freiburg. These rolls are of inestimable value for the analysis of late-romantic piano performance practice; while the reproductive fidelity of these rolls in respect of dynamic and tone color is certainly limited, assertions as to the dubious reliability of the encoded timing of note beginnings and endings must be qualified; in general the relationship of timing of notes to one another is quite reliable, if we allow for a slight margin of error in the punching of duplicate rolls and for the technical exigencies of paper rolls as a recording medium. Particularly interesting are rolls cut between 1905 and 1907, at the beginning of the full Welte production. The rolls present a wealth of material which has been shown to respond well to computer-aided analysis. Study of early rolls show consistently that pianists of the generation in maturity by the last third of the nineteenth century were expressing hierarchical relationships not so much in the sense of a stress accentuation, as in the sense that "strong" and "weak" are expressed as longer and shorter time-spans in relationships between complementary pairs in the phrase structure. For example, Camille Saint-Saëns's performance of the Chopin Nocturne in F♯ Major, Op. 15, No. 2, Welte-Mignon Roll No. 807, recorded in November 1905, reveals intricate balancing of complementary units at the half-bar, whole-bar, two-bar and four-bar phrase levels. Noteworthy, too, are four ritardandos in which Saint-Saëns nests complementary units in very pronounced short-long relationships. Welte-roll research places late-romantic performance practice in a new light: an analyzable formal control in interpretation clearly belies the negative reputation of late-romantic musicianship as purely subjective and irrational. Contrary to this popular view, we must see performances such as Saint-Saëns's as reflecting an awareness and control of expression of form such as is well beyond the scope of classical musicianship today. For a graphic representation of the Saint-Saëns performance with accompanying explanation by Hermann Gottschewski (University of Freiburg, Germany), see the *Neues Handbuch der Musikwissenschaft*, Band 11: Interpretation, ed. Hermann Danuser (Wiesbaden: Akademische Verlagsgesellschaft Athenaion, 1992), pp. 318–19. Gottschewski completed in 1993 a dissertation entitled "Theorie und Analyse der musikalischen Zeitgestaltung: Neue Wege der Interpretationsforschung gezeigt an Welte-Mignon-Aufnahmen aus dem Jahre 1905." The CD Archiphon ARC-106, *The Closest Approach to 19th Century Piano Interpretation* (1992), published by the Verein für musikalische Archiv-Forschung, Großherzog-Friedrich-Straße 62, Kehl am Rhein, Germany, includes six Welte-roll performances by Saint-Saëns, two by Carl Reinecke, and four by Theodor Leschetizky, with informative liner notes by Hermann Gottschewski.

33 One model on which to base our reconstruction is the violin playing of Joseph Joachim (1831–1907). Joachim is among the oldest musicians to have recorded the classical instrumental repertory shortly after 1900. He was highly regarded in his own time, on close terms with "non-Wagnerian" musicians and composers (including Mendelssohn, Schumann, and Brahms), and a central figure in instrumental pedagogy, to name just some of his qualifications. His discreet quality of tempo rubato was often praised by his contemporaries, for example Paderewski (see note 19 above). The complete recordings of Joachim are available together with those of Pablo Sarasate on the LP Opal 804, published by Pavilion Records (48 High Street, Pembury, Kent TN2 4NU, Great Britain). For an example of late nineteenth-century declamation, see the recording of the twenty-third Psalm made in New York on 27 February 1897 (the speaker is believed to be Len Spencer), reissued on the CD Symposium 1058, *Emile Berliner's Gramophone: The Earliest Discs 1888–1901*. J. Alfred Johnstone used the playing of Joachim to exemplify his ideal of tempo rubato: "Flexibility, as opposed to stiffness, is one of the essentials of eloquent playing. And *tempo rubato* is the soul of flexibility. Not the modern *tempo rubato* of the ultra-romantic school, which plays havoc with both form and time, but that delicate *tempo rubato* which recognises the inadequacy of our fixed note values to give voice to the varying shades of impassioned eloquence which issue from the human heart. This device, which consists in the almost imperceptible lengthening and shortening of certain notes, this instrument of expressive beauty used invariably in the declamation of verse, this vitalising method of treating the otherwise too rigid and mechanical record of music in our notation, this essential medium for the attainment of eloquence, is astonishingly neglected by our pianists. Joachim produced wonderful effects by its use; and I have known many students of little talent or attainment develop rapidly in taste and style by its judicious adoption. Until this device is used freely and wisely, until it is used adequately when rendering the music of Beethoven, his impassioned spiritual revelations will remain more or less a sealed book both to those who play and those who hear." J. Alfred Johnstone, *Essentials in Piano-Playing and Other Musical Studies* (London: W. Reeves, n.d.), pp. 45–46.

34 Take for example the following remarks by Christian Friedrich Daniel Schubart, dating from 1784–85: "The expressive range of music appears to me to be entirely an invention of recent times. I say *appears*, because one cannot maintain with certainty that the ancients were merely painting in one color. . . . The great Jommelli was the first to specify the coloration of music, and since his time we have gone so far, that even the finest nuances are now specified for the player. . . . [Nonetheless,] many nuances and fine shadings of music can be noticed, which are not so much in the province of the notator of music as in the heightened realm of the musical mind.

Portamento, . . . the half or whole trill, the sudden interruption of a piece, tempo rubato, where the performance wants to hold back, yet goes forward – this tender hesitation of a lover who must leave his mistress, and a hundred other ancillary arts are only effective in the hands of a master." (Das musikalische Kolorit scheint mir ganz eine Erfindung neuerer Zeiten zu sein. Ich sage *scheint*, denn so zuverlässig kann man doch nicht behaupten, daß die Alten bloß mit einer Farbe gemalt haben sollten. . . . Der große Jommelli war der erste, der die *musikalische Farbengebung* bestimmte, und seit dieser Zeit ist man so weit gegangen, daß man dem Spieler auch die feinsten Nuancen vorzeichnet. . . . Es lassen sich noch viele Nuancen und feine Schattierungen der Tonkunst bemerken, die aber nicht in die Sphäre des Skribenten, sondern in den Lichtkreis des musikalischen Kopfs gehören. Das *Portamento* oder der Träger, der *halbe* oder *ganze Triller*, die plötzliche Unterbrechung des Tonstücks, das Tempo rubato, wo der Vortrag nicht fort will und doch fort geht – dies zärtliche Zögern eines Liebhabers, der eben von seinem Mädchen gehen will, und hundert andere Nebenzüge sind nur unter dem Faust des Meisters wirksam.) See Christian Friedrich Daniel Schubart, *Ideen zu einer Ästhetik der Tonkunst*, ed. Jürgen Mainka (Leipzig: Reclam, 1977), pp. 274–77.

35 About ten years before Schubart's comments, Johann Friedrich Reichardt reported on the famous Adagio playing of the violinist Franz Benda (1709–86): "It is true, the genuine performing style of Benda has a quality all its own. Its main character is noble, charming and extremely moving. . . . It achieves these qualities through the manner of bowing . . . the particular emphasis with which a note is occasionally brought out, the always readily discernible relationship between strong and weak . . . the moderate ornamentation, chosen with a pure taste . . . and finally some negligences, of the utmost significance, in the length of notes, which remove any forced quality from the melody, and make the ideas appear to be the player's own, so that the melody seems to be the individual expression of the feelings of the soloist himself." (Es ist wahr, die ächte Bendaische Spielart hat ganz etwas eigenes. Ihr Hauptcharakter ist: Adel, Annehmlichkeit, und äusserst rührend. . . . Jenes eigene bestehet nun aber in der Führung des Bogens . . . der besondere Nachdruck, mit dem zuweilen eine Note herausgehoben wird, das stets vor Augen habende Verhältniß der Stärke und Schwäche . . . die mäßigen, und mit edler Wahl gewählten Verzierungen . . . und endlich einige äusserst bedeutende Nachläßigkeiten in dem Zeitmasse der Noten, die dem Gesange das Gezwungene benehmen, und den Gedanken mehr dem Spieler eigen machen, daß er gleichsam scheint der eigene Ausdruck von der Empfindung des Solospielers selbst zu seyn.) See Johann Friedrich Reichardt, *Briefe eines Aufmerksamen Reisenden die Musik Betreffend. An seine Freunde Geschrieben*, vol. 1 (Frankfurt a.M. and Leipzig, 1774), in *Der Critische Musicus an der Spree: Berliner Musikschrifttum von 1748 bis 1799. Eine Dokumentation*, ed. Hans-Günter Ottenberg (Leipzig: Reclam, 1984), p. 265. Thus, a late-eighteenth century ideal was to perform works not of one's own composition in such a way as to make them appear *as if they were one's own.*

36 Thirty years later, in 1805, Reichardt reviewed a Berlin concert in which the young .violinist Ludwig Spohr (1784–1859) played two of his own violin concertos. Besides criticizing Spohr's "modern" string-playing mannerisms (portamento, playing in high positions on the lower strings, avoidance of *mesa da voce* in sound production), Reichardt objected to a new fashion in tempo modification: ". . . finally, [one would wish] that he would not partake of the fatal habit of the newer virtuosi, now having become a

fashion, of entirely changing the tempo of those cantabile passages that alternate with difficult ones. It is not a mere gradual slowing of the movement, which is so advantageous to beautiful expression and so natural to a performance with feeling, and which allows itself to be easily and graciously led back to the actual movement of the piece, to which the greatest singers and masters of earlier times who excelled in beautiful and expressive performance conscientiously limited themselves, rather it is the exaggeration, the caricature of that beauty. From the first note of such a passage, Mr. Spohr changes the tempo entirely, changing it again in the more lively, difficult passages according to the characteristics of the figuration, so that an allegro movement has three or four different tempi. . . . The soloist himself also suffers thereby – and entirely avoidably – the inconvenience of being badly accompanied by any orchestra not fully accustomed to him and that does not know his concerti practically as well as he himself." (. . . endlich noch [wünschte man] das er nicht nach der so fatal zur Mode gewordenen Gewohnheit neuerer Virtuosen zum Vortrage jeder kantablen Stelle, die mit Schwierigkeiten wechselt, das Tempo so gänzlich ändern möchte. Es ist nicht ein bloßes allmähliches Aufhalten der Bewegung, welches dem schönen Ausdruck so vorteilhaft und dem gefühlvollen Vortrage so natürlich ist und welches sich leicht und graziös wieder in die eigentliche Bewegung des Stücks zurückführen läßt, worauf sich auch die größten Sänger und Meister früherer Zeit, die gerade im schönen und gefühlvolle Vortrage exzellierten, gewissenhaft beschränkten, es ist vielmehr die Übertreibung, die Karikatur jener Schönheit. Von der ersten Note einer solchen Stelle an verändert Herr Spohr das Tempo gänzlich und verändert es wieder in den lebhafteren, schwierigen Stellen nach B[eschaffenheit] der Figuren, so daß ein solches Allegro drei, vier verschiedene Tempi bekommt. . . . Der Konzertspieler selbst erlebt dadurch auch noch ganz unvermeidlich die Unannehmlichkeit, daß er von jedem Orchester, welches ihn nicht ganz gewohnt ist und seine Konzerte nicht fast ebenso genau kennt als er selbst, schlecht begleitet wird.) See Johann Friedrich Reichardt, "Konzert des Herrn Louis Spohr und der Demoiselle Alberghi im Saale des Königl. Nationaltheaters, am 3. März," *Berlinische Musikalische Zeitung* 1 (1805), repr. in *Johann Friedrich Reichardt: Briefe, die Musik Betreffend. Berichte, Rezensionen, Essays*, ed. Grita Herre and Walther Siegmund-Schultze (Leipzig: Reclam 1976), pp. 245–48.

37 Carl Ludwig Junker (1748–1797), *Einige der vornehmsten Pflichten eines Capellmeisters oder Musikdirektors* (1782), cited by Richard Taruskin in "Resisting the Ninth", *19th Century Music* 12/3 (Spring 1989), pp. 241–56.

38 Johann Nepomuk Hummel, *Ausführlich theoretisch-practische Anweisung zum Piano-forte Spiel* (1828; facs. repr. of 1838 edn Geneva: Minkoff, 1981), esp. pt 3 chap. 2.

39 T. Lindsay, *The Elements of Flute-Playing* (London, 1828), cited by David Charlton in *Performance Practice: Music after 1600*, ed. Howard Mayer Brown and Stanley Sadie, The Norton/Grove Handbooks in Music (London: Norton, 1989), p. 410: "In passages of excitement or rising passion (which are generally of the ascending series), requiring animation and energy, the time should be rather accelerated; and in those of subdued feeling or depression . . . the time should be correspondingly retarded."

40 Carl Czerny, *Vollständige theoretisch-practische Pianoforte-Schule*, Op. 500 (Vienna: Diabelli, [1839]), esp. pt 3.

41 Georg Schünemann, *Geschichte des Dirigierens* (Leipzig: Breitkopf & Härtel, 1913; facs. repr. Hildesheim: Olms, 1965), pp. 64–65.

42 Quoted by M. Ruhnke in his article "Friderici, Daniel" in *MGG* and *NG*.

43 Thomas Mace, *Musick's Monument* (1676; facs. repr. Paris: Edition du Centre Nationale de la Recherche Scientifique, 1958), p. 81.

44 Roger North, "As to Musick" (MS, ca. 1695), in *Roger North on Music*, ed. John Wilson (London: Novella, 1959), pp. 27–28. See also pp. 151f.

45 Admonitions to keep strict time dating from before the modernist period must be seen within the context of a performance practice in which the ability to maintain a steady beat (whatever that might mean for a specific period or performance tradition) was considered difficult to acquire and a mark of professionalism. But these admonitions must be seen as warnings against *unintended* modifications of the beat; the admonitions as such tell us nothing positive about the writer's attitude toward *intended* modifications.

46 Thus, I disagree with Neal Zaslaw (*Mozart's Symphonies: Context, Performance Practice, Reception* [Oxford: Clarendon, 1989], pp. 508–09), when he asserts neo-classicism as the only interpretive mode possible for classical period orchestral music today: "The implications are clear: a 'neo-classical' performance may be lively poignant, acute, clear, refined. It cannot have the ongoing shaping, the personal interpretation, that we treasure in performances of romantic and modern orchestral music by great modern conductors; nor would it have been practical to create such performances in the single rehearsal usually allotted symphonies in the eighteenth century. Let it be clearly stated, however, that even without a baton conductor, *there can never be no interpretation*, [italics Zaslaw's] for all performance, competent or otherwise, implies interpretation. . . . the music will have to speak for itself more than it will under a 'post-romantic' conductor. The results are bound to be more neutral and less personal, more objective and less subjective." Zaslaw's assertion that individuated performance is not possible in brief rehearsal time is based, no doubt, on his assumption of modern conventions of rehearsal practices and goals.

47 Walter Benjamin, "Das Kunstwerk im Zeitalter seiner technischen Reproduzierbarkeit," first version, in *Walter Benjamin: Gesammelte Schriften*, ed. Rolf Tiedemann and Hermann Schweppenhäuser (Frankfurt a.M.: Suhrkamp, 1974), vol. 1, part 2, p. 438.

4 LEHRSTÜCK: AN AESTHETICS OF PERFORMANCE

1 Kurt Weill, "Aktuelles Zwiegespräch über die Schuloper," *Die Musikpflege* 1 (1930); reprinted in Kurt Weill, *Musik und Theater: Gesammelte Schriften*, ed. S. Hinton and J. Schebera (Berlin: Henschelverlag, 1990), pp. 306–07: "Dieses Lehrstück soll ein vollwertiges Kunstwerk werden, kein Nebenwerk . . . Einfache Musik kann nur der einfache Musiker schreiben. Für ihn ist der einfache Stil kein Problem, sind die einfachen Werke keine Nebenwerke, sondern Hauptwerke."

2 "Kurt Weill has secured a niche of his own at 35" (interview), *New York World Telegram*, 21 December 1935.

3 A list and description of the principal writings on the Lehrstück are contained in the following books: Reinhold Grimm, *Bertolt Brecht* (Stuttgart: Metzler, 3rd edn 1971); Jan Knopf, *Bertolt Brecht: Ein kritischer Forschungsbericht* (Frankfurt a.M.: Suhrkamp, 1974); Juliane Eckhardt, *Das epische Theater* (Darmstadt: Wissenschaftliche Buchgesellschaft, 1983), esp. pp. 78–104; Rekha Kamath, *Brechts Lehrstück-Modell als Bruch mit den bürgerlichen Theatertraditionen*, Europäische Hochschulschriften 605 (Frankfurt a.M.: P. Lang, 1983); and Matthias-Johannes Fischer, *Brechts Theatertheorie: Forschungsgeschichte –*

Forschungsstand – Perspektiven, Europäische Hochschulschriften, 1115 (Frankfurt a.M.: P. Lang, 1989).

4 Jacob und Wilhelm Grimm, *Deutsches Wörterbuch*, vol. 12 (Leipzig: S. Hirzel, 1885), p. 578.

5 The Lehrstück entry in Wahrig's *Deutsches Wörterbuch* (Munich: Mosaik-Verlag, 3rd edn 1980) offers the following definition, which is specific about genre but not about authorship: "Theaterstück, das eine Lehre oder Erkenntnis vermitteln soll." The *Brockhaus Wahrig Deutsches Wörterbuch* (Wiesbaden: Brockhaus, 1982) also restricts itself to drama but gives Brecht as an example: "Drama, das belehren will, dramatische Lehrdichtung; die Lehrstücke Brechts." The *Wörterbuch der deutschen Gegenwartssprache* (Berlin: Akademie Verlag, 1969), produced in the former German Democratic Republic, defines Lehrstück as "didactic theater" (*belehrendes Theater*); it does not mention Brecht, but it does list the term as a "neologism" (*Neuprägung*).

6 In his study of *Brecht und das Fastnachtspiel* (Göttingen: Arbeitstille für Renaissanceforschung am Seminar für deutsche Philologie der Universtität Göttingen, 1978), which draws parallels between Brecht's plays and sixteenth-century religious dramas, Thomas Habel remarks how Brecht often uses the terms "episch" and "lehrhaft" as synonyms (p. 32).

7 See note 3.

8 Johann Balthassar Schupp, *Lehrreiche Schriften* (Frankfurt, 1677): "Lasse dir Gottes Exempel in dieser Sach ein Lehrstück sein" (p. 755); "sollen meine Schäden dein Lehrstück sein" (p. 756).

9 For example, Yizhak Ahren, *Das Lehrstück "Holocaust": zur Wirkungspsychologie eines Medienereignisses* (Opladen: Westdeutscher Verlag, 1982); Fritz Schweighofer, *Das Privattheater der Anna O.: ein psychoanalytisches Lehrstück: ein Emanzipationsdrama* (Munich: E. Reinhardt, n.d. [?1987]).

10 Ingrid Craemer-Ruegenberg, "Die Seele als Form in einer Hierarchie von Formen: Beobachtungen zu einem Lehrstück aus der De-Anima-Paraphrase Alberts des Großen," in *Albertus Magnus Doctor Universalis 1280/1980*, ed. G. Meyer *et al.* (Mainz: Matthias-Grünewald, 1980), p. 64. This is also the earliest sense of the word cited in Grimms' *Deutsches Wörterbuch*: "Unter des Plato alten Lehrstücken war auch dieses, das anders nichts von den Göttern solle gebeten werden, als: zu geben dasjenige, was dem Menschen am nützlichsten" (Samuel von Butschky, *Hochdeutsche Kanzeley* [Leipzig, 1659]: p. 347).

11 See, for example, the entry "Lehrstück-Katechismus" in the *Lexikon für Theologie und Kirche*, 6 vols. (Freiburg: Herder, 1961).

12 This general sense is conveyed in Christian Achelis's absorbing historical study of the utilization of the decalogue in catechistic teaching: *Der Dekalog als katechetisches Lehrstück* (Gießen: Alfred Töppelmann, 1905). Achelis is concerned with the decalogue's didactic status as such rather than with its particular mode of presentation in the type of catechism known as *Lehrstück-Katechismus*.

13 The first part of Carl Philip Emanuel Bach's *Versuch über die wahre Art das Clavier zu spielen* (Berlin: C.F. Henning, 1753; repr. Leipzig: Breitkopf & Härtel, 1981), for example, is divided into three "Hauptstücke" (fingering, ornamentation and performance), which comprise the foundation of keyboard musicianship.

14 Martin Luther, *Werkausgabe*, vol. 19, p. 76: "Diese [sic] Unterricht oder Unterweisung weiß ich nicht schlechter oder besser zu stellen, denn sie bereit gestellt ist von Anfang der Christenheit und bisher blieben, nämlich die drei Stücke: die zehn Gebote, der

Glaube und das Vaterunser. In diesen drei Stücken steht schlicht und kurz fast alles, was einem Christen zu wissen not ist."

15 "The common people, especially those who live in the country, have no knowledge whatever of Christian teaching, and unfortunately many pastors are quite incompetent and unfitted for teaching." Luther's Preface to *The Small Catechism*, in *Three Reformation Catechisms: Catholic, Anabaptist, Lutheran*, ed. Denis Janz (New York and Toronto: E. Mellen, Press 1982), p. 182.

16 The so-called *Hessische Fragestücke*, first published in 1574 and intended expressly for such instruction, were later incorporated into the widely used *Darmstädter Katechismus*.

17 See "Katechismus", in *Die Religion in Geschichte und Gegenwart*, vol. 3 (Tübingen: J. C. B. Mohr, 1959), p. 1184.

18 A cogent summary of these issues can be found in Bernhard Truffer, *Das material-kerygmatische Anliegen in der Katechetik der Gegenwart: Zur Geschichte der inneren Stoffgestaltung des Lehrstück-Katechismus* (Freiburg: Herder, 1963).

19 From an unpublished paper of 1860, quoted in Henry Tristram, "On Reading Newman," *John Henry Newman: Centenary Essays* (London: Burns, Oates and Washburne, 1945), p. 226.

20 Franz Michel Willam, *Die Erkenntnis-Lehre Kardinal Newmans: systematische Darlegung und Dokumentation* (Bergen-Enkheim: Gerhard Kaffke, 1969)

21 See Willam's article "Lehrstück-Katechismus," in the *Lexikon für Theologie und Kirche*.

22 In the Foreword to his *Vollständige Katechesen für die untere Klasse der katholischen Volksschule* (Freiburg: Herder, 1911; 13th edn 1971), Gustav Mey explained the nature of his reforms as follows: "Auch in den Reimsprüchen, welche jeder Katechese beigefügt sind, erhalten die Benützer dieses Buches das, was ich meinen Schülern gebe. An puren Moralsprüchen, welchen die historische oder dogmatische Grundlage fehlt, habe ich kein Gefallen. Nach solchen Sprüchen dagegen, welche mit den behandelten Lehrstücken in einen organischen Zusammenhang gebracht werden könnten, namentlich nach Sprüchen, worin die Ereignisse der heiligen Geschichte kurz und sinnig verwertet wären, habe ich mich in den Spruchsammlungen, welche mir zu Gebote stehen, umsonst umgesehen. Darum habe ich es selbst versucht, Sprüche zum Gebrauch für meine Katechumenen zu verfassen." (p. v)

23 E. Chr. Achelis, *Der Dekalog als katechetisches Lehrstück* (Gießen: Alfred Töppelmann, 1905), p. 75: "Sie werden . . . darin übereinstimmen, daß das Prinzip der religiösen Begründung aller christlichen Sittlichkeit und daß das Ziel, zu *autonomer* Sittlichkeit die Schüler zu befähigen, unveräußerlich sind."

24 Karl Laux, "Skandal in Baden-Baden," *Hindemith-Jahrbuch* 2 (1972), pp. 166–80.

25 Cited in *Brecht in der Kritik*, ed. Monika Wyss (Munich: Kindler, 1977), p. 97: "Unwillkürlich kam der Gedanke angesichts dieser Schinderei, die allen Gesetzen der Ästhetik und Moral Hohn sprach: ein Schubert ist am Hungertyphus gestorben, ein Kleist elend zugrunde gegangen, und ein Brecht, absoluter Nichtskönner und Bluffer, genießt die 'Segnungen der Kultur,' wie das schöne Wort heißt."

26 The text of the opening chorus of *Lehrstück* is identical to the closing chorus of *Der Lindberghflug*.

27 Reiner Steinweg, "*Das Badener Lehrstück vom Einverständnis*: Mystik, Religionsersatz oder Parodie?" in *Bertolt Brecht II*, Sonderband aus der Reihe Text und Kritik, ed. Heinz Ludwig Arnold (Munich: Edition Text & Kritik, 1973), pp. 109–30. See also Andreas Lehmann, "Hindemiths Lehrstück," *Hindemith-Jahrbuch* 11 (1982), pp. 36–76.

28 Ernst Schumacher, *Die dramatischen Versuche Bertolt Brechts 1918–1933* (Berlin: Verlag Rütter und Loening, 1954), p. 329.

29 Steinweg, *Das Badener Lehrstück*, p. 110.

30 Thomas O. Brandt, "Brecht und die Bibel," *Proceedings of the Modern Language Association*, 79 (1964), pp. 171–76; Hans Pabst, *Brecht und die Religion* (Graz: Verlag Styria, 1977); G. Ronald Murphy, *Brecht and the Bible: A Study of Religious Nihilism and Human Weakness in Brecht's Drama of Mortality and the City* (Chapel Hill, N.C., University of North Carolina Press, 1980); Eberhard Rohse, *Der frühe Brecht und die Bibel: Studien zum Augsburger Religionsunterricht und zu den literarischen Versuchen des Gymnasiasten* (Göttingen: Vandenhoeck und Ruprecht, 1983).

31 I am deeply indebted here to the painstaking research of Eberhard Rohse, whose study *Der frühe Brecht* reconstructs the entire curriculum of Brecht's religious education at grammar school in Augsburg. In the segment of religious instruction called "Catechism and Faith" each *Hauptstück* was treated in turn. The year 1908–09 was devoted to the first *Hauptstück* and the first and second articles of faith (the second *Hauptstück*). The following year concentrated on the second article, while introducing the third *Hauptstück* and so on, until the fourth year, when all six *Hauptstücke* were reviewed.

32 "Da das Lehrstück nur den Zweck hat, alle Anwesenden an der Ausführung eines Werkes zu beteiligen und nicht als musikalische und dichterische Äußerung in erster Linie bestimmte Eindrücke hervorrufen will, ist die Form des Stückes dem jeweiligen Zwecke nach Möglichkeit anzupassen. Der in der Partitur angegebene Verlauf ist demnach mehr Vorschlag als Vorschrift. Auslassungen, Zusätze und Umstellungen sind möglich."

33 Bertolt Brecht, *Versuche*, vol. 2 (Berlin: Gustav Kiepenheuer Verlag, 1930), p. 148: "Selbst wenn man erwartete, daß . . . hier auf musikalischer Grundlage gewisse geistige formale Kongruenzen entstehen, wäre eine solche künstliche und seichte Harmonie doch niemals imstande, den die Menschen unserer Zeit mit ganz anderer Gewalt auseinander zerrenden Kollektivbildungen auf breitester und vitalster Basis auch nur für Minuten ein Gegengewicht zu schaffen."

34 Ibid: "An diesem Mißverständnis ist wohl hauptsächlich meine eigene Bereitwilligkeit, einen unabgeschlossenen und mißverständlichen Textteil, wie es die in Baden-Baden aufgeführte Fassung des Lehrstücks war, zu rein experimentalen Zwecken auszuliefern, schuld, so daß tatsächlich der einzige Schulungszweck, der in Betracht kommen konnte, ein rein musikalisch formaler war."

35 Bertolt Brecht, "Aus der Musiklehre," in *Schriften*, vol. 1, ed. W. Hecht as vol. 21 of *Große kommentierte Berliner und Frankfurter Ausgabe* (Berlin and Weimar: Aufban-Verlag, 1992), pp. 268: "Musik, *lautes Fühlen* (wobei es gleichgültig ist, ob gesungen wird oder ob das 'werkzeugmachende Tier' Instrumente benützt), gibt dem Fühlen des einzelnen, soweit es allgemein werden will, eine allgemeine Form, ist als Organisation von Menschen auf Grundlage der Organisation von Tönen."

36 Cited in Reiner Steinweg (ed.), *Brechts Modell der Lehrstücke: Zeugnisse, Diskussion, Erfahrungen* (Frankfurt a.M.: Suhrkamp, 1976), p. 38. The text is written with lower-case letters throughout: "im verfolg des grundsatzes; der staat soll reich sein, der mensch soll arm sein, der staat soll verflichtet sein vieles zu können, dem menschen soll es erlaubt sein weniges zu können, soll der staat, was die musik betrifft, alles hervorbringen, was besonderes studium, besondere apparate und besondere fähigkeiten verlangt, aber der einzelne soll alles das lernen, was zum genuss nötig ist. freischwebende gefühle

anlässlich von musik, besondere gedanken ohne folgen wie sie beim anhören von musik gedacht werden, erschöpfung des körpers wie beim blossen anhören von musik leicht eintritt sind ablenkungen von der musik und verringern den genuss an der musik. um diese ablenkungen zu vermeiden, beteiligt sich der denkende an der musik, hierin auch dem grundsatz folgend: tun ist besser als fühlen, indem er die musik mitliest und in ihr fehlende stimmen mitsummt oder im buch mit den augen verfolgt oder im verein mit anderen laut singt. so gibt der staat eine unvollkommene musik aber der einzelne macht sie vollkommen."

37 The first edition of *Lehrstück* has been recently published in Paul Hindemith, *Szenische Versuche*, Sämtliche Werke, 1/6, ed. R. Stephan (Mainz: Schott, 1982). The latest edition of Brecht's works (*Große kommentierte Berliner und Frankfurter Ausgabe*) curiously reprints *Das Badener Lehrstück vom Einverständnis*, despite its declared policy of publishing "as a matter of principle the authorized and established [*wirksam gewordene*] first editions." During the period 1929–33 there are thirteen productions of the first version of *Lehrstück* on record and none of the revised version.

38 Heinrich Strobel, "Musikerziehung – die Forderung der Zeit," *Berliner Börsen-Courier*, 8 August 1929. See also Dorothea Kolland, *Die Jugendmusikbewegung: "Gemeinschafts-musik" – Theorie und Praxis* (Stuttgart: J. B. Metzler, 1979) and Heide Hammel, *Die Schulmusik in der Weimarer Republik: Politische und gesellschaftliche Aspekte der Reformdiskussion in den 20er Jahren* (Stuttgart: J. B. Metzler, 1990).

39 On several occasions Besseler acknowledged an intellectual debt to Martin Heidegger, his philosophy teacher. In Heideggerian terms *Gebrauchsmusik* belongs to the more immediate, primordial realm of *Zeug* (equipment) as opposed to that of *Ding* (thing). *Zeug* is *zuhanden* (ready-to-hand), an object of manipulation (or *umgangsmässig*, as Besseler says), in contrast to objects of bare perceptual cognition or reflection, which Heidegger describes as *vorhanden* (present-at-hand).

40 Originally published in the *Zeitschrift für Musik*, Laux's review was reprinted as part of his article "Skandal in Baden-Baden:" "Wir leben in einer neuen Zeit. Auch das musikalische Weltbild hat sich verändert. Worin bestand, vor zwanzig Jahren noch, das Musikleben einer Stadt? In ihren Symphoniekonzerten, in ihren Chorkonzerten, in den Solistenabenden. Man ging hin, weil man sich an den Darbietungen anderer erfreuen wollte, auch weil es zum guten Ton gehörte, dabeigewesen zu sein. Man war dabei, körperlich gewiß. Wie weit die seelische Anteilnahme ging, konnte nicht festgestellt werden. Man konnte eine Symphonie gleichgültig über sich ergehen lassen oder man konnte sie innerlich erleben, als Sturm über die Seele, als Kampf mit geistigen Mächten. Aber dies war Sache des Individuums. Das Konzert war eine Angelegenheit mehr oder minder großer Passivität.

Das ist anders geworden. So wie sich die soziologische Schichtung des Publikums veränderte – die arbeitende Masse drängte nach oben, will Anteil an den Kulturgütern – so veränderte sich die innere Struktur. Man sitzt nicht mehr einsam auf dem Klappstuhl seines Abbonements. Man sitzt in einer Reihe mit vielen anderen, man möchte sich zu einer Gemeinschaft zusammenschließen. Mehr noch. Diese Gemeinschaft beschränkt sich nicht mehr auf ein bloßes Hören. Man will selbst musizieren. Die innere Anteilnahme soll damit gewährleistet sein. An die Stelle der Passivität des Individuums tritt die *Aktivität der Gemeinschaft*.

Es ist ein Neues, aber auch das ist schon da gewesen.

Heinrich Besseler hat in einem Aufsatz 'Grundfragen des musikalischen Hörens' (im Jahrbuch der Musikbibliothek Peters für 1925) der *umgangsmäßigen Gebrauchsmusik die eigenständige Konzertmusik* gegenübergestellt. Diese tritt dem Dasein 'in irgend einer Weise als in sich begründet' gegenüber, bei jener liegt der Schwerpunkt 'durchaus auf dem aktiven Vollziehen der Musik.' Diese ist 'wesentlich geknüpft an ein umgangsmäßiges Verhalten des Daseins, an Gebet, Bekenntnis, Arbeit, Erholung in Tanz und Gemeinschaft, Eingehen in ein mythischen oder magischen Weltzusammenhang: es tritt stets als Schmuck oder Steigerung, als spezifisch 'musikalische' Ausformung dieses Verhaltens auf."

Solche *Gebrauchsmusik* – dies ist das Wort, das heute in aller Mund ist – hat es (nach Besseler) immer schon gegeben: beim Tanz, in den Arbeitsgesängen, in den Gesellschaftsliedern, den Bekenntnisliedern, der liturgischen Musik, im Mythischen und Magischen, in der sprachmelodischen Erhöhung des Vortrags beim Märchenerzählen, bei Schlummerliedern und Zaubergesängen.

Die musikalische Jugendbewegung und mit ihr die junge Komponistengeneration will diese Gebrauchsmusik erneuern. Sie wollen nicht mehr das Konzert, das den Hörer *vom* Alltag befreit, sondern das Musizieren, das den Spieler *im* Alltag erlöst. Im Sommer 1927 entschloß man sich, gemeinsam zu handeln. Die alljährliche '*Deutsche Kammermusik Baden-Baden*' sollte mit der Jahrestagung der Jugendbewegung zusammenfallen. Man wollte 'Förderung der Laienmusik in jeder Gestalt.'

Im Jahre 1929 standen drei solcher *Zweckformen* der heutigen Musik in Baden-Baden zur Diskussion."

41 The article originated from a lecture Besseler gave as part of his "Habilitation" ritual at the University of Freiburg. See my dissertation *The Idea of Gebrauchsmusik* (University of Birmingham, 1984; New York: Garland, 1989), pp. 6–23, and monograph "Gebrauchsmusik," *Handwörterbuch der musikalischen Terminologie*, vol. 15 (Wiesbaden: F. Steiner, 1988).

42 Hans Joachim Moser openly attacked Besseler's essay in *Archiv für Musikwissenschaft* 7 (1926), p. 380. Besseler responded in the same issue with a "critical remark," in which he commented that the "Jugendbewegung" had "been strongest and most decisive in preparing the ground".

43 *Der Jasager* received more than 300 performances in Germany prior to the seizure of power by the National Socialists in January 1933.

44 Weill's statement on the matter, which examines among other things the relationship between *Gebrauchskunst* and state subvention, was published in his article "Musikfest oder Musikstudio," *Melos* 9 (1930), pp. 230–32; it is reprinted in Weill, *Gesammelte Schriften*, pp. 88–90. An abbreviated version of Eisler's open letter to the festival's committee was published as "Offener Brief an die künstlerische Leitung der neuen Musik Berlin 1930" in the *Berliner Börsen-Courier*, 13 May 1930; it is published in full in Hanns Eisler, *Musik und Politik: Schriften 1924–1948* (Leipzig: Dentscher Verlag für Musik, 1973), pp. 102–5.

45 "Über meine Schuloper *Der Jasager*," *Die Scene* 20 (1930), pp. 232–3; reprinted in *Gesammelte Schriften*, pp. 91–92: "Eine Oper kann zunächst Schulung für den Komponisten oder für eine Komponisten-Generation sein . . . Eine Oper kann auch Schulung für die Operndarstellung sein . . . so wäre ein solches Werk auch geeignet, die Opernsänger . . . im Gesang und in der Darstellung zu jener Einfachheit und Natürlichkeit zu zwingen, die wir in den Opernhäusern noch so oft vermissen. . . . Die dritte Interpretation des Wortes 'Schuloper' ist diejenige, die die beiden ersten in sich schließt:

es ist die Oper, die für den Gebrauch in den Schulen bestimmt ist. Sie ist einzureihen unter die Bestrebungen zur Schaffung einer musikalischen Produktion, in der die Musik nicht mehr Selbstzweck ist, sondern in den Dienst jener Institutionen gestellt wird, die Musik brauchen und für die gerade eine neue Musikproduktion einen Wert darstellt."

46 n.n., "Der 'Jasager' in Arnstadt: Freunde und Gegner," *Melos* 10 (1931), p. 86: "Wochenlang wurde über den 'Jasager' gestritten, und nicht nur in der Schulgemeinde, sondern in allen musikalisch interessierten Kreisen. Der Kritiker, ein feiner musikalischer Kopf, bekennt sich zum ersten Male vorbehaltlos zur neuen Musik. Musikalisch Gleich-gültige sind geweckt. Abseits stehende Erwachsene, nicht nur Eltern von Mitwirkenden, treten in den Kampf für die neue Musik ein. Als Zentren der Gegenbewegung stellen sich heraus: die völkische Bewegung, der Wagner-Jugend-Bund (an unserer Anstalt von einem Philologen geleitet) und die orthodoxe Richtung der Kirche (des unchrist-lichen Gedankenkreises wegen)."

47 See, for example, the review by Frank Warschauer, originally published in *Die Weltbühne* (8 July 1930): "In this school opera young people are inculcated with a philosophy that finely mixes in, while still effectively containing, all the evil ingredients of reac-tionary thought based on senseless authority." Reprinted in Bertolt Brecht, *Der Jasager und Der Neinsager: Vorlagen, Fassungen und Materialien*, ed. Peter Szondi (Frankfurt a.M.: Suhrkamp, 15th edn 1978), p. 73. By way of responding to such criticisms, Brecht made two separate revisions – one small, the other major. In the first, the changes mainly serve to stress the autonomy of the boy's decision. In the second, *Der Jasager* is complemented by *Der Neinsager*. In this alternative version the boy actively contravenes convention by declining to jump. The additional music supplied by Weill for the first revision has never been published, no doubt because it disrupts his original design. Nor is there any musical setting of *Der Neinsager* by Weill.

48 Hans Gutman, "Eine Schuloper von H.J. Moser," *Melos* 10, pp. 425–26.

49 Sergei Tretjakov, "Hanns Eisler," in *Die Arbeit des Schriftstellers*, ed. H. Boehnke (Reinbek bei Hamburg: Rowohlt, 1972), p. 182: "Es ist ein politisches Seminar besonderer Art zu Fragen der Strategie und Taktik der Partei. . . . Das Lehrstück ist nicht für den Konzertgebrauch gemacht. Es ist nur ein Mittel der pädagogischen Arbeit mit Studenten marxistischer Schulen und proletarischen Kollektiven."

50 See Werner Fuhr, *Proletarische Musik in Deutschland 1928–1933* (Göppingen: Verlag Alfred Kümmerle, 1977).

51 The fate of the German New Music festivals in the years immediately preceding and subsequent to the Nazi seizure of power is extensively documented in Werner Zintgraf's study *Neue Musik 1921–1950* (Horb am Neckar: Geiger-Verlag, 1987).

52 The designation "Thingspiel" was suggested by the drama professor Carl Niessen, who had in mind the ancient concept of a judicial-cum-political meeting at which free men assembled in order to deliberate over matters of state. Especially significant for the Nazi tradition was the function of the "Thing" as the highest judicial authority at which the assembled company made a collective judgment. See Johannes M. Reichl, *Das Thingspiel: über den Versuch eines nationalsozialistischen Lehrstück-Theaters* (Frankfurt a.M.: Dr Misslbeck, 1988).

53 Letter from Weill to Hans Heinsheimer (Universal-Edition) dated 14 October 1929. Quoted by permission of the Kurt Weill Foundation, New York. "Fast alles, was zu der Baden-Badener Fassung hinzugekommen ist, ist in einem vollkommen reinen,

durchaus verantwortungsbewußten Stil geschrieben, von dem ich fest annehme, daß er länger bestehen wird, als das meiste, was heute produziert wird."

54 A analogous kind of musical symbolism (jazz vs neo-baroque) pervades the *Lehrstücke* of Eisler: while *Die Maßnahme* (1930) keeps the dualism in balance, *Die Mutter* (1931) tends more towards the austere neo-baroque.

55 Recounting the genesis of *Down in the Valley*, Weill wrote: "I remembered the wonderful experience I had had with a school opera in Europe years ago and it occurred to me that the [new] piece . . . would be readily adaptable for an American school opera." (*New York Times*, 5 June 1949)

56 For a fuller account of the points summarized here, see my article "Hindemith: pedagogy and personal style," *Hindemith-Jahrbuch* 17 (1988), pp. 54–67.

57 Heinrich Strobel, *Paul Hindemith* (Mainz: Schott, 3rd edn 1948), p. 54.

58 See note 56.

59 Quoted in Steinweg, *Das Lehrstück*, p. 87: "Diese Bezeichnung gilt nur für Stücke, die für die *Darstellenden* lehrhaft sind. Sie benötigen so kein Publikum."

60 Julius Bab, "Lehrstück in Gegenwart und Vergangenheit," *Die Literarische Welt*, 19 February 1932; reprinted in Bertolt Brecht, *Die Maßnahme: Kritische Ausgabe mit einer Spielanleitung von Reiner Steinweg* (Frankfurt a.M.: Suhrkamp, 1972), p. 407: "Es ist merkwürdig, und es ist wichtig, daß nach dem Katholizismus nun auch der Kommunismus ein Lehrstück entwickelt."

5 SINGING BRECHT VERSUS BRECHT SINGING: PERFORMANCE IN THEORY AND PRACTICE

1 "Wir sprachen in der letzten Stunde von der Umwandlung der Oper in das Musikdrama, und ich erklärte euch den Begriff des Gesamtkunstwerkes. Ich schreibe noch einmal an die Tafel die Namen

Richard Wagner,
Richard Strauss,

damit keiner eine Ausrede hat.

Wir kommen nun zu einem neuen Kapitel. Ihr erinnert euch, daß ich euch aus den Texten Wagners vorlas. Da ging es immer um Götter und Helden und merkwürdige Begriffe, wie Waldesweben, Feuerzauber, Gralsritter usw., die euch ganz fremd vorkamen. Dann gab es da schwierige Gedankengänge, denen ihr nicht folgen konntet, und auch gewisse Dinge, von denen ihr noch nichts versteht und die euch auch noch nichts angehen. Das alles hat euch wenig interessiert. . . . Ich habe euch auch aus der Musik Wagners und seiner Nachfolger vorgespielt. Ihr habt gesehen, daß es in dieser Musik soviel Noten gab, daß ich sie gar nicht alle greifen konnte. Ihr hättet gern einmal eine Melodie mitgesungen, aber das ging nicht. Ihr habt auch gemerkt, daß diese Musik auf euch einschläfernd oder berauschend wirkte wie Alkohol oder andere Rauschgifte. Ihr wollt aber nicht eingeschläfert sein. Ihr wollt eine Musik hören, die ihr auch versteht, ohne daß sie euch erklärt wird, die ihr gleich aufnehmt und die ihr bald nachsingen könnt. . . . Heute gibt es wieder große Gebiete, für die sich alle interessieren, und wenn die Musik nicht in den Dienst der Allgemeinheit gestellt werden kann, so hat sie heute keine Daseinsberechtigung mehr.

Aufschreiben!:
Die Musik ist nicht mehr eine Sache der Wenigen."

2 Kurt Weill, "Der Musiker Weill," *Berliner Tageblatt*, 25 December 1928; repr. in Weill, *Musik und Theater: Gesammelte Schriften*, ed. Stephen Hinton and Jürgen Schebera (Berlin: Henschelverlag, 1990), pp. 52–54; partially repr. and trans. in *The Musical Times* 70 (1 March 1929), p. 224. Complete Eng. trans. and facs. of original clipping with Arnold Schoenberg's marginal commentary in Alexander Ringer, "Schoenberg, Weill and Epic Theater," *Journal of the Arnold Schoenberg Institute* 4 (June 1980), pp. 77–98; repr. as "Relevance and the Future of Opera: Arnold Schoenberg and Kurt Weill" in Ringer, *Arnold Schoenberg: The Composer as Jew* (Oxford: Clarendon Press, 1990), pp. 83–102. For additional commentary on the essay, see David Drew's Letter to the Editor in the *Kurt Weill Newsletter* 5 (Autumn 1987), p. 3; and Kim H. Kowalke's notes in *A New Orpheus: Essays on Kurt Weill* (New Haven: Yale University Press, 1986), pp. 150–51. The cliché comparing the effects of Wagner's music to those of alcohol was far from new in 1928: Nietzsche had already so characterized it in *Der Fall Wagner* in 1888.

3 "Er hat sich darum jener Theaterbewegung angeschlossen, die am stärksten die künst- lerischen Forderungen unserer Zeit erfüllt und die von Bertolt Brecht – Klammer auf: Bertolt Brecht, der Begründer des epischen Dramas; Klammer zu – begründet worden ist. Weill hat erkannt, daß es innerhalb dieser Bewegung für den Musiker eine Fülle neuer, überraschender Aufgaben gibt. Brecht und Weill haben die Frage untersucht, welche Rolle der Musik auf dem Theater zukommt. Sie haben erkannt, daß die Musik nicht die Handlung des Stückes fördern oder untermalen darf, sondern daß sie nur dann richtig zur Geltung kommt, wenn sie die Handlungen an den geeigneten Stellen unterbricht. Schreibt euch als wichtigstes Ergebnis der bisherigen Arbeit Weills das Wort 'gestischer Charakter der Musik' auf, über das wir im nächsten Jahr im Fach- kursus noch ausführlich sprechen werden, wenn diejenigen unter euch, die sich dem Kritikerberuf zuwenden wollen, uns verlassen haben werden.

    Aufstehen! Wir singen jetzt Nr. 16.

[Der Mensch lebt durch den Kopf, der Kopf reicht ihm nicht aus, versuch' es nur, von deinem Kopf lebt höchstens eine Laus.]"

4 The songs, billed on the label of Orchestrola 2131 as "Moritat" and "Ballade von der Unzulänglichkeit," were recorded in May 1929 and released shortly thereafter. Carola Neher's "Barbara Song" and "Seeräuberjenny" were recorded at the same time and appeared as Orchestrola 2132. In both cases, the orchestra was unidentified; although similar in instrumentation to the Lewis Ruth Band, conducted by Theo Mackeben in the original production, the recorded arrangements are not Weill's. Brecht's renditions, said to have been strongly influenced by the Bavarian clown Karl Valentin's, have been re-released most recently on compact disc (Mastersound DFCDI–100). One suspects that Weill suggested coupling the two ballads; in composing *Kleine Dreigroschenmusik* in December 1928, he had already combined the closely related songs within a single movement, and it was one of the four Otto Klemperer had recorded shortly after the official premiere in February 1929.

5 Bernhard Reich has noted: "Brecht picked from the deep impressions left by the barrel-organ singer one major element – one might call this the naïveté of represen- tation. . . . The composers of fairground Moritaten neither allow themselves to be led astray by reflections on the material, nor do they let themselves be overly specific through the use of minute naunces in the material. This fairground theater strives to present things in an unmistakable and coarse way (they represent only the basics)." Trans.

John Fuegi in *Bertolt Brecht: Chaos, According to Plan* (Cambridge: Cambridge University Press, 1987), p. 25.

6 A teenage friend recalled that "Brecht did not sing in a polished way, but with a passion that swept others along, drunk from his own verses, ideas, and creations as other people would be drunk from wine, and his singing made those who heard him drunk also." Carl Zuckmayer remembered that when "Brecht picked up the guitar, the hum of conversation ceased, while all around him people sat as though caught up in a magic spell." Another close friend, Arnolt Bronnen, also attested to Brecht's charisma: 'Did he sing? He created magic. . . . It was uncanny how . . . people became lemurs; he alone was human." Trans. Fuegi, *Chaos*, pp. 4, 26, 40.

7 John Willett deemed the maxim so central to an understanding of Brecht's work that it appears as the epigram for *Brecht on Theatre* (New York: Hill & Wang, 1964). Fuegi has noted (*Chaos*, pp. 16, 49) that as a director Brecht could and did demonstrate to his actors nuances of any role and as a lyricist he tried to show to his musical collaborators what he expected from a song.

8 Bertolt Brecht, "Ueber reimlose Lyrik mit unregelmässigen Rhythmen," *Das Wort* 3 (March 1939); repr. in *Gesammelte Werke*, 20 vols, ed. Elisabeth Hauptmann and Werner Hecht (Frankfurt a.M.: Suhrkamp, 1967), vol. 19, pp. 395–403.

9 "It is hard to think of another example anywhere, by an author, which has had an equally potent or misleading effect. . . . The problem is not only how to read and evaluate Brecht's theoretical works, but how to deal with the confusions that these have created in the ranks of his interpreters." Hilda Meldrum Brown, *Leitmotiv and Drama: Wagner, Brecht, and the Limits of 'Epic' Theatre* (Oxford: Clarendon, 1991), pp. 68–69. Although Brecht's theoretical writings about theater are voluminous, they are unsystematic and inconsistent. The shifts in both theory and practice over the four decades of his career cohere only if one considers the very different resources available to him at different stages in his life and his ever-changing world views. The fact, for example, that *Verfremdung* is routinely applied to production and criticism of Brecht's entire œuvre even though he did not invoke the concept until 1935 should serve as ample warning to those who would attempt to assemble a unified aesthetic code by combining statements from different periods. As Fuegi has observed (*Chaos*, p. 51): "It is worth remembering that many of the slogans that Brecht used in the heat of political battle in the late twenties and early thirties were responses to a specific set of extremely dire political circumstances, and not slogans that would work just as well in other very different political circumstances such as, to cite one example, the socialist section of Berlin in the very early 1950s. . . . We must be wary of taking Brecht's statements out of their original historical context and at their apparent face value."

10 Brecht, "Ueber die Verwendung von Musik für ein episches Theater," *Gesammelte Werke*, vol. 15, pp. 472–82; repr. in Joachim Lucchesi and Ronald K. Shull, *Musik bei Brecht* (Berlin: Henschel, 1988), pp. 157–58; trans. as "On the use of music in an epic theatre," in Willett, *Brecht on Theatre*, pp. 84–90.

11 Hans Mersmann, "Die neue Musik und ihre Texte," *Melos* 10 (May/June 1931), p. 171. Eisler recalled, however, that "Brecht was interested in music only in how it might be useful for his theater." Lucchesi/Shull, *Musik bei Brecht*, p. 86.

12 Normative obstacles to translations are dwarfed by those that Brecht's musico-dramatic works present, and the most recent edition of the texts of these works [*Bertolt Brecht*

Werke: Grosse Kommentierte Berliner und Frankfurter Ausgabe, ed. Werner Hecht, Jan Knopf, Werner Mittenzwei, and Claus-Detlef Müller (Berlin: Aufbau; Frankfurt a.M.: Suhrkamp, 1988)] demonstrates the editorial complications posed by musical settings of Brecht's texts, in that the "authorized" literary versions differ markedly from those published and performed with the musical scores.

13 See, for example, these recent books and extended essays on the comprehensive topic of Brecht and music: Fritz Hennenberg, ed., *Das grosse Brecht-Liederbuch* (Frankfurt a.M.: Suhrkamp, 1984); Jürgen Engelhardt, *Gestus und Verfremdung: Studien zum Musiktheater bei Strawinsky und Brecht/Weill* (Munich: Emil Katzbichler, 1984); John Willett, "Brecht and the musicians," in *Brecht in Context: Comparative Approaches* (London: Methuen, 1984), pp. 151–77; Ulrich Weisstein, "Von reitenden Boten und singenden Holzfällern: Bertolt Brecht und die Oper," in *Brechts Dramen: neue Interpretationen*, ed. Walter Hinderer (Stuttgart: Reclam, 1984), pp. 266–99; Albrecht Dümling, *Lasst euch nicht verführen: Brecht und die Musik* (Munich: Kindler, 1985); Michael John T. Gilbert, *Bertolt Brecht's Striving for Reason, Even in Music: A Critical Assessment* (New York: P. Lang, 1988); Jost Hermand, "Kurt Weill und andere 'Brecht-Komponisten'," in *Beredte Töne: Musik im historischen Prozess* (Frankfurt a.M.: P. Lang, 1991), pp. 157–72. Notable exceptions include Lucchesi and Shull's *Musik bei Brecht*, which, apart from its lengthy introduction, has few critical aspirations. The short monograph of Kenneth Fowler, *Received Truths: Bertolt Brecht and the Problem of Gestus and Musical Meaning* (New York: AMS, 1991), confronts this issue head-on. In his perceptive survey of Eisler's music ("Eisler and Austrian Music: Notes for the Almeida Festival," *Tempo* [June/September 1987], pp. 24–35), David Drew pointed out a corollary of this critical approach to "Brecht's composers": "For many years the parallactic view of Brecht's musical collaborators that rendered them figuratively and even functionally indistinguishable from Brecht himself was supposed to justify the idea that resemblances between (for instance) the music of Weill and of Eisler were simply attributable to the influence of Brecht." (For the most blatant exposition of such a naïve view, see Willett's "Brecht and the musicians," pp. 176–77.) Drew continued: "Today [1987] it is perhaps permissible to suggest that Weill was one of the means whereby Eisler temporarily freed himself from Vienna."

14 Bertolt Brecht, *Arbeitsjournal*, 3 August 1938; quoted in Lucchesi/Shull, *Musik bei Brecht*, p. 175. Brecht's brother Walter could read and write music and was frequently called on by Brecht to notate his melodies and guitar chords for the early poems. Brecht's own primitive notation utilized no time signature or barlines, as the rhythm was to follow that of the words, which were not to be distorted when sung. Some of Brecht's texts are hardly more than tropes on songs by Wedekind; compare, for example, Wedekind's "Ich war ein Kind von fünfzehn Jahren" (*Lautenlieder: 53 Lieder mit eigenen und fremden Melodien* [Munich: Drei Masken Verlag, 1920]) with Brecht's "Surabaya Johnny" and "Nannas Lied" ("Meine Herren, mit siebzehn Jahren"), the latter set by both Eisler and Weill.

15 Zuckmayer's description of Brecht's cabaret performances is quoted by Willett in *Brecht in Context*, p. 152.

16 Quoted by Willett in *Brecht in Context*, p. 152. Willett identifies a number of popular tunes Brecht borrowed, including most incongruously both "There's a tavern in the town" and "Un bel di" for the "Benares Song."

17 Bertolt Brecht, *Tagebuch*, 26 August 1920; quoted in Lucchesi/Shull, *Musik bei Brecht*, p. 97.

18 *Berlin Börsen-Courier*, 9 December 1923; trans. Fuegi, *Chaos*, p. 15. See also Hanns Henry Jahn's description of the 1926 Berlin production of *Baal*, pp. 54–55.

19 Brecht, "Ueber die Verwendung von Musik für ein episches Theater"; trans. Willett, *Brecht on Theatre*, p. 84.

20 Eisler's comment was recorded by Hans Bunge in *Fragen Sie mehr über Brecht: Hanns Eisler im Gespräch* (Munich: Rogner and Bernhard, 1970), p. 210. Brecht introduced the descriptive term "dialectic" in the "Anmerkungen zur *Die Dreigroschenoper*," *Versuche* 3 (1931), but seldom used it thereafter until the end of his career. See Willett, *Brecht on Theatre*, p. 46.

21 For a biographical sketch of Bruinier, who was a student of Egon Petri and a friend of Klabund (Carola Neher's husband), see Joachim Lucchesi, "Franz S. Bruinier: Brecht's erster Komponist," *Das Magazin* [Berlin] 1 (January 1985), pp. 66–70. Bruiner's settings of nine songs survive in the Bertolt Brecht Archive, Berlin.

22 Weill previewed and reviewed the production for *Der deutsche Rundfunk* in March 1927; both are reprinted in Weill, *Musik und Theater*, pp. 248–50.

23 When Brecht published a revised text of the *Lehrstück* in 1930, he retitled it *Das Badener Lehrstück vom Einverständnis*. Hindemith also set Brecht's poem "Ueber das Frühjahr" for male chorus in 1929. Brecht vehemently disagreed with Hindemith's emphasis on the opportunity for collective amateur music-making (*Gemeinschaftsmusik*) within the new genre of the learning play and his de-emphasis of the text's content and significance. Their confrontation at the 1930 New Music Festival in Berlin over *Die Maßnahme* precluded the possibility of any further collaboration. See Gilbert, *Bertolt Brecht's Striving for Reason, Even in Music*, pp. 89–96.

24 "Deine Kompositionen fühle ich sogleich mit meinen Liedern identisch: die Musik nimmt nur, wie ein einströmendes Gas, den Luftballon mit in die Höhe. Bei andern Komponisten muß ich erst aufmerken, wie sie das Lied genommen, was sie daraus gemacht haben." Letters from Zelter to Goethe (7 April 1820) and Goethe to Zelter (11 May 1820) quoted by Wilhelm Bode in *Die Tonkunst in Goethes Leben* (Berlin: E. G. Mittler, 1912), pp. 180–81.

25 Eisler's Brecht-compositions are only one component within a large and diverse œuvre, and the Eisler of the String Quartet (1938) differs from the composer of *Die Mutter* (1931) as much as the Weill of Symphony No. 2 (1933–34) from the composer of *Lady in the Dark* (1940). David Drew has observed that "neither the power nor the extra-ordinary durability of Eisler's collaboration with Brecht would have been attainable but for the self-awareness and the mastery he had first achieved within Schoenberg's orbit and then developed on the tangential path he took in 1927. Theoretically, the post-Schoenbergian tangent presupposed the possiblity of re-entry. Eisler repeatedly availed himself of that possibility." See Drew, "Eisler and Austrian music," p. 29.

26 The scores on which Brecht collaborated for the original productions of *Mutter Courage und ihre Kinder* (1941), *Der kaukasische Kreidekreis* (1948), and *Der gute Mensch von Sezuan* (1943) achieved little identity after the plays' premieres and are seldom used in performances today. Paul Dessau subsequently wrote new scores for all of them, as well as for *Die Ausnahme und die Regel* (1948) and *Herr Puntila und sein Knecht Matti* (1949). It is important to distinguish between those works on which Brecht collaborated with composers (almost exclusively Weill and Eisler) in the actual planning and drafting and those to which the composer contributed only *ex post facto* incidental music subsequent to the conception and execution of the overall dramatic structure and content of the work. In

the case of the former – "joint" works from the *Mahagonny Songspiel* (1927) through *Die Rundköpfe und die Spitzköpfe* (1936) – it would be inconceivable to substitute a new score for the original, something which has now become common practice for the latter group.

27 Brecht's comment about Eisler is quoted in Willett, *Brecht in Context*, p. 162; his appraisal of Weill appears in the *Arbeitsjournal*, 7 October 1940; repr. in Lucchesi/Shull, *Musik bei Brecht*, p. 182. Other than the two "cantatas" *Vom Tod im Wald* and *Das Berliner Requiem*, outside the theater Weill composed only two songs with texts by Brecht. Eisler, in contrast, was a prolific composer of self-standing lieder, many with texts by Brecht.

28 Bertolt Brecht and Peter Suhrkamp, "Anmerkungen zur Oper *Augstieg und Fall der Stadt Mahagonny*, *Versuche* 2 (1930); trans. Willett, *Brecht on Theatre*, p. 37. Brecht continued: "So long as the arts are supposed to be 'fused' together, the various elements will all be equally degraded, and each will act as a mere 'feed' to the rest. The process of fusion extends to the spectator, who gets thrown into the melting pot too and becomes a passive (suffering) part of the total work of art. Witchcraft of this sort must of course be fought against. Whatever is intended to produce hypnosis, is likely to induce sordid intoxication, or creates fog, has got to be given up." Later, in "Kleines Organon für das Theater" (1948), Brecht subdivided the elements further and demotes music to lower status within the hierarchy. Note that the question "Which is the pretext for what?" is precisely the one which also occupied Wagner throughout his career; his own changing verdict prompted him to reverse the thesis of *Oper und Drama* (that music is the means and drama the end) and to disown the expression "music drama" by formulating the alternative "ersichtlich gewordene Taten der Musik" (events in music made visible) in *Ueber die Benennung "Musikdrama"* (1872). For an extended discussion of this point, see, with caution on musical issues, Brown, *Leitmotiv and Drama: Wagner, Brecht, and the Limits of "Epic" Theatre*.

29 Letter from Marc Blitzstein to Stella Simon, 28 January 1930; quoted by Eric A. Gordon in *Mark the Music: The Life and Work of Marc Blitzstein* (New York: St Martin's, 1989), p. 55.

30 "Ueber die Verwendung von Musik für ein episches Theater," in *Gesammelte Werke*, vol. 15, p. 480.

31 Ibid; trans. Willett, *Brecht on Theatre*, p. 87.

32 Brecht, "Texte für Musik," in *Gesammelte Werke*, vol. 19, p. 406; repr. in Lucchesi/Shull, *Musik bei Brecht*, pp. 150–51. The short essay is undated, but probably originated *ca.* 1934/35.

33 During the last decades, Brecht's objections to denying music social meaning and ascribing to it transcendental significance have been taken up and extended by numerous critics. See, for example, Susan McClary's foreword to Catherine Clément's *Opera or the Undoing of Women*, trans. Betsy Wing (Minneapolis: University of Minnesota Press, 1988), pp. ix–xviii.

34 Brecht, "Texte für Musik." Brecht even complained that "very seldom have I found my name on gramophone recordings and concert programs, and when it is there, then it's printed very small."

35 Edward T. Cone, *The Composer's Voice* (Berkeley: University of California Press, 1974), p. 45.

36 Hanns Eisler, "Bertolt Brecht und die Musik," *Sinn und Form* (1957), pp. 439–41; trans. Marjorie Meyer in *A Rebel in Music: Selected Writings*, ed. Manfred Grabs (New York:

International, 1978), pp. 173–74. Eisler concluded the essay: "Writing these lines I recall that Brecht accused me of having a skeptical and condescending attitude towards *Misuk*, his invention. Unfortunately he was right." See also Alexander Ringer, "*Kleinkunst* and *Küchenlied* in the socio-musical world of Kurt Weill," in *A New Orpheus*, pp. 37–59.

37 Felix Jackson, "Portrait of a quiet man: Kurt Weill, his life and his times," unpub. biography (photocopy in Weill-Lenya Research Center, New York), p. 110.

38 Bertolt Brecht, *Arbeitsjournal*, 16 October 1940; repr. in Lucchesi/Shull, *Musik bei Brecht*, p. 183.

39 'That was the time!' *Theatre Arts* (May 1956); repr. as "August 28, 1931," the foreword to Desmond Vesey and Eric Bentley's translation of *The Threepenny Opera* (New York: Grove Press, 1964), p. ix. George Davis derived the essay from interviews with Lenya and Elisabeth Hauptmann; the transcripts of those interviews and the typescript of the essay are now in the Weill-Lenya Research Center. The nature and extent of the few documented musical "borrowings" by Weill from Brecht are discussed by David Drew in *Kurt Weill: A Handbook* (London: Faber, 1987), pp. 201–05.

40 Ole Winding, "Kurt Weill i Exil," *Aften-Avisen* (Copenhagen), 21 June 1934; Ger. trans. in Weill, *Musik und Theater*, pp. 314–17.

41 Weill refers to *gestische Musik*. Eisler recalled that Brecht used the term *Gestus*, as opposed to *Geste*, as early as 1924, but it does not appear in his writings with reference to music until *ca.* 1930. For a chronological survey of Brecht's usage of *Gestus*, social *Gestus*, and *Grundgestus*, see Fowler, *Received Truths*, pp. 40–46.

42 In the absence of unambiguous definition by either Weill or Brecht, many critics have been forced to derive their own definitions on the unstable base of changing usage in their writings, thereby running the risk of combining statements from different periods that are, in fact, mutually exclusive. Martin Esslin has defined *Gestus* very simply, as "the clear and stylized expression of the social behaviour of human beings towards each other." (*Brecht: The Man and His Work* [Garden City, N.Y.: Doubleday, 1961], p. 134.) More recently Renate Voris has attempted to reconcile the conflicts inherent in Brecht's usage: she claims that *Gestus* "weaves together *Gest* (gesture) and *Grundgestus* (gist) . . . in an attempt to distance the signifier from the signified, the sign from the referent." See "Brecht's *Gestus*: the body in recess," paper delivered at 1989 MLA-IBS session, Washington, D.C.; abstract published in *Communications* 19 (Winter 1990), pp. 19–22. Shubei Hosokawa maintains that "*Gestus* condenses the narrative to be interpreted by the spectators, assigns a comprehensible form to the amorphous mass of the social process and interpersonal relationship, unravelling themselves on stage, and articulates the progressive development of the production of the multilinear network of events over the whole strata of the stage." See "Distance, Gestus, Quotation: *Aufstieg und Fall der Stadt Mahagonny* of Brecht and Weill," *International Review of the Aesthetics and Sociology of Music* 16 (1985), pp. 181–99. Perhaps the most valuable English-language discussion of problems presented by Gestus in Patrice Pavis, "On Brecht's notion of Gestus," trans. Susan Melrose, in *Semiotics of Drama and Theatre: New Perspectives in the Theory of Drama and Theatre*, ed. Herta Schmidt and Aloysius van Kesteren (Amsterdam: John Benjamins, 1984), pp. 292–303. For specific insight into *gestische Musik*, see Michael Morley, "Suiting the action to the word: some observations on *Gestus* and *Gestische Musik*," in *A New Orpheus*, pp. 183–201.

43 Brecht, *Arbeitsjournal*, 2 February 1941; reprinted in Lucchesi/Shull, *Musik bei Brecht*, p. 185.

44 Igor Stravinsky, *An Autobiography* [1936] (New York: Norton, 1962), pp. 150–51.

45 Weill, "Ueber den gestischen Charakter der Musik," *Die Musik* 21 (March 1929), pp. 419–23; trans. in Kim H. Kowalke, *Kurt Weill in Europe* (Ann Arbor: UMI Research Press, 1979), pp. 491–96. Although Weill claimed that "gestic music is, of course, in no way bound to the text," his examples tend to contradict this assertion.

46 "Ueber die Verwendung von Musik für ein episches Theater," *Gesammelte Werke*, vol. 15, p. 476.

47 "Vorwort zum Regiebuch der Oper *Aufstieg und Fall der Stadt Mahagonny*," *Anbruch* 12 (January 1930), p. 6.

48 Brecht had "borrowed" the name Mahagonny, as well as specific word-play for "Auf nach Mahagonny," from a popular song by Krauss-Elka and O. A. Alberts from 1921 entitled "Komm nach Mahagonne," subtitled in various publications and recordings either as an "Afrikanischer-" or "Amerikanischer-Shimmy." See Andreas Hauff, "Mahagonny. . . . Only a Made-Up Word?," *Kurt Weill Newsletter* 9 (Spring 1991), pp. 7–9. Weill's notation of Brecht's melody differs from both the *Taschenpostille* and *Hauspostille* versions; there is also a word inversion: "We must now say goodbye."

49 Theodor W. Adorno, ["Mahagonny"], *Anbruch* 14 (February–March 1932), p. 53.

50 Weill had already inserted a similar coloratura embellishment in the vocal part used by Irene Eden at the premiere in Baden-Baden. In a cast originally comprising only opera singers, Lenya had been an eleventh-hour substitute. See Drew, *Kurt Weill: a handbook*, p. 172. In the opera, the "Alabama Song" recurs in the finales to both Act I and Act II, where, according to Adorno, "it is revealed as the lament of the creature in the face of its isolation."

51 See, for example, Adorno's review of *Die Dreigroschenoper* ("Zur Dreigroschenoper," *Die Musik* 21 [March 1929], pp. 424–28; trans. Stephen Hinton in *Kurt Weill: The Threepenny Opera* [Cambridge Opera Handbook, Cambridge University Press, 1990], pp. 129–33) and the Berlin production of *Aufstieg und Fall der Stadt Mahagonny* (1932) (trans. [with many errors] by Jamie Owen Daniel, *Discourse* 12 [Fall–Winter 1989–90], pp. 70–77).

52 In "Der Messingkauf," the 200-page, unfinished "four-sided conversation about a new way of making theatre," Brecht described his company: "The Augsburger's theatre was very small. It performed very few plays. It trained very few actors. The chief actresses were Weigel, Neher, and Lenya. The chief actors were Homolka, Lorre, and Lingen. The singer Busch likewise belonged to this theatre, but he seldom appeared on the stage. The chief scene designer was Caspar Neher, no relation to the actress. The musicians were Weill and Eisler." See Willett, *Brecht on Theatre*, p. 173.

53 For a comprehensive discography of these recordings, see Bernd Meyer-Rähnitz, "Drei Groschen und mehr: Werke von Brecht-Weill auf 78er-Schallplatten," *Fox auf 78* (Autumn 1987), pp. 44–50; (Spring 1988), pp. 24–28. Also Jürgen Schebera, "Kurt Weill's early recordings: 1928–1933," *Kurt Weill Newsletter* 4 (Spring 1986), pp. 6–9. The principal re-releases of these early recordings on compact disc are Mastersound DFCDI–100 and Capriccio 10346 & 10347. Two of Lenya's recorded renditions of the "Alabama Song" are included on Capriccio 10347; especially revelatory is the "Querschnitt aus der Oper *Aufstieg und Fall der Stadt Mahagonny*" conducted by Hans Sommer.

54 Those works that Weill composed on Brecht texts he had assembled without collaboration, including *Das Berliner Requiem* and *Vom Tod im Wald*, were left untouched, of course.

55 "Anmerkungen zur Oper *Mahagonny*," trans. Willett, pp. 41–42. For a comparison of Weill's and Brecht's comments on *Mahagonny*, see Stephen Hinton, "The concept of epic opera: theoretical anomalies in the Brecht-Weill partnership," in *Festschrift Carl Dahlhaus* (Laaber: Laaber, 1988), pp. 285–94.

56 In an interview with himself dating from *ca.* 1933, Brecht answered the question, "What, in your opinion, accounted for the success of *Die Dreigroschenoper*? I'm afraid it was everything that didn't matter to me: the romantic plot, the love story, the music. . . ." See Kim H. Kowalke, "Accounting for success: misunderstanding *Die Dreigroschenoper*," *The Opera Quarterly* 6 (Spring 1989), pp. 18–38; and Hinton, "Misunderstanding *The Threepenny Opera*" in Cambridge Opera Handbook, pp. 181–192.

57 Hinton, Cambridge Opera Handbook, pp. 19, 57. The description of the piece as a "comic literary operetta" is the original producer's, Ernst Josef Aufricht.

58 Brecht, "Anmerkungen zur *Die Dreigroschenoper*," trans. Willett, *Brecht on Theatre*, pp. 44–45. Note that Brecht is so advising all the actors, not just those playing Peachum and the Streetsinger, whose roles lend themselves to this sort of delivery because of the nature and limitations of the musical demands placed on them.

59 See Carolyn Abbate, *Unsung Voices: Opera and Musical Narrative in the Nineteenth Century* (Princeton: Princeton University Press, 1991), pp. 10–11. Nicholas Deutsch has suggested another basis for objecting to operatically-trained voices: "We perceive the vibrational richness of classically trained singing as an expression of the human soul; it, in turn, connects the listener to a direct sense of transcendental reality, which is calmer, more serene, more compassionate, more impersonal (in the positive sense) than the emotional, mental, and physical struggles of our daily existence. . . . Warm and compassionate tone is filled with an unspoken certainty that unconditional love stands ready to suffuse our hearts and minds in a potentially transformational way. What could possibly be more inappropriate to Mr. Peachum and *Die Dreigroschenoper*? . . . The world of the piece is haunted by the *absence* of transcendental connectedness, whether to a higher power or between human beings. . . . So the strengths of an opera singer are not only irrelevant, but a hindrance to a convincing portrayal." See *Kurt Weill Newsletter* 9 (Spring 1991), pp. 25–26.

60 "Im orchester, klein wie es sein mag, liegt Ihre chance als musiker, die melodie mußten Sie dem unmusiker, dem schauspieler, ausliefern, was können Sie sich von diesem menschen erwarten? Ihr orchester ist Ihre truppe, Ihr gang, Ihr fester punkt, es ist wahr, es muß dem unmusiker oben auch noch die stützpunkte geben, sonst fällt er um, aber jedes instrument, das Sie freikriegen von diesem dienst, ist für Sie gewonnen, für die musik, herr! bedenken Sie, die instrumente sprechen nicht per 'ich', sondern per 'er' oder 'sie', was zwingt Sie, die gefühle des 'ich' auf der bühne zu teilen? wo sind seine eigenen? Sie sind berechtigt, Ihre eigene stellung zu dem thema des liedes einzunehmen, selbst die unterstützung, die Sie leihen, kann sich anderer argumente bedienen, emanzipieren Sie Ihr orchester!" Brecht, *Arbeitsjournal*, 2 February 1941; reprinted in Lucchesi/Shull, *Musik bei Brecht*, p. 185. In his notes to *Mahagonny*, Brecht had asserted that "the orchestral apparatus needs to be cut down to thirty specialists or less." For a concise history of the term "lyrische Ich" and a comparison with Cone's use of "persona" in *The Composer's Voice*, see Ann Clark Fehn and Jürgen Thym, "Who is speaking? Edward T. Cone's concept of persona and Wolfgang von Schweintz's setting of poems by Sarah Kirsch," *Journal of Musicological Research* 11 (1991), pp. 1–3, 18–19.

61 Brecht, "Anmerkungen zur Oper *Mahagonny*," trans. Willett, *Brecht on Theatre*, p. 38. Because often the performer is "reporting" rather than experiencing first-hand, many of Brecht's songs may be sung interchangeably by various characters within a given play or even in different plays. Thus, at different times in the run of the original production of *Die Dreigroschenoper*, Polly and Lucy both sang the "Barbarasong," and in later years Lenya appropriated "Seeräuber-Jenny" for Jenny's role. For a practical application of Brecht's theories to her own renditions of five songs by Weill, see Roswitha Trexler (with collaboration by Fritz Hennenberg), "Was der Sänger von Brecht lernen kann oder meine Auffassung von Weill," *Brecht-Jahrbuch 1979*, ed. John Fuegi, Reinhold Grimm, and Jost Hermand (Frankfurt a.M.: Suhrkamp, 1979), pp. 30–45.

62 The Berliner Ensemble's "Bühnenfassung" of *Mahagonny* was credited to Manfred Karge and Matthias Langhoff, but the musical arrangements by Dieter Hosalla were uncredited, and thus subject to confusion with Weill's almost unknown originals. "Das kleine Mahagonny" has been preserved on recording, Litera 8 60 034–035. For further details of the production and its subsequent influence, see Drew, *Kurt Weill: A Handbook*, pp. 174–75.

63 Thomas Mann, "Ueber die Kunst Richard Wagners," *Gesammelte Werke* (Frankfurt a.M.: Suhrkamp, 1974), pp. 841–42; trans. Brown, *Leitmotiv and Drama*, p. 28. See also Marianne Kesting, "Wagner/Meyerhold/Brecht oder die Erfindung des 'epischen Theaters'," in *Brecht-Jahrbuch 1977*, pp. 111–30.

64 Fuegi, *Chaos*, p. 16–17. Brecht was, of course, paraphrasing Goethe's *Faust*, Part I, verses 2038–9, where Mephistopheles observes to the student: "Grau, teurer Freund, ist alle Theorie/Und grün des Lebens goldner Baum."

65 Johann Harrer's recollection, quoted by Gilbert, *Bertolt Brecht's Striving for Reason*, p. 11.

6 GERMAN MUSICOLOGY AND EARLY-MUSIC PERFORMANCE

1 W.L. Guttsman, *Workers' Culture in Weimar Germany* (New York: Berg, 1990), p. 158.

2 Government support in Prussia went only so far as to establish the Preußische Volksliedkommission, which in 1924 co-sponsored the publication of *Landschaftliche Volkslieder* (edited by Johannes Bolte, Max Friedländer, and John Meier) along with the private Vereine deutscher Volksliedkunde. Friedländer was then appointed chairman of the Staatliche Kommission für das deutsche Volkslied-Buch, but this organization produced no editions.

3 For a discussion of isolationism, see my article "The Deutsche Musikgesellschaft, 1918–1938," *Journal of Musicological Research* 11 (1991), pp. 151–76.

4 Berlin (1904), Munich (1909), Bonn (1915), Halle (1918), Breslau (1920), Göttingen (1920), Leipzig (1920), Heidelberg (1921), Kiel (1928), Freiburg (1929), and Cologne (1932).

5 Fritz Ringer, *The Decline of the German Mandarins: The German Academic Community, 1890–1933* (Cambridge, Mass.: Harvard University Press, 1969), pp. 67–75.

6 Sächsisches Ministerium für Volksbildung to Philosophische Fakultät Leipzig, 25 April 1932, and Dekan der Philosophischen Fakultät to Ministerium, 12 May 1932, Universitätsarchiv Leipzig (UAL) PA 661, pp. 21–23, Dekan to Kroyer, 20 January 1933, UAL B2/20[21], pp. 112–15, and Dekan to Minister, 13 February 1933, UAL B2/20[21], pp. 156–157a; Engel to Sandberger, 20 September 1933, and draft of Sandberger's

answer to Engel, 22 September 1933, Adolf Sandberger Papers (Ana 431), Manuscript Division, Bavarian State Library, Munich.

7 The first cut, introduced in December 1930, reduced salaries by 6%, then by 10% in June 1932, and ended in an overall reduction of 15% by July 1932. Form letters from Verwaltungsdirektor of the university to Max Friedländer, 24 January 1931, 11 February 1931, 1 July 1931, 2 June 1932, and 27 July 1932, Universitätsarchiv Berlin (UAB), Friedländer file.

8 Preußischer Minister für Wissenschaft, Kunst und Volksbildung to Moser, 4 June 1933, UAB Moser file; to Wolf, same date, UAB Wolf file.

9 Hermann Kretzschmar, *Musikalische Zeitfragen* (Leipzig: Peters, 1903), p. 79.

10 Arnold Schering, "Musikwissenschaft und Kunst der Gegenwart," in *Bericht über den I. Musikwissenschaftlichen Kongress der Deutschen Musikgesellschaft in Leipzig* (Leipzig: Breitkopf & Härtel, 1926), pp. 13–14.

11 Mersmann, "Volk und Musik," *AM* 45 (1918), pp. 511–13.

12 Egon Wellesz, "Die sozialen Grundlagen der gegenwärtigen Musikpflege," *Der Friede* 3 (1919), pp. 300–01.

13 Hans Joachim Moser, "Die neue Reichsmusikzunft," *AM* 49 (1922), pp. 704–05, and Hermann Unger, "Musikprobleme der Zeit," *Deutsches Musikjahrbuch* 1 (1923), pp. 36–37.

14 Johannes Wolf, "Musikwissenschaft und musikwissenschaftlicher Unterricht," in *Festschrift Hermann Kretzschmar zum 70. Geburtstag* (Leipzig: Peters, 1918), pp. 174–79.

15 *AM* 45 (1918), pp. 531–33. This tactic of seeking the attention of a broader audience through the popular press was facilitated in the post-war period by the growing number of non-academic music journals.

16 Georg Schünemann, *Geschichte der deutschen Schulmusik* (Leipzig: Kistner & Siegel, 1927).

17 Ernst Bücken, ed., *Handbuch der Musikerziehung* (Potsdam: Akademische Verlagsgesellschaft Athenaion, 1931).

18 Hans Joachim Moser, "Zum Musikunterricht an den Volksschulen," *Die Musik* 20 (1928), pp. 669–70; and Hans Albrecht, "Zur inneren Lage im Privat-Musikunterricht," ibid, pp. 671–72.

19 Moser, "Aus musikalischer Volksbildungsarbeit," *AM* 50 (1923), pp. 683–84.

20 Moser, *Das musikalische Denkmälerwesen in Deutschland* (Kassel: Bärenreiter, 1952), pp. 20–22.

21 Bücken to "Herr Geheimrat," 25 April 1922, Universitätsarchiv Köln (UAK) Zug. 9/285. Later that year, Bücken also enumerated for the Prussian authorities the activities of the institute that served the interests of the Rhineland, including Beethoven research (responding specifically to Belgian claims that Beethoven had Belgian lineage); cataloging of music performance in the Rhineland in the past century in order to study the "musicality of the Rhineland Germans"; and public lectures and performances. Bücken to Eckert (Kuratorium), 20 December 1922, UAK Zug. 9/285.

22 Hermann Matzke, "Bericht über die zweite Jahresversammlung," *Archiv für Musikwissenschaft* 2 (1919–1920), pp. 444–45.

23 Ibid, p. 22.

24 "Mitteilungen," *ZfM* 7 (1924–25), pp. 252–53.

25 . . . daß auch die Musikwissenschaft an der großen, allen Universitätswissenschaften obliegenden gemeinsamen Aufgabe teilhat, die Menschheit aus der gegenwärtigen

Zersplitterung zu einem einheitlichen, ganzen Leben zu erziehen. Staat und Stadt haben uns diese Stätte der Arbeit gegeben – auch wir arbeiten für Staat und Volk!" Theodor Kroyer, "Die Wiedererweckung des historischen Klangbildes in der musikalischen Denkmälerpraxis," *Mitteilungen der Internationalen Gesellschaft für Musikwissenschaft* 2 (1930), p. 80.

26 Max Seiffert's activities of the 1920s in the *DDT* commission had remedied the problem of regional imbalance to some extent by supervising a more even distribution of local research. Moser, *Das musikalische Denkmälerwesen,* pp. 24–25.

27 *Bericht über den I. Musikwissenschaftlichen Kongress der Deutschen Musikgesellschaft in Leipzig,* pp. 3–6, 381–404.

28 "Mitteilungen," *ZfM* 12 (1929–30), p. 645.

29 "Mitteilungen," *ZfM* 15 (1932–33), p. 287.

30 "Mitteilungen," *ZfM* 14 (1931–32), p. 384.

31 "Mitteilungen," *ZfM* 15 (1932–33), pp. 191–92.

32 "Mitteilungen," *ZfM* 7 (1924–25), p. 604.

33 Hans Engel, "Organisationsfragen der Musikwissenschaft," *Zeitschrift der Deutschen Musik-gesellschaft* 14 (1931–32), pp. 272–76.

34 Engel, "Organisationsfragen," pp. 274–75.

35 Gustav Becking's collegium at the university in Erlangen was praised in 1929 for its successes in Bayreuth, Würzburg, Coburg, Munich, and other cities. (Ludwig Unterholzner, "Um das musikwissenschaftliche Seminar der Universität Erlangen," *AM* 56 [1929], p. 478).

36 Philosophiche Fakultät to Kulturministerium, 21 June 1915, UAL PA 925, p. 35.

37 Dekan (Philosophische Fakultät) to Kulturministerium, 20 December 1919, UAL PA 272, p. 17.

38 Krueger (Psychologisches Institut der Universität Leipzig) to Philosophische Fakultät, 27 July 1931, UAL PA 661, p. 14.

39 *Chronik der Rheinischen Friedrich-Wilhelms-Universität zu Bonn* (1919–1920), p. 70.

40 See Hans Joachim Moser, "Noch ein Wort zur musikalischen Jugendbewegung," *AM* 53 (1926), pp. 381–82, and the response by Karl Hasse, "Zur Frage der Führung in der Jugendmusik," ibid, pp. 527–28.

41 *DJD,* pp. 1009, 1016–18.

42 Ibid, pp. 168–69, 393.

43 Ibid, pp. 170, 748, 752, 895.

44 Ibid, p. 195.

45 Ibid, p. 318.

46 Walther Hensel, "Von Gregorianischen Melodien," *Frankensteiner Liederbuch* 1 (1928); repr. in *DJD,* pp. 337–38.

47 Fritz Jöde, "Alte Madrigale und andere a cappella Gesänge aus dem 16. und 17. Jahrhundert," *Hausmusik* 14/16 (1921); repr. in *DJD,* p. 329.

48 Wilhelm Thomas, "Lied am Alltag," *Die Singgemeinde* 2/29; repr. in *DJD,* pp. 352–54.

49 Hermann Reichenbach, "Unsere Stellung zu Bach," *Musikantengilde* 7/25; repr. in *DJD,* pp. 330–34; Felix Messerschmid, "Von Johann Sebastian Bach, unserem Meister," *Die Schildgenossen* 6/24; repr. in *DJD,* pp. 335–37.

50 Wilhelm Kamlah, "Nach dem zweiten deutschen Heinrich-Schütz-Fest in Celle 15.–17. März 1929," *Die Singgemeinde* 4/29; repr. in *DJD,* pp. 348–52.

51 Hermann Erpf, "Anmerkungen zur Bearbeitung und Wiedergabe alter Musik," *Musikantengilde* 3/27; repr. in *DJD*, pp. 341–43; Reinhold Heyden, "Alte Chorpraxis heute," *Melos* 5/29; repr. in *DJD*, pp. 343–47.

52 See Robert Treml, "Wie können wir Lauten und Gitarren erfolgreich in unser Musizieren einbeziehen?" *Collegium Musicum* 2/32, repr. in *DJD*, pp. 358–60; "Österreichische Blockflöten- und Gambenspieltage, Ostern 1932," *Collegium Musicum* 5/32, repr. in *DJD*, p. 361; Bruno Lehmann, "Abendspielwoche für Gitarre und Laute in Kassel," *Zeitschrift für Schulmusik* 1/31, repr. in *DJD*, pp. 362–63; Herman Reichenbach, "Blasinstrument," *Der Kreis* 1932/33, repr. in *DJD*, pp. 364–67; Fritz Reusch, "Von unseren Blockflöten," *Der Kreis* 7/29, repr. in *DJD*, pp. 367–68; W. Kurka, "Blockflötentagung," *Der Kreis* 2/31, repr. in *DJD*, pp. 370–71; Karl Gofferje, "Blockflöten, die große Mode," *Die Singgemeinde* 5/31, repr. in *DJD*, pp. 371–74; Peter Harlan, "Bärenreitergamben und Bärenreiterfideln aus den Peter Harlan-Werkstätten, Markneukirchen," *Lied und Volk* 8/31, repr. in *DJD*, pp. 375–76; "Das Klavichord," *Die Singgemeinde* 6/27, repr. in *DJD*, pp. 377–79; Herbert Just, "Die Barockinstrumente in der Gegenwart," *Musik und Gesellschaft* 1/30, repr. in *DJD*, p. 383; and Konrad Ameln, "Alte Musik auf alten Instrumenten," *Die Singgemeinde* 6/31, repr. in *DJD*, pp. 384–86.

53 Rudolf Steglich, "Hugo Riemann als Förderer der Hausmusik durch Neuausgaben alter Tonwerke," *Zeitschrift für Musik* 86 (1918), pp. 178–81.

54 Rudolf Steglich, "Hugo Riemann als Wiedererwecker älterer Musik," *ZfM* 1 (1918–1919), pp. 605–07.

55 Eugen Schmitz, "Die Zukunft der Hausmusik," *Hochland* 17 (1919–20), pp. 254–56.

56 Fritz Jöde, "Jugendmusikbewegung und Hausmusik," *Die Musik* 24 (1932), pp. 564–69.

57 Georg Schünemann, "Die Lage der Hausmusik," ibid, pp. 561–64.

58 Peter Raabe, "Wege zur Belebung der Hausmusik," *AM* 60 (1933), pp. 353–55.

59 Schünemann, "Lage der Hausmusik," pp. 562–63.

60 *DJD*, pp. 460–61.

61 Karl Blessinger, "Repertoirebildung und Gebrauchsmusik," *AM* 56 (1929), p. 311; Schünemann, "Lage der Hausmusik," p. 561.

62 Edward Yarnell Hartshorne, Jr., *The German Universities and National Socialism* (Cambridge, Mass.: Harvard University Press, 1937), pp. 49–52, 101–05, 127–30.

63 Ibid, pp. 106–25.

64 For a detailed account of the transformation, see chapter 5 of my "Trends in German musicology, 1918–1945: the effects of methodological, ideological, and institutional change on the writing of music history," (Ph.D. diss., Yale University, 1991).

65 Heinrich Besseler, "Die Neuordnung des musikalischen Denkmalwesens," *Deutsche Wissenschaft, Erziehung und Volksbildung: Amtsblatt des Reichs- und Preußischen Ministeriums für Wissenschaft, Erziehung und Volksbildung und der Unterrichtsverwaltung der anderen Länder* 1 (1935), pp. 187–89.

66 Besseler and Sandberger to Reichs- und Preußischer Minister für Wissenschaft, Erziehung und Volksbildung [n.d.], p. 3, Archive of the Staatliches Institut für Musikforschung-Preußischer Kulturbesitz.

67 Hans Engel, "Die Leistungen der deutschen Musikwissenschaft," *Geistige Arbeit* 6 (1939), p. 7.

68 "Der einzelne Musikhistoriker kann und darf nicht mehr abseits stehen und seinen eigenen Forschungsneigungen nachgehen. Die Stunde ist da, wo die Gesamtheit der deutschen Musikwissenschaft und der ihr Nahestehenden Hand anlegen muß, um das 'Erbe der deutschen Musik' vollständig und im wissenschaftlichen Sinne zu erfassen und es in seinen charakteristischen Leistungen dem Volk zugänglich zu machen." Rudolf Gerber, "Die Aufgaben der Musikwissenschaft im Dritten Reich," *ZfM* 102 (1935), p. 500.

69 "Die deutsche Musikwissenschaft hat eines der edelsten Güter der deutschen Kultur zu hüten. Von je ist die Musik eine der lebendigsten und eigenartigsten Prägungen des deutschen Geistes gewesen. Das deutsche Volk hat sich und seinem Schicksal in der Musik seit Jahrhunderten eine 'Siegesallee' großartigster Denkmäler gesetzt. Mit dieser Tatsache ist einer Musikforschung, die es mit ihren Pflichten gegen Volk und Staat ernst nimmt, die Ausrichtung vorgezeichnet. Das Erbe der deutschen Musik diktiert seinen Auftrag." Friedrich Blume, "Deutsche Musikwissenschaft," *Deutsche Wissenschaften. Dem Führer und Reichskanzler zum 50. Geburtstag* (Leipzig 1939), p. 16.

70 Eugen Schmitz applauded the revival of early lute music, which provided access to one of the forms of *Hausmusik* that would be economically feasible by virtue of the inexpensive production of guitars. Schmitz, "Zukunft der Hausmusik," pp. 254–55.

71 Blessinger, "Repertoirebildung," p. 311.

72 Engel, "Leistungen," p. 8.

73 Richard Petzoldt, "Musikwissenschaft als Hemmschuh?" *AM* 65 (1938), pp. 67–68.

7 JAZZ RECEPTION IN WEIMAR GERMANY: IN SEARCH OF A SHIMMY FIGURE

1 By "legitimate jazz" I mean the music now called such by jazz historians, involving solo or group improvisation, a New Orleans-style instrumental ensemble, a rhythmic basis of triplet swing, and a repertoire of New Orleans "standards" and 1920s popular songs. This is to be distinguished from the clipped duplet style of ragtime or the many commercial imitations, which, however, were all known as jazz at the time. For the purposes of this essay, "jazz" refers to these commercial surrogates, whether American or German. One author who well understands the distinction and avoids the word jazz entirely in favor of "dance music" is Kim Kowalke, in *Kurt Weill in Europe* (Ann Arbor: UMI Research Press, 1979).

2 The leisure habits of young working-class Germans are admirably analyzed in Detlev J. K. Peukert, *Jugend zwischen Krieg und Krise: Lebenswelt von Arbeiterjungen in der Weimarer Republik* (Cologne: Bund-Verlag, 1987). The remaining socio-historical statistics will be documented below as necessary.

3 Paul Bernhard, *Jazz: eine musikalische Zeitfrage* (Munich: Delphin-Verlag, 1927), the first book-length study of jazz in German. This fascinating mixture of historical myth-making, impassioned advocacy, and practical suggestions for the dance-band arranger, written in the wake of Paul Whiteman's first European tour, is thought to have been the work of the musicologist Bernhard Diebold.

4 Ernst Krenek, *Jonny spielt auf*, piano-vocal score (Vienna: Universal, 1926), pp. 26ff. The *Holztrommel*, called simply *Holz* in the autograph score (Vienna, Nationalbibliothek, Leihg. 1 UE 641, p. 53), is often given to a tom-tom or slit drum today. In fact, as a glance at Egg's contemporary dictionary of jazz terminology confirms, it was simply

the 1920s German term for a woodblock. (See Bernhard Egg, *Jazz-Fremdwörterbuch* [Leipzig: Ehrler, 1927], p. 47.)

5 Herbert Peyser, "Jonny over there", *Modern Music* 6 (January–February 1929), pp. 32–34.

6 See T. Dennis Brown's definitive *History and Analysis of Jazz Drumming to 1942* (Ph.D. diss., University of Michigan, 1976). Jazz woodblock patterns differ fundamentally from the Jonny figure, nor is there anything resembling this figure in the ragtime drumming of Buddy Gilmore.

7 Karol Rathaus, *Der letzte Pierrot*, piano-vocal score (Vienna: Universal, 1927), p. 30.

8 *Duke Bluebeard's Castle* (1911) and *The Wooden Prince* (1914–16).

9 Wilhelm Grosz, *Baby in der Bar*, Op. 23, piano score (Vienna: Universal, 1927). Anticipating a possible hit along the lines of *Jonny's Blues*, Universal published the shimmy separately in 1928. Example 7.4 is taken from bars 23ff. of this separate print, Example 7.5 from the first page of the piano score.

10 Wilhelm Grosz, *Achtung, Aufnahme!* Op. 25, piano-vocal score (Vienna: Universal, 1930), p. 5.

11 Pencil sketch in Weill-Lenya Research Center, Beineke Rare Book Library, Yale University, Box 24, Folder 359; see also David Drew, *Kurt Weill: a Handbook* (Berkeley and Los Angeles: University of California Press, 1987), pp. 165–66.

12 Kurt Weill, *Aufstieg und Fall der Stadt Mahagonny*, piano-vocal score, ed. David Drew (Leipzig: Peters, 1969), p. 236.

13 It is tempting to speculate whether Weill deliberately drew on the Krenek figure and recast it into a negative counterpart, just as he drew on *Götterdämmerung* for the rhythmic pattern (and the final conflagration) of the finale. The stylistic similarities – an isolated "thematic" rhythm, a solo percussion instrument taken from the jazz trap set – are striking enough. But even more so are the almost deliberate dissimilarities: the figure introduces Jonny as a vital and impulsive *Naturkind*, a panacea for the stricken culture of post-war Europe, but takes leave of the defeated Jimmy, and with him the commercialized post-war German culture for which he and the Mahagonny of Act 2 stand. Krenek's mindless shimmy, it would seem, has become a pensive dirge in a process that reflects not only the fundamental difference between these two operas, but also the changes in the reception of American dance music as a whole during the Weimar period.

14 Kurt Weill, "Lied der Seeräuber-Jenny" in *Die Dreigroschenoper*, quoted from *Brecht Liederbuch*, ed. Fritz Henneberg (Frankfurt a.M.: Suhrkamp, 1984), pp. 56ff.

15 The German term *Kunstjazz* was coined at the time for mixtures of art and commercial music; see especially Alfred Baresel ("Kunst-Jazz," *Melos* 7 [1928], p. 356), who went to some lengths to elaborate the concept and distinguish it from symphonic jazz à la Gershwin and Whiteman. It deserves to be accepted in academic parlance today. For its commercial counterpart, the term *Tanzjazz*, coined by Heinrich Strobel and Frank Warschauer in "Interessante Jazzschallplatten" (*Melos* 9 [1930], p. 482), might be adopted.

16 It is seldom noticed that Ansermet's celebrated paean of 1919 to Sidney Bechet was originally published in a minor Swiss literary journal, and only became well known after its republication in Paris in 1938. It therefore had no effect on the jazz reception of the 1920s. Though this great jazz soloist had at least two long tenures in Berlin, leading a band at Haus Vaterland and even appearing (anonymously) in an early

German "talkie", he was unknown by name to the public. Only one reviewer of Bechet's Berlin appearances among Josephine Baker's retinue thought his name worth mentioning: Ottomar Starke, "Revue Nègre," *Der Querschnitt* 6 (1926), pp. 118–20.

17 Strobel and Warschauer, "Interessante Jazzschallplatten." This short review belatedly introduced the Weimar public to Ellington and Armstrong and clearly set them apart from commercialized white – and black – *Tanzjazz*.

18 Kurt Weill, "Tanzmusik," *Der deutsche Rundfunk* 411 (14 March 1926), pp. 732–33. Weill apparently drew his notion of black–American jazz from the "revue bands" of Wooding and Hopkins. There is no indication that he was aware of the then leading practitioners of legitimate jazz: indeed, he explicitly denies its potential as a vehicle for individual expression.

19 *Zeugen des Jahrhunderts: Porträts aus dem Musikerleben – Hans Heinz Stuckenschmidt, Ernst Krenek, Rolf Liebermann*, ed. Karl B. Schnelting (Frankfurt: Fischer, 1987), p. 60: "Der wirkliche Jazz war noch gar nicht bekannt in Europa. Aber wir haben alles, was aus Amerika kam, als Jazz klassifiziert."

20 For a superb study of the non-musical meanings of the term "jazz" in Weimar Germany's mass media see Reinhard Fark, *Die missachtete Botschaft: Publizistische Aspekte des Jazz im soziokulturellen Wandel* (Berlin: Spiess, 1971).

21 Weill-Lenya Research Center, Beineke Rare Book Library, Yale University, Box 35, Folder 522, and Box 36, Folder 547. The former, rather than being an incomplete draft (as David Drew claims), consists of two complete numbers in piano score, the second of which is texted. The latter, dating somewhat later, bears a close stylistic resemblance to rehearsal number 84 of *Aufstieg und Fall der Stadt Mahagonny* ("Das sind die Jimmies, Jimmies, Jimmies aus Alaska"), which it preceded by half a decade.

22 David Drew, *Kurt Weill: A Handbook* (Berkeley and Los Angeles: University of California Press, 1987), pp. 129–30 and 157–8. The extremely early date of 1921 given to the first example, justified by biographical considerations, would make Weill's interest in jazz antedate Krenek's, who did not take up lighter forms until one year later.

23 For import figures see Dietrich Schulz-Köhn, *Die Schallplatte auf dem Weltmarkt* (Berlin: Verlag Reher, 1940). In 1926, for example, at the peak of the jazz craze in Germany, a total of only 15,747 records were imported from the USA, of which only a fraction were related to jazz (pp. 152–53).

24 Alfred Baresel, the leading practical authority on German jazz, argued unheeded for years that jazz violinists should take up the saxophone, saying that "lead violins are characteristic of Viennese dance music, not jazz" (Führende Geigen sind ein Merkmal der Wiener Tanzmusik, nicht des Jazz). See *Das Jazz-Buch* (Leipzig: Zimmermann, 4th edn 1926), p. 33.

25 Horst H. Lange, *Die deutsche "78er"-Diskographie* (Berlin: Colloquium, 1966; rev. 2nd edn 1978).

26 Surprisingly, jazz reception continued unabated in Germany during the Nazi years under the name of Swing. Records by Armstrong and many others on the Okeh and Vocalion labels were sent via the matrix-exchange program to the German company Odeon, where they appeared in a special "Odeon Swing Music Series". See also *"Swing Heil!": Jazz im Nationalsozialismus*, ed. Bernd Polster (Berlin: Transit, 1989).

27 Jelly Roll Morton, *The Chant*, German Electrola EG. 383, recorded in Chicago, 1926.

28 A superficial reading of Lange's catalogue misled so reputable a historian as Susan C. Cook, who found that "German audiences could . . . obtain American records with little trouble" and that "interested composers and musicians would have had access to the top-quality early recordings of King Oliver, Louis Armstrong and his Hot Five, Mamie Smith, and Bix Beiderbecke"; see her *Opera for a New Republic: The Zeitopern of Krenek, Weill, and Hindemith* (Ann Arbor: UMI Research Press, 1988), p. 60. In fact, only four Mamie Smith recordings were pressed in Germany, all of them under the collective pseudonym "American Jazz Band" for sale to undiscriminating consumers in department stores. Hence there was no way to order a Mamie Smith recording under her name, or to recognize a recording as hers. Of Armstrong's fifty-odd Hot Five titles only six appeared in Germany during the 1920s.

29 The inner workings of the matrix-exchange program and the international recording conglomerates during the 1920s are revealingly described by Schultz-Köhn (*Die Schallplatte*), an insider with access to figures and sources that no longer exist today.

30 Mezz Mezzrow and Bernard Wolfe, *Really the Blues* (London: Secker & Warburg, 1946), p. 195.

31 The *Hauptverzeichnis der Parlophon-, Beka-, Lindström American Record-, Lindex-Musikplatten* for 1925–26 is dominated by Sam Lanin, Eddie Elkins, "Markel's Orchestra," and, as always, Vincent Lopez. Its two discs of legitimate jazz, by King Oliver and Erskine Tate, in no way stand out from the hundreds of commercial titles. The "American-Jazz-Band" heading in Odeon's *Deutsches Hauptverzeichnis 1926/27*, issued at the height of the German jazz craze by the leading German participant in the matrix-exchange program, has nothing of jazz interest at all apart from one disc by the Arkansaw [sic] Travellers and two by the Goofus Five.

32 Theodor Adorno, "Über Jazz" [1937], *Musikalische Schriften* 4 (Frankfurt a.M.: Suhrkamp, 1982), p. 83: "die Haut der Neger [ist] so gut wie das Silber der Saxophone ein koloristischer Effekt."

33 These figures and the following were obtained in a telephone conversation on 6 October 1988 with Horst Lange in Berlin, who had access to the companies' files in the years following World War II. The files were destroyed when these companies transferred from Berlin to the West following the partition of Germany. For comparison purposes, American race records were issued in runs of 11,000 for sale to the black-American market alone; see Klaus Kuhnke, Manfred Miller and Peter Schultze, *Geschichte der Pop-Musik*, vol. 1 (Lilienthal-Bremen: Eres Verlag, 1976), and Paul Oliver, *Songsters and Saints: Vocal Traditions on Race Records* (Cambridge: Cambridge University Press, 1984).

34 Amusing but by no means untypical examples of the low quality of jazz programming in Weimar Germany's radio broadcasts are provided by the Münster station ("moderne Tänze für Balalaika-Jazz-Band") and the Hamburg station ("Im Rhythmus des Jazz: Verstärktes Fledermaus-Orchester"). See Fark, *Die missachtete Botschaft*, pp. 159–60.

35 Krenek himself began work on *Jonny spielt auf* during a floor show in the Zurich luxury hotel Baur au Lac, which pioneered the live broadcasting of dance music; see *Zeugen des Jahrhunderts*, p. 60, and Heinrich Baumgartner, *"Jazz" in den zwanziger Jahren in Zürich: Zur Entstehung und Verwendung einer populärkulturellen Bezeichnung* (Zurich: Hug, 1989). This kind of prettified jazz, known in certain circles as "Hotelmusik", became part of the dramaturgical stock-in-trade of Weimar opera composers, from Weill's *Royal Palace* to Eugen d'Albert's *Die schwarze Orchidee*.

36 See Bernd Hoffmann, "Jazz im Radio der frühen Jahre," in *Rock/Pop/Jazz: Vom Amateur zum Profi*, ed. Helmut Rösner (Hamburg: Arbeitskreis Studium populärer Musik e.V., 1987), pp. 43–59.

37 Henry Ernst, "Meine Jagd nach der 'Tschetzpend'," *Der Artist*, No. 2134 (12 November 1926), pp. 4–5. The otherwise unknown author undoubtedly anglicized his name for commercial reasons, as did many other German dance musicians of the time. "Noch zu Beginn des Jahres 1920, also zu einer Zeit, die im Reich weite hinter uns liegt, wußte in ganz Deutschland kaum *ein* Musiker, was denn eigentlich eine Jazzband oder ein Shimmy sei. Wer das bezweifelt, dem möchte ich den Beweis für diese Behauptung aus eigenem Erlebnis bringen. Vorweg sei betont, daß dem deutschen Musiker diese Unkenntnis nicht zum Vorwurf gemacht werden soll! Der Hauptgrund für das Manko lag vielmehr in der traurigen Tatsache, daß Deutschland zu jener Zeit immer noch für das 'feindliche' Ausland abgeschlossen blieb, obwohl die große Hirnfermate, auch Weltkrieg genannt, seit Jahr und Tag beendet war. Unser Urteil über das Wesen und Eigenart der Jazzband basierte darum auf sehr unbestimmten und dunklen Gerüchten. . . .

Mit unseren Ave Marias und Serenaden heimsten wir in St. Moritz viel Ehren und Whiskysodas ein. Nur bei den 'Fuchstänzen' machten die Leute ein verlegenes Gesicht. Als nun eines Abends, an dem wir vorwiegend unsere Fuchstänze zum besten gaben, ein Engländer an das Podium herantrat und höflich um einen Foxtrott bat, da war ich sehr erstaunt und fragte ihn ebenso höflich, ob er denn nicht bemerkt habe, daß wir schon fast eine Stunde lang nur Foxtrots gespielt hätten. Er wiederum meinte, verlegen lächelnd, daß er unserem Spiel stets aufmerksam gefolgt sei; *was* wir gespielt hätten, wisse er zwar nicht, daß aber kein Foxtrott darunter gewesen wäre, das könne er mit Bestimmtheit behaupten. . . . Nur zu bald sollte ich erfahren, daß der Engländer recht hatte und unsere damaligen deutschen Foxtrots sich bei näherem Zusehen als verkappte, nur etwas exotisch synkopierte Gavotten und Rixdorfer entpuppten. . . .

Vor Kriegsausbruch besaß ich mehrere Jahre hindurch ein Abonnement bei dem Londoner Musikverlag Francis and Day, der mir gegen ein Jahresfixum anglo-amerikanische Novitäten reichlich zusandte. Die Erneuerung dieses Abonnements *nach* dem Kriege, *von Dortmund aus*, mißlang kläglich: meine Briefe wurden überhaupt nicht beantwortet, da es damals noch jeder Engländer unter seiner Würde hielt, mit einem Deutschen in Geschäftsverbindung zu treten. (Auch eine Nachwirkung oben erwähnter Hirnfermate!) *Von St. Moritz* aus erfolgte dagegen der Abschluß des Abonnements reibungslos, und schon nach wenigen Tagen erhielt ich einen solchen Stapel der neuesten englischen und amerikanischen Foxtrots zugeschickt, daß dem Granatverschlag eine Zwiebackkiste beigelegt werden mußte. . . .

Die Foxtrottklippe war für uns eben glücklich umschifft, da drohte schon neue Gefahr! Eines Tages eröffnete mir der Hotelier, daß er uns für die kommende Hauptsaison im Winter zu reengagieren wünsche. Der Kontrakt könne gleich abgeschlossen werden. Allerdings knüpfte er daran eine Bedingung: *ich müßte Jazzband spielen*. Er sagte: 'Tschetzpend.' Ich hörte dieses exotische Wort zum erstenmal in meinem Leben und hatte keine blasse Ahnung, was es bedeute. Da aber mein Grundsatz stets das Horazische 'nil admirari' (nichts verblüffen lassen) war, antwortete ich mit dem ehernen Gesicht eines assyrischen Sichelwagenlenkers 'Selbsverständlich,

Herr Direktor, wir spielen Tschetzpend' . . . Gemacht! Wir unterschrieben gegenseitig die Kontrakte, worin meine Verpflichtung schwarz auf weiß verklausuliert stand, daß ich Tschetzpend zu spielen habe. . . . Die Jagd nach der Tschetzpend begann! . . .

Wir rasten im Derbygaloptempo, daß das Podium nur so staube. Das Publikum machte verdutzte Gesichter. Aha, dachte ich, die riechen schon den Jazzbraten! Als aber von verschiedenen Seiten angefragt wurde, was ich denn da spiele und ich stolz darauf erwiderte, wir hätten eben Jazz gespielt, da tauchte wieder das mir nur zu bekannte verlegene Lächeln auf. Und als ein nervöser Gast, der mit Wein und Wahrheit vollgesogen war, zurücksagen ließ, das wäre ein Blödsinn aber kein Jazz, da flüsterte mir mein Daimonion zu: der Mann hat recht, es scheint doch nichts zu sein mit dem Berliner Jazz! Meine Verlegenheit erreichte ihren Höhepunkt, als nun auch noch eine kleine Pariserin uns Shimmy zu spielen bat. Sie käme, sagte sie, direkt aus Paris und dort sei jetzt Shimmy mit Jazzband die große Mode. . . . Ich bedauerte achselzuckend und die kleine Pariserin rümpfte spöttisch die grellrot bemalten Lippen. . . .

Ich hatte in einem Buchladen eben meine gewohnte Morgenzeitung gekauft, da bemerkte ich auf dem Nebentisch einen Stoß Musikalien: französische und englische Tanzmusik für Klavier, mit buntdrolligen Titelbildern. Ich blätterte ahnungslos darinnen. Plötzlich stieß ich auf einen Foxtrot, dessen Titelseite die Photographie eines Orchesters zeigte mit der erklärenden Ueberschrift: daß dies die berühmte Londoner Jazzband N.N. sei, zu deren Repertoireschlager obiger Foxtrot gehöre. Kein Aegyptologe hat seinen neu entdeckten Papyrus liebevoller in die Hand genommen und intensiver studiert, als ich diese Jazzband-Photographie! . . . Da sah ich nun endlich, was eine Jazzband ist. Sieben Männeckens in Sportdreß: Klavier, Geige, zwei Banjos, Saxophon, Posaune und Schlagwerk. Das, meinerseits diplomatisch geführte, Zwiegespräch mit dem Buchhändler, der ein begeisterter Anhänger der neuen Jazzmusik war, tat ein übriges, um mich über das kleinste Detail einer Jazzband aufzuklären. Ich war gerettet! Alles das, was heute bezüglich Jazz jedem Musiker selbstverständlich geworden, damals aber noch unklar und rätselhaft war, wurde mir nun offenbar."

38 The latter four composers all wrote jazz-related operas in the late 1920s that did not reach the stage until after World War II, in most cases posthumously: Dessau's *Orpheus und der Bürgermeister* (*ca.* 1930, performed 1991), Blacher's *Habemeajaja* (1929, performed 1987), Hartmann's *Wachsfigurenkabinett* (1928–29, performed 1988), and Wagner-Régeny's *Die Fabel vom seligen Schlächtermeister* (1930, performed 1964). All reveal the strong influence of Kurt Weill, providing clear evidence of what a "Weill tradition" in German opera might have looked like if economic and political events had not intervened.

39 George Grosz, *Ein kleines Ja und ein grosses Nein* (Hamburg: Rowohlt, 1955), p. 97. Grosz's observation, as many writers, including Cook, (*Opera for a New Republic*), have overlooked, refers to the years 1912–14.

40 Proof that Stravinsky was fully aware of American popular music before Ansermet's well-known visit is provided by the composer himself; see C. Stanley Wise, "'American music is true art' says Stravinsky," *New York Times* (16 January 1916), Section 5, p. 3.

41 Kurt Weill, *Alabama-Song aus der Oper "Aufstieg und Fall der Stadt Mahagonny,"* *Spezialarrangement von Richard Etlinger* (Vienna: Universal, 1930).

42 No. 14 in *Zum 5 Uhr Tee (Five O'Clock Tea): eine Sammlung 19 ausgewählter Tanz-, Operetten- und Liederschlager*, vol. 4 (Leipzig and Milan: Anton J. Benjamin; Vienna, Berlin and New York: Wiener Bohême-Verlag, 1924).

43 Eric Borchard, *Mama loves Papa – Papa loves Mama* (Grammophon 14803), recorded in Berlin, 1924.

44 Alex Hyde, *Mama Loves Papa, Papa Loves Mama* (Vox 01622), recorded in Berlin, June 1924. Hyde, whose appearance in Germany five years after the onset of the German jazz craze created a sensation among commercial musicians, led one of the many franchise bands that toured American cities under the nominal leadership of Paul Whiteman. See H. J. P. Bergmeier and Rainer E. Lotz, *Alex Hyde Bio-Discography* (Menden: Der Jazzfreund, 1985).

45 No. 11 in *Zum 5 Uhr Tee.*

46 A good example, recorded in September 1925 in Berlin, is provided by Julian Fuhs' *Look Who's Here* (Homokord B1887), where the trumpeter plays the same plunger-mute solo chorus twice, note for note, evidently as proof of his mastery of the style.

47 A good discussion of Seiber's jazz seminar can be found in Peter Cahn, *Das Hoch'sche Konservatorium 1878–1978* (Frankfurt: Waldemar Kramer, 1979). Amazingly, a number of radio performances by Seiber's class have survived in air-shot recordings from the late 1920s; see Rainer E. Lotz, "Amerikaner in Europa," in *That's Jazz: Der Sound des 20. Jahrhunderts* (Darmstadt: Jazz-Institut, 1988), p. 296.

48 Mátyás Seiber, *Leichte Tänze: Eine Querschnitt durch die neuen Tanzrhythmen für instruktive Zwecke* (Mainz: Schott, 1933; 2nd edn 1965).

49 Mátyás Seiber, *Schule für Jazz-Schlagzeug* (Mainz: B. Schott's Söhne, 1929). An indication of the inordinately high opinion of this work in the German intellectual press can be obtained from the reviews by Böttcher in *Die Musik* 12/8 (May 1930), pp. 630–31, and Schoen in *Melos* 8/8 (1929), pp. 322–23.

50 See Adorno's apologetic confession of his reliance on Seiber as a jazz authority in "Vorrede," *Musikalische Schriften*, vol. 4 (Frankfurt a.M.: Suhrkamp, 1982), pp. 10–11. Seiber's theory of jazz syncopation and its relation to Brahms, echoes of which can be found in Adorno's jazz writings, was carried to almost comic extremes in "Rhythmic freedom in jazz? A study of jazz rhythms," in *Music Review* 6 (1945), pp. 30–41, 89–94, 160–71.

51 A short list of Baresel's major jazz-related publications would include: "Kulturwert des Jazz," *Der Artist* no. 2134 (12 November 1926), pp. 8–9; "Die Jazz als Rettung," *Der Auftakt* 6/10 (1926), pp. 213–16; "Entwicklungsmöglichkeiten der Jazzmusik," *Der Artist* no. 2183 (21 December 1927), pp. 4–5; "Kunst-Jazz," *Melos* 7 (1928), p. 356; *Schule des Rhythmus* (Leipzig: Zimmermann, 1930); Reinhard Wenskat: *Schule für Jazz-Schlagzeug*, ed. Baresel (Leipzig: Zimmermann, *ca.* 1930); "Ethos des Jazz," *Der Artist* no. 2305 (21 March 1930), pp. 1–2; *Schule des Rhythmus* (Leipzig: Zimmermann, [1930]); 77 *Klavier-Breaks/Jazz-Breaks for Piano* (Leipzig: Zimmermann, *ca.* 1930); *Der Klavierdoktor: 45 Konzentrationsübungen . . . mit erstmaliger Berücksichtung des Jazz und der modernen Musik* (Leipzig: Zimmermann, 1931).

52 *Das Jazz-Buch: Anleitung zum Spielen, Improvisieren und Komponieren moderner Tanzstücke mit besonderer Berücksichtigung des Klaviers* (Leipzig: Zimmermann, 1925).

53 *Das neue Jazz-Buch: Ein praktisches Handbuch für Musiker, Komponisten, Arrangerer, Tänzer und Freunde der Jazzmusik* (Leipzig: W. Zimmermann, 1929).

54　See *Das neue Jazz-Buch*, p. 26. Over the years the various editions of Baresel's *Jazz-Buch* record a gradual slowing-down of dance tempos. This same fact was confirmed by contemporary observers, who felt that German jazz, like German culture as a whole, was going through a period of *Neue Sachlichkeit* after leaving its expressionist stage of the early 1920s.

55　Listed in *Der Artist* no. 2163 (3 June 1927), p. 1. For these authorities, jazz tempos were as follows, expressed 4/4 bars per minute: Foxtrott 58–60, Charleston 54, Black Bottom 45, Slow Fox 42, Blues 33, Tango 27, with the English Waltz at 43 bars per minute.

56　Blues also involved what we would call a "four-beat" accompaniment in block chords (as opposed to a two-beat "stride" accompaniment) and a flexible melodic line, often with triplet subdivisions. Latter-day attempts to derive European blues from black-American rural blues – especially when carried to such extremes as in Heinrich W. Schwab, "Zur Rezeption des Jazz in der komponierten Musik," *Dansk Årbog for Musikforskning* 10 (1979), pp. 127–177 – are singularly unrevealing. Central European composers derived their notion of the blues not from Charley Patton or Blind Lemon Jefferson but from America's Tin Pan Alley, which used the term as an evocative label for any pop songs in moderate tempo.

57　*Das neue Jazz-Buch*, p. 74. The same figure appears in the first edition of 1925 as the defining rhythm of the foxtrot.

58　See, for example, A. von Gizycki-Arkadjew, "Von deutschen Bearbeitern," *Der Artist* no. 2134 (12 November 1926), p. 5, where Lange is recommended to German commercial musicians as the "most popular American [dance band] arranger, who also obliges practically all notable English publishers with his expertise" ("der . . . populärste amerikanische Bearbeiter, der auch fast ausnahmslos allen namhaften englischen Verlegern mit seiner Kunstfertigkeit beispringt").

59　See, for example, Max Harrison, "Around Paul Whiteman," in *A Jazz Retrospect* (Newton Abbot: David and Charles, 1976), pp. 185–94.

60　Arthur Lange, *Arranging for the Modern Dance Orchestra* (New York: Arthur Lange, Inc., 1926), p. 91.

61　See Gizycki-Arkadjew, "Von deutschen Bearbeitern," which appeared a mere six months after the book's private publication in New York.

62　*Der Artist* no. 2341 (31 October 1930).

63　Eugen Rosenkaimer, "Ein Lehrwerk über Jazz-Instrumentation aus der Feder des amerikanischen Meister-Arrangeurs Arthur Lange," *Der Artist* no. 2341 (31 October 1930), serialized weekly to no. 2349 (26 December 1930).

64　The waning fascination with America and jazz among Weimar Germany's intellectuals is exhaustively traced in Albrecht Dümling, "Symbol des Fortschritts, der Dekadenz und der Unterdrückung. Zum Bedeutungswandel des Jazz in den zwanziger Jahren," in *Angewandte Musik, Zwanziger Jahre: Exemplarische Versuche gesellschaftsbezogener musikalischer Arbeit für Theater, Film, Radio, Massenveranstaltung*, ed. Dietrich Stern (Berlin: Argument-Verlag, 1977), pp. 81–100.

65　Egon Wellesz, *Die neue Instrumentation* (Berlin: M. Hesse, 1928–9), vol. 2, p. 172. "Endlich wäre noch des Jazzorchesters zu gedenken, wie es Wilhelm Grosz im 'Baby in der Bar,' Kurt Weill in der 'Dreigroschenoper' und Max Brand im 'Maschinist Hopkins' verwendet haben. Diese Übernahme erfordert die Kenntnis der Eigenarten der Jazzkapellen und ihrer Spielmanieren, welche, wie bereits erwähnt, am ausführlichsten in der Arbeit von Arthur Lange 'Arranging for the dance orchestra' [*sic*] (New York 1926) behandelt sind."

66 Ibid, appendix, pp. 20 and 21.

67 *Zeugen des Jahrhunderts*, p. 60.

68 Cook, *Opera for a New Republic*, pp. 190–91.

69 See David Drew, *Kurt Weill*, p. 433. Weill's stylistic exercises mainly concentrate on Tin Pan Alley harmony, which, with its preponderance of ninths and elevenths and many chromatic passing chords, differed considerably from its European counterpart.

70 See for example Willi Reich's review in *Die Musik*, 12/6 (March 1930), p. 466. The choice of reviewer (Reich was a close friend and early biographer of Alban Berg) provides a further indication that Baresel's book was well-known in Viennese *avant-garde* circles.

71 The first is bar 26 from "Die Ballade vom angenehmen Leben" as reprinted in *Brecht Liederbuch*, ed. Fritz Henneberg (Frankfurt a.M.: Suhrkamp, 1984), p. 77. The second is taken from the present author's personal copy of Art Shefte, *Up-to-the-Minute Jazz Breaks, Tricks, Blues, Endings, Etc. for the Amateur and Professional Pianist* (Chicago: Forster, [1925]), p. 18, formerly in the possession of Adolf Stauch, Berlin. Weill's piano textures, especially the remarkable piano solo in *Royal Palace*, suggest a close familiarity with the novelty piano style represented by Zez Confrey in America and Billy Maierl in England.

72 Österreichische Nationalbibliothek, Alban-Berg-Fond, Box 21 Berg 80/IV. Interestingly, Berg consulted the fourth edition of 1926 rather than any of the later editions or the *Neue Jazz-Buch* of 1929. This suggests that his practical interest in jazz had begun earlier than is generally assumed.

73 Berg may have met Weill as early as 1926, before the success of the *Mahagonny-Songspiel* and *Die Dreigroschenoper* had made him famous: his appointment calendar (Österreichische Nationalbibliothek, F 21 Berg 432/23, fol. 44) has the name "Weill" entered during 19–21 December 1926. *Jonny spielt auf* is entered twice, on 12–21 December 1926 (fol. 44) and on 31 December 1927 (fol. 151). Work on *Lulu* began in early 1928.

74 *Das Jazz-Buch*, 4th edn, p. 10.

75 A good summary of the autobiographical and constructive significance of the number 23 in Berg's music can be found in Douglas Jarman, *The Music of Alban Berg* (Berkeley and Los Angeles: University of California Press, 1979), pp. 228ff.

76 For Tempo di Tango see Alban Berg, *Der Wein: Konzertarie für Sopran*, score (Vienna: Universal, 1966), bar 39 and *passim*; for *Hauptzeitmass* see bar 17.

77 *Das Jazz-Buch*, 4th edn, p. 24: "Eine raffinierte Art der Synkopierung." Baresel was ever at pains to legitimize jazz by pointing out features in common with historical dance forms; see particularly his *Schule des Rhythmus* (Leipzig: Zimmermann, [1930]).

78 Alban-Berg-Fond, 21 Berg 80/IV, fol. 40.

79 *Das Jazz-Buch*, 4th edn, p. 21: "Wenn eine Singstimme vorgesehen ist, beschränkt sich Synkopierung und Auszierung auf die begleitenden Mittelstimmen."

80 Modern-day attempts to add a jazz flavor to, say, the melody line of the "Alabama Song" by syncopating or swinging the rhythm are thus stylistically *outré*.

81 See, for instance, Baresel's Examples 14 and 22, both circled by Berg.

82 *Das Jazz-Buch*, 4th edn, Example 7, p. 14.

83 77 *Klavier-Breaks*, p. 10.

84 The vibraphone is, however, listed in *Das neue Jazz-Buch* of 1929 – one year before its first recorded use as a jazz instrument (by Lionel Hampton on Armstrong's *Confessin'*, 19 August 1930).

85 *Das Jazz-Buch*, 4th edn, p. 35.

86 In the 1920s, a decade before the introduction of electric amplification, the jazz violin was equipped with a megaphone-like contraption called a *Jazz-Trichter* to increase its volume. Berg, anticipating the acoustical demands of the opera house, preferred to set the violin part *à tre* as well as calling for *Jazz-Trichter*.

87 *Das Jazz-Buch*, 4th edn, p. 34. As mentioned above in connection with Krenek's *Holztrommel*, a *Holz-Trom* was merely another term for a woodblock.

88 *Lulu*, ed. H. E. Apostel (Vienna: Universal, 1963), p. 240: "gr[osse] u[nd] kl[eine] Trom[mel] und Beck[en] (freihängend), gr[osser] u[nd] kl[einer] Tempelblock und Stahlbesen". The vibraphone remains in the orchestra pit, presumably to be played by a second percussionist.

89 Not until much later did Berg assemble these instruments into the familiar jazz trap set. On the back of an envelope dated 1 November 1932 (Alban-Berg-Fond, 21 Berg 80/IV, fol. 43) he sketched a trap set with bass and snare drum, woodblock, suspended cymbal and "gedämpfter Becken" which, on closer inspection, turns out to be a hi-hat. This instrument, though long familiar in Germany as a *Charleston-Maschine*, was apparently new to Berg at the time.

90 The parallels are more than dramaturgical. Just as the dance scene in the first *Don Giovanni* finale involves overlapping meters, the 2/2 trio of Berg's ragtime in *Lulu* (Act I, bars 1155ff.) conflicts with the 3/4 of the orchestra. The *Don Giovanni* minuet is also quoted by an onstage band in *Wozzeck* (Act II, bar 441).

91 Hans F. Redlich, *Alban Berg: The Man and His Music* (London: John Calder, 1957), pp. 156f.

92 See 77 *Klavier-Breaks*, no. 42, p. 13.

93 See Wellesz, *Die neue Instrumentation*.

94 Adorno, "Abschied vom Jazz," *Europäische Revue* 9 (1933), pp. 313–16. The other lasting achievement was the singing of the Revellers, a novelty vocal group remembered today, if at all, as a predecessor of the more famous Comedian Harmonists.

95 In 1925 Gruenberg sacrificed his status as an authority by rashly proclaiming the superiority of *Kitten on the Keys* to all music post-dating the *B Minor Mass* (see his letter to the editor in *Musikblätter des Anbruch* 7 [June-July 1925], pp. 337–38). Even so, his collection of negro spirituals, published by Universal in 1926, was long considered definitive among the Austro-German intelligentsia.

96 Alban-Berg-Fond, 21 Berg 80/IV, fols. 39–39' and 40–40'.

8 THE IDEA OF *BEWEGUNG* IN THE GERMAN ORGAN REFORM MOVEMENT OF THE 1920S

1 Günther Ramin, *Gedanken zur Klärung des Orgelproblems* (Kassel: Bärenreiter, 1929), p. 4. "Unsere Zeit schreitet schnell in Bezug auf Wertung und Umschichtung künstlerischer Komplexe und man ist fast betroffen, wie groß und umfassend in einer Frist von etwa 6 Jahren die Orgel-Erneuerungsbewegung geworden ist. Möchte dies

kein Zeichen dafür sein, daß diese Renaissance als eine der vielen geistigen Modeströmungen der Nachkriegsepoche in Aufnahme gekommen ist, sondern möge der echte Kern und die reine Glut dieses Wandlungsprozesses erhalten bleiben."

2 E.g. Albert Schweitzer, *Deutsche und französische Orgelbaukunst und Orgelkunst* (Leipzig: Breitkopf & Härtel, 1906), *plus* "Nachwort über den gegenwärtigen Stand der Frage des Orgelbaues," (ibid 2nd edn, 1927). A good, recent summary of Schweitzer's thinking is Harald Schützeichel, "Orgelbau und Kulturreform: Albert Schweitzer in neuer Sicht," in *Berliner Orgel-Colloquium* 1988, ed. Hans Heinrich Eggebrecht (Murrhardt: Musikwissenschaftliche Verlags-Gesellschaft, 1990), pp. 45–64; Wilibald Gurlitt, "Die Wandlungen des Klangideals der Orgel im Lichte der Musikgeschichte," in *Bericht über die Freiburger Tagung für deutsche Orgelkunst vom 27. bis 30. Juli 1926*, ed. W. Gurlitt (Augsburg: Bärenreiter, 1926), pp. 11–42, and "Zur gegenwärtigen Orgel-Erneuerungsbewegung in Deutschland," *Musik und Kirche* 1 (1929), pp. 90–102; reprinted in W. Gurlitt, *Musikgeschichte und Gegenwart: eine Aufsatzfolge*, 2 vols., ed. H. H. Eggebrecht (Wiesbaden: Steiner, 1966). Also Christhard Mahrenholz, "Orgel und Liturgie," in *Bericht über die Dritte Tagung für deutsche Orgelkunst in Freiberg in Sachsen vom 2. bis 7. Oktober 1927*, ed. C. Mahrenholz (Kassel: Bärenreiter, 1928), pp. 13–37, and "Fünfzehn Jahre Orgelbewegung: Rückblick und Ausblick," *Musik und Kirche* 10 (1938), pp. 8–28.

3 On Rupp, see the preface by Joachim Dorfmüller to the facsimile edition of Emile Rupp, *Die Entwicklungsgeschichte der Orgelbaukunst* (Einsiedeln, 1929; repr. Hildesheim: Olms, 1981). On Schweitzer, see Schützeichel, "Orgelbau," esp. pp. 49–50.

4 Luigi Ferdinando Tagliavini, "Mezzo secolo di storia organaria," *L'Organo* 1 (1960), pp. 70–86.

5 For Danish, Dutch, and East German accounts, see Frans Brouwer, *Orgelbewegung und Orgelgegenbewegung: eine Arbeit über die Ursprünge und die Entwicklung der dänischen Orgelreform bis heute* (Utrecht: Joachimsthal, 1981), esp. pp. 13–35; Hans Kriek, *Organum novum redivivum* (Buren: Knuf, 1981), esp. pp. 21–32; *Wege zur Orgel: Instrument, Musik und Spieler im Wandel von zehn Jahrhunderten*, ed. Christoph Krummacher (Berlin: Evangelische Verlagsanstalt, 1987), esp. pp. 74–78. In Denmark, Marcussen made mechanical-action sliderchests from 1930 (Kriek, *Organum novum*, p. 25).

6 According to Friedrich Högner, "Die deutsche Orgelbewegung," *Zeitwende* 7 (1931), pp. 56–71.

7 In "Karl Straube als Vorkämpfer der neueren Orgelbewegung," in *Karl Straube zu seinem 70. Geburtstag: Gaben der Freunde* (Leipzig: Peters, 1943), reprinted in Gurlitt, *Musikgeschichte*, pp. 74–89. For Gurlitt's remarks on Straube's rev. edn of 1929 see Gurlitt, p. 97.

8 In particular, Ludwig Burgemeister, *Der Orgelbau in Schlesien* (Strasbourg: Heitz, 1925), and Ernst Flade, *Der Orgelbauer Gottfried Silbermann: ein Beitrag zur Geschichte des deutschen Orgelbaues im Zeitalter Bachs* (Leipzig: Kistner & Siegel, 1926). As instances of both the geographical claims of Germany in the 1920s (Silesia as part of the Reich) and its musical assumptions (Silbermann important as a contemporary of J. S. Bach), these two titles are characteristic.

9 In particular, *Les grandes orgues des églises de Paris et du Département de la Seine* (Paris: Fischbacher, 1927).

10 For the French cases, see e.g. Félix Raugel, *Les anciens buffets d'orgues du Département de*

Seine-et-Marne (Paris: Fischbacher, 1928). For a belated appreciation of Hill's significance, see W. Heise, "Ueber die Entdeckung des Orgelgehäuses," *Ars organi* 4 (1956), pp. 106ff.

11 Walter Kaufmann, *Die Orgeln Ostfrieslands: Orgeltopographie* (Aurich: Ostfriesländische Landschaft, 1968), pp. 19–20.

12 H. H. Eggebrecht, *Die Orgelbewegung* (Stuttgart: Musikwissenschaftliche Verlags-Gesellschaft, 1967), pp. 10–12.

13 Wilhelm Kamlah, "Die deutsche Musikbewegung," *Musik und Volk* 1 (1933) and *Monatshefte für Gottesdienst und kirchliche Kunst* 38 (1933): in Eggebrecht, *Die Orgelbewegung*, p. 11. "[In diesem Sinne sei] die deutsche Musikbewegung durch den Vorstoß des Nazionalsozialismus erst ganz zu sich selbst gekommen . . ."

14 See remarks by L. F. Tagliavini, "L'organo nel mondo musicale contemporaneo – Note in margine ad uno scritto di H. H. Eggebrecht," *L'Organo* 6 (1968), pp. 221–30, here p. 225.

15 Tagliavini, "Mezzo secolo," p. 80; cf. Tagliavini, "L'organo nel mondo," p. 224.

16 Arnold Dolmetsch, *The Interpretation of the Music of the XVII and XVIII Centuries* (London: Novello [1915]), pp. 436–37.

17 The "High Pressure Party" attacked in Emile Rupp's book of 1929 (*Die Entwicklungsgeschichte*, p. 339) is even accused by Rupp of being politically active, denouncing opponents "during the first inflammatory war psychosis."

18 Mahrenholz, "Orgel und Liturgie," p. 22, and "Fünfzehn Jahre," p. 11. Of course, the sixteenth-century orchestra, with its large proportion of winds (as so understood by *Aufführungspraxis* musicologists of the 1920s) was more suitable for imitation than that of the string-and-brass-based orchestra of the nineteenth century.

19 E.g. sliderchests in Mahrenholz, "Füntzehn Jahre," pp. 22–23, where there is also a hint, an unformed view, on the need for rethinking temperament.

20 Quoted by Gurlitt in "Orgel-Erneuerungsbewegung": see *Musikgeschichte*, p. 98. "Indem die Musik unserer Tage . . . nähert sie sich in vielen Punkten dem Grundzuge der Barockmusik . . . die alte Orgel wird zum Symbol einer Musikerfassung, deren Auswirkung der Zukunft gehört."

21 Cf. the descriptions of *Sprechgesang* in terms of primitive, Jewish, and Gregorian musics, made by Robert Haas in *Aufführungspraxis der Musik* (Potsdam: Academische Verlagsgesellschaft, 1931), during the period in which Schoenberg was working on *Moses und Aron*.

22 Arnold Schering, "Historische und nationale Klangstile," *Jahrbuch der Musikbibliothek Peters* 35 (1927), pp. 31–43, here 42. "Denn wenn wir den erdennahen Klang einer barocken Orgel mit dem erdenfernen einer romantischen vergleichen, so muß . . . als unabweislich angenommen werden, daß der Protestantismus der Romantik von dem des Barock in entscheidenden Punkten des religiösen Erlebens in ebendemselben Maße abstand wie das eine Klangideal vom andern."

23 Cf. also the title of F. T. Arnold's book on figured-bass playing (see below, note 30).

24 Alexander J. Ellis's papers from the *Journal of the Royal Society of Arts* (March and April, 1880); reprinted in Arthur Mendel, *Studies in the History of Musical Pitch* (Amsterdam: Knuf, 1931).

25 Such as the Flemish harpsichord, in Grant O'Brien, *Ruckers: a Harpsichord and Virginal Building Tradition* (Cambridge: Cambridge University Press, 1990), esp. pp. 175ff.

26 Curt Sachs, *Handbuch der Musikinstrumentenkunde* (Leipzig: Breitkopf & Härtel, 1919; 2nd edn, 1930). Sachs gives no critique of e.g. the high wind-pressure of modern organs and what it leads to, in his reference to it and other parts of the organ (final section of the *Handbuch*). One cannot say he avoids it: rather, the question does not arise in such a book.

27 E.g. Friedemann Hellwig, *Atlas der Profile an Tasteninstrumenten vom 16. bis zum frühen 19. Jahrhundert* (Frankfurt: Bochinsky, 1985).

28 A good example is C. Mahrenholz's *Die Berechnung der Orgelpfeifen-Mensuren vom Mittelalter bis zur Mitte des 19. Jahrhunderts* (Kassel: Bärenreiter, 1938), the medieval section of which was fundamentally questioned in Klaus-Jürgen Sachs, *Mensura fistularum: die Mensurierung der Orgelpfeifen im Mittelalter*, 2 vols. (Murrhardt: Musikwissenschaftliche Verlags-Gesellschaft, 1970/1980). On p. 16 of vol. 2 Sachs points out that the second edition of *Die Berechnung* in 1968 "appeared without the slightest indication of a possibly altered state of knowledge" in thirty years: an omission of the publisher, perhaps?

29 Dolmetsch, in *Interpretation*, pp. 342–63; A. Schering, *Aufführungspraxis alter Musik* (Leipzig: Quelle & Meyer, 1931), pp. 147–62.

30 Schering, *Aufführungspraxis*, pp. 148–49; cf. F. T. Arnold, *The Art of Accompaniment from a Thorough-Bass as Practised in the XVIIth and XVIIIth Centuries*, 2 vols. (Oxford: Oxford University Press, 1931).

31 Max Schneider, "Der Generalbass Johann Sebastian Bachs," *Jahrbuch der Musikbibliothek Peters* (1914/15), pp. 27–42.

32 Also a topic of interest to the canonic writers: cf. E. Rupp, *Abbé Vogler als Mensch, Musiker und Orgelbautheoretiker* (Ludwigsburg: Walcker, 1932), and the Freiburg dissertation of Hertha Schweiger, *Abbé G. J. Voglers Orgellehre* (Vienna: Knoch, 1938).

33 Terms reviewed by Erwin R. Jacobi, ed., in A. Schweitzer, *Zur Diskussion über Orgelbau (1914)* (Berlin: Merseburger, 1977), pp. 33–34.

34 Ibid, pp. 41–42.

35 Eggebrecht, *Die Orgelbewegung*, pp. 21–22. Reviews of the 1921 organ when it was new speak of its "fabulous stops", the "originality of sound", etc.

36 Ramin, *Gedanken*, p. 20. "Betrachtet man die Entwicklungsgeschichte der Kirchenmusik, so wird klar, daß die große Erscheinung Joh. S. Bachs ein Ziel, eine Erfüllung bedeutet, und daß die wesentlichen Stufen der Entwicklung *vor* ihn zu suchen sind." On p. 35 is the description of Bach as the "highest perfection of a wide-ranging Christian music-culture" (höchste Vollendung einer umfassenden christlichen Musikkultur), showing the division then made between the decadent concert-hall organ and the newly classical church organ.

37 On French-Alsatian styles in general: Schützeichel, "Orgelbau," pp. 49–50, 56, 60ff. On the Kronenburg organ of 1908: Bernhard Billeter, "Albert Schweitzer und sein Orgelbauer," *Acta organologica* 11 (1977), pp.173–225, here 176f.

38 *Der Orgelbauer, Gottfried Silbermann*. In its preface, Flade says the "outward" reason for writing his book was the comments of the Alsatian Organ Reform on the "advantages and disadvantages" of Silbermann organs.

39 E.g. the *Sonatas* and the *Orgelbüchlein* were both from the Cöthen years: Freiburg Conference report (see note 2), pp. 75 (Flade) and 69 (Fischer).

40 Ibid, pp. 156 (Mahrenholz) and 160 (Gurlitt). The Conference's papers on Reger (Karl Hasse, pp. 122–29) and post-Reger (Hermann Keller, pp. 130–38) give an instructive view of many musicians' preoccupations at the period.

41 Flade, *Der Orgelbauer Gottfried Silbermannn*, p. 157.

42 J. S. Bach, *Acht kleine Präludien und Fugen für die Orgel*, ed. Karl Straube (Leipzig: Peters, 1934).

43 Ramin, *Gedanken*, p. 3. Jahnn's technical papers in the Freiburg and Freiberg Conferences were in part prompted by his knowledge of the *Jakobiorgel*. On the whole, his nineteen essays over the period 1922–39 (as listed in Rudolf Reuter, *Bibliographie der Orgel: Literatur zur Geschichte der Orgel bis 1968* [Kassel: Bärenreiter, 1973], p. 103), have not received the attention they deserve.

44 See facs. edn of *Die Entwicklungsgeschichte*, pp. 6*–7*. Rupp, for whom German behavior in Strasbourg during the war still rankled, rejoiced at the failure of certain German firms in the inflationary years (p. 359) – a rare reference in organ literature to other problems of the 1920s.

45 E.g. *Die Tagung für Orgelbau in Berlin 1928*, ed. Johann Biehle (Kassel: Bärenreiter, 1929). If there had been basic rivalries between the personnel and the universities of the Upper Rhineland and those of Prussia in the 1920s, as one imagines there were, they would not have easily survived the West German monopoly of literature after the Second War.

46 In the Freiberg Conference papers, Friedrich Blume, Ernst Flade, Karl Straube and Christhard Mahrenholz spoke around the subject but never quite made it clear that e.g. the organ parts are notated at a lower pitch.

47 Tagliavini, "L'organo nel mondo," p. 225, points out that it was not the nineteenth century as such that the *Orgelbewegung* resisted (as suggested in Eggebrecht, *Die Orgelbewegung*, p. 15) but the factory production of organs during that period.

48 For Burgemeister, see *Der Orgelbau in Schlesien*. Walter Haacke's *Die Entwicklungsgeschichte des Orgelbaus im Lande Mecklenburg-Schwerin* (Wolfenbüttel: Kallmeyer, 1935) originated as a Freiburg dissertation under Gurlitt.

49 E.g. M. Tremmel, "Die neue Passauer Domorgel," *Musica sacra* 56 (1926), pp. 129–33. This was less than a generation after the building of the Hamburg Michaeliskirche organ, the then biggest, a "milestone in German organ-art" as it was called (Alfred Sittard, *Das Hauptorgelwerk und die Hilfsorgel der Grossen St Michaelis-Kirche in Hamburg* [Hamburg: Bösen & Maasch, 1912]). Straube's only publication on organs was a booklet on the giant Breslau organ (1914).

50 Paul Walcker, *Die Direkte, Elektrische, Funkenfreie Orgeltraktur* (Frankfurt a.O.: Bratfisch, 1914).

51 Freiberg conference papers, (see note 2), p. 116.

52 Ibid, p.149.

53 Karl Gustav Fellerer, *Beiträge zur Choralbegleitung und Choralverarbeitung in der Orgelmusik des ausgehenden 18. und beginnenden 19. Jahrhunderts* (Straßburg: Heitz, 1932), and *Studien zur Orgelmusik des ausgehenden 18. und frühen 19. Jahrhunderts* (Kassel: Bärenreiter, 1932).

54 Spanish (Ramin, *Gedanken*, pp. 14, 26), Italian (Mahrenholz at Freiberg – see note 2 – pp. 23f., 31), American (Gurlitt, *Musikgeschichte*, pp. 91f., 100).

55 Fritz Piersig and Richard Liesche, *Die Orgeln in Bremer Dom* (Bremen: n.p., 1939), p. 16.

56 E.g. Hermann J. Busch, "Historismus und historisches Bewußtsein in der deutschen Orgelmusik zwischen den Weltkriegen," *Acta organologica* 17 (1984), pp. 169–83, esp. 181.

57 Haacke, *Die Entwicklungsgeschichte*, pp. 8, 9. Haacke's Freiburg dissertation was presented in January 1934, a few months after Heidegger's famous rectoral address at the university apparently offering support to Hitler.

58 J. Müller-Blattau, preface to Ingeborg Rücker, *Die deutsche Orgel am Obberrhein um 1500* (Freiburg: Albert, 1940).

59 Nevertheless, standard terms can signify politically: references to *das echte deutsche Volk* in *Die Meistersinger* had an electrifying effect in Leipzig and Dresden in the 1960s.

60 Gurlitt, "Orgel-Erneuerungsbewegung": see *Musikgeschichte*, p. 100.

61 Hasse in the Freiberg Conference papers, p. 56. On Schweitzer, see Schützeichel, "Orgelbau," pp. 62–63.

62 Letter given in Rüdiger Wagner, *Hans Henny Jahnn: der Revolutionär der Umkehr* (Murrhardt: Musikwissenschaftliche Verlags-Gesellschaft, 1989), pp. 106–10, here 107.

63 Ibid, pp. 101–04. Also, R. Wagner, *Der Orgelreformer Hans Henny Jahnn* (Stuttgart: Musikwissenschaftliche Verlags-Gesellschaft, 1970), p. 51.

64 Ibid, pp. 18, 29, 53 *et passim*.

65 Gurlitt 1935, regarding the *Schützbewegung*: see *Musikgeschichte*, p. 140.

66 Quoted in Friedhelm Krummacher, "Dietrich Buxtehude. Musik zwischen Geschichte und Gegenwart," in *Dietrich Buxtehude und die europäische Musik seiner Zeit*, ed. Arnfried Edler and F. K. (Kassel: Bärenreiter, 1990), pp. 9–30, here 13: *beispiellos gesunden Musik*.

67 For a certain sympathy towards Günther Ramin's own involvement with the Nazis ("Hitler's organist") and convenient references to the *Entjüdung* of German evangelical church-music in the mid-1930s, see Manfred Mezger, "Inquisition: der 'Nationalsozialist' Günther Ramin," *Musik und Kirche* 59 (1989), pp. 289–91.

68 Gurlitt, "Karl Straube" and "Orgel-Enneuerungsbewegung": see *Musikgeschichte*, pp. 84, 91. The latter speaks of world leadership passing to *Amerika* and of the cultural implications of there now being "twice the number of mankind with coloured skins in the world of the whites."

69 Cf. Fritz Lehmann in the Freiburg conference papers (see note 2), p. 111.

70 Title of a Freiberg conference paper (see note 2), p. 4.

71 "Die Orgelbewegung ist in ihren Anfängen selbstverständlich ein Kind ihrer Zeit, der Zeit nach dem großen Weltkriege und dem Zusammenbruch unseres Volkes . . . Vieles von dem, was die zivilisierte Welt vor 1918 mit Stolz besessen hatte, erschien hohl . . ." Mahrenholz, "Fünfzehn Jahre," p. 10.

72 Conferences summary, in *Bericht über die zweite Freiburger Tagung für Deutsche Orgelkunst*, ed. J. Müller-Blattau (Kassel: Bärenreiter, 1939), p. 146. Discussion in Albrecht Rieth-müller, "Die Bestimmung der Orgel im Dritten Reich," in *Orgel und Ideologie*, ed. H. H. Eggebrecht (Murrhardt: Musikwissenschaft Verlags-Gesellschaft, 1984), pp. 28–60. "Die große Orgel zieht als das umfassendeste Instrument unserer Musikkultur ein in die großen Hallen unserer politischen Feste und Feiern . . . ein Gesamtmusikreich . . . das symbolische Instrument der Gemeinschaft. Sie ist ein im höchsten Sinne 'politisches' Instrument."

73 E.g. Origen in his psalm-commentary (*Patrologiae cursus completus, series graeca*, ed. J. P. Migne [Paris, 1857], 12.1684).

74 Any more than it did, according to Mahrenholz, when the Third Reich reintroduced an inheritance-legislation, which was a former law whose principle had gradually been lost (Mahrenholz, "Fünfzehn Jahre," p. 13). This was not historicism but advance.

75 Thus the kind of organ put in former churches (now turned into something else) in Russia: ibid, p. 14.

76 See Riethmüller, "Bestimmung," p. 48f.

77 E.g. Rupp, *Die Entwicklungsgeschichte*, pp. 92, 329, 360–70; Tagliavini, "Mezzo secolo," p. 84.

78 I have taken the phrase from Karl Geiringer, *Johann Sebastian Bach: The Culmination of an Era* (New York: Oxford University Press, 1966), but the idea is (or was) common and takes various forms. For example, it lies behind Willi Apel's remark in the preface to his *Geschichte der Orgel- und Klaviermusik bis 1700* (Kassel: Bärenreiter, 1967) that he does not include Bach because "earlier compositions would . . . be seen . . . in the lesser light of a preparation or of first steps" (English translation by Hans Tischler, *The History of Keyboard Music to 1700* [Bloomington: Indiana University Press, 1972], p. xiv).

79 But at that same period, Harvey Grace in *The Organ Works of Bach* (London: Novello, *ca*1922) did not totally ignore French elements, being responsive to hints dropped half a century earlier by Spitta.

80 Hans Klotz, *Über die Orgelkunst der Gotik, der Renaissance und des Barock* (Kassel: Bärenreiter, 1934; rev. edn, 1975). Klotz was another Straube pupil, and Straube's key position as both the most powerful figure in church music of the period and someone who (for whatever motive) joined the NSDAP, is clear from Günter Hartmann's *Karl Straube und seine Schule: "Das Ganze ist ein Mythos"* (Bonn: Verlag für systematische Musikwissenschaft, 1991). Hartmann's sharp criticisms of the man, his colleagues, and his period (in turn sharply reviewed in *Musik und Kirche* 62 [1992], pp. 154–59), include documentation for the thesis that Straube's "cult of the Old Masters" and Gurlitt's "Praetorius researches" had – "laughingly" – a kind of official status through their appeal to the three ruling concepts: *German, national,* and *ecclesiastical* (p. 269).

81 See e.g. Hartmann, *Karl Straube,* or Jörg Fischer, "Evangelische Kirchenmusik im dritten Reich. 'Musikalische Erneuerung' und ästhetische Modalität des Faschismus," *Archiv für Musikwissenschaft* 46 (1989), pp. 185–234.

82 E.g. Wolfgang Auler, "Die Anfänge der Orgelbewegung in Berlin und die Krise des Jahres 1933," *Musik und Kirche* 35 (1965), pp. 126–33.

83 E.g. the later and respected Bach scholar Walter Blankenburg wrote in the same year (1933) that political life and church life had a common goal, and went on to use the metaphor of *cleanliness* for certain music (see above, apropos Buxtehude). Thus J. N. David's language was "much more native, real and pure" *(viel urwüchsiger, echter und reiner)* than what one usually heard, just as the old pentatonic music of the *Volk* had shunned the sentimental–chromatic. (W. Blankenburg, "Hugo Distler's 'Jahrkreis' ", *Zeitschrift für Hausmusik* 5/6 [1933] , pp. 81–87.)

84 Fischer, "Evangelische Kirchenmusik," pp. 189, 191.

INDEX